MARK WAID
J C

# ARCHIE®



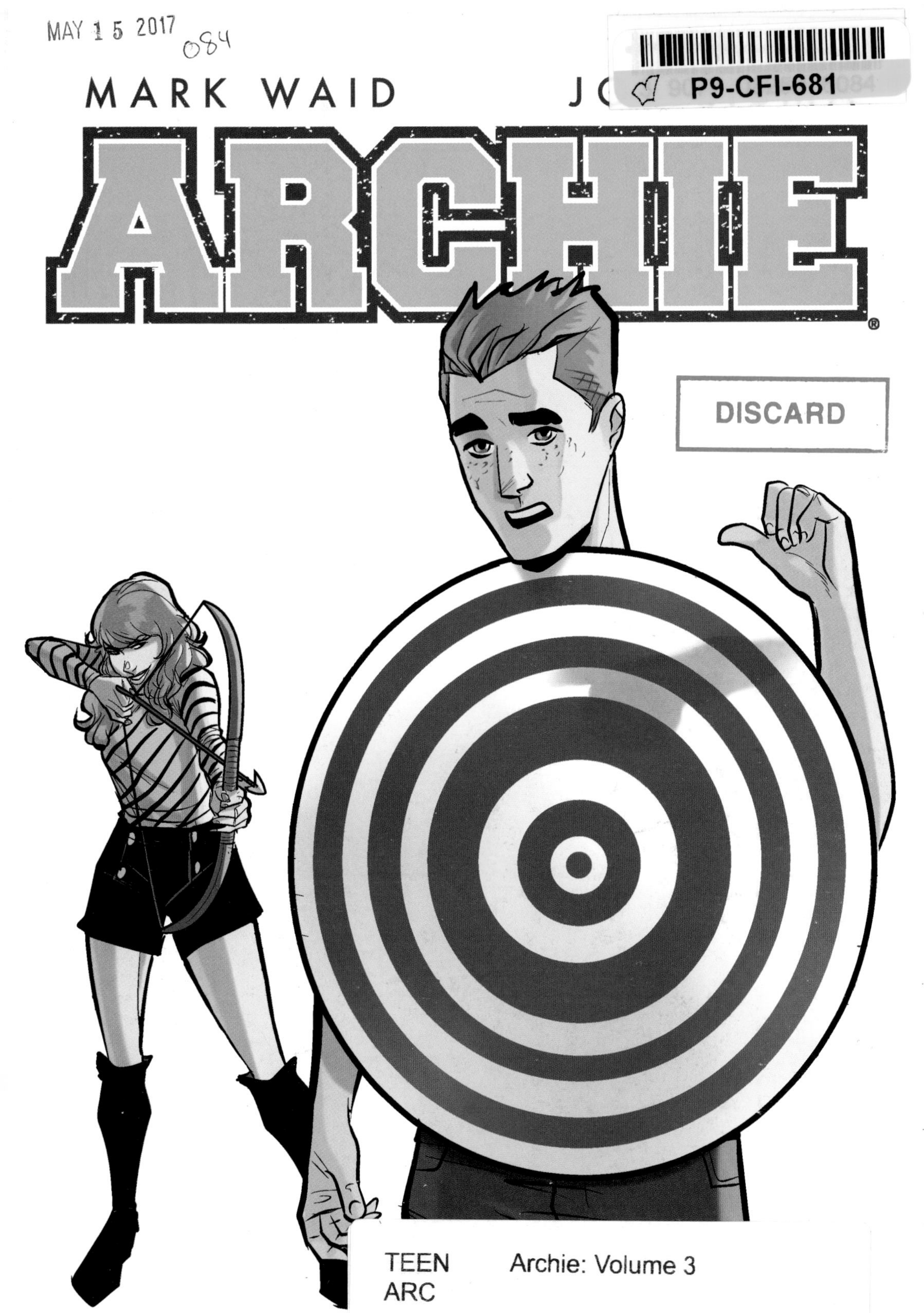



## VOLUME THREE

**STORY BY**
# MARK WAID
WITH LORI MATSUMOTO

**ART BY**
# JOE EISMA

**COLORING BY**
## ANDRE SZYMANOWICZ

**LETTERING BY**
## JACK MORELLI

**COVER ART BY**
### CAMERON STEWART

**GRAPHIC DESIGN BY**
### KARI McLACHLAN

**EDITOR**
## MIKE PELLERITO

**ASSOCIATE EDITOR**
STEPHEN OSWALD

**ASSISTANT EDITOR**
JAMIE LEE ROTANTE

**EDITOR-IN-CHIEF**
## VICTOR GORELICK

**PUBLISHER**
# JON GOLDWATER

# PREVIOUSLY IN...

## by MARK WAID

Veronica's dad, the obscenely wealthy Hiram Lodge, ran for Mayor of Riverdale. At the last minute, his campaign crashed aflame to the ground, and for once, his torment wasn't Archie's fault.

But Archie got punished anyway.

In his cruelest moment yet, Mr. Lodge—mortified at his political loss—announced that the family would be moving out of Riverdale and that Veronica would be shipped off to a private boarding school in Europe.

Wait. It gets worse.

*Lodge deliberately left Ronnie no time to tell any of her friends where she was headed.* Now, as we begin this volume, Archie and Veronica are both struggling with their greatest fear: life without each other.

As a writer, I've gotten pretty good at putting the Riverdale kids through their paces. On the other hand, I'm not especially gifted at writing about the trials and tribulations of young women negotiating their way through boarding school, so I turned to my friend Lori Matsumoto and asked her to take point on the Veronica scenes. Together, we wrote and polished many of the issues in this collection. Lori was very good at explaining to me why girls at a private school would say certain things and how they would act towards one another. I, on the other hand, never really managed to explain articulately to Lori how it's not really an Archie story unless he somehow ends up with a bucket over his head, but that's on me.

So that should bring you up to speed except to say: you're about to meet Ms. Cheryl Blossom, one of Archie Comics' greater latter-day characters and a force of nature. Cheryl is to Veronica as Reggie is to Archie, except for—well, you'll see.

And, yes, I know full well that no one's sold molasses by the barrel since Lincoln was president, but I don't care, shut up.

# ISSUE THIRTEEN

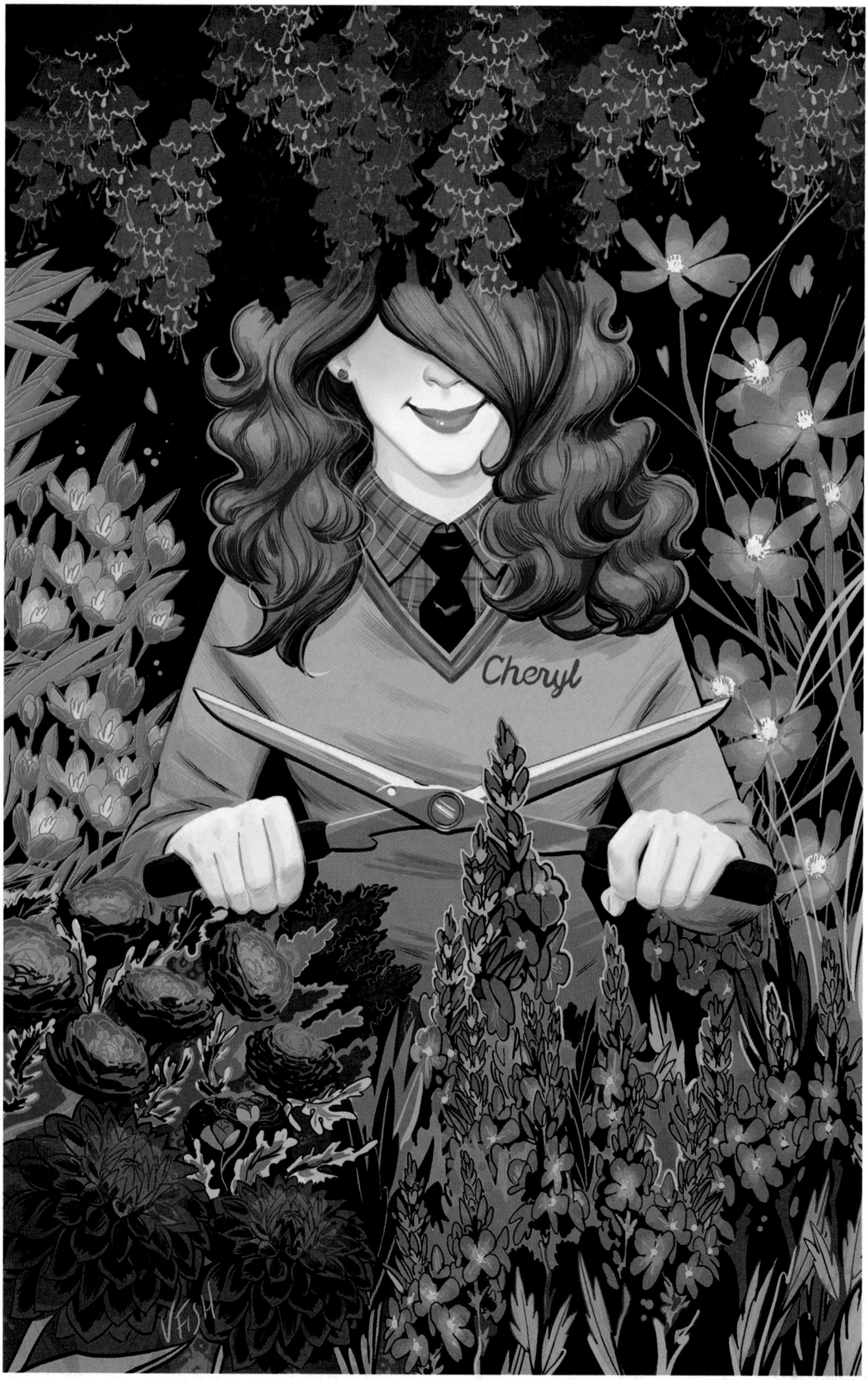
Cheryl
VFISH

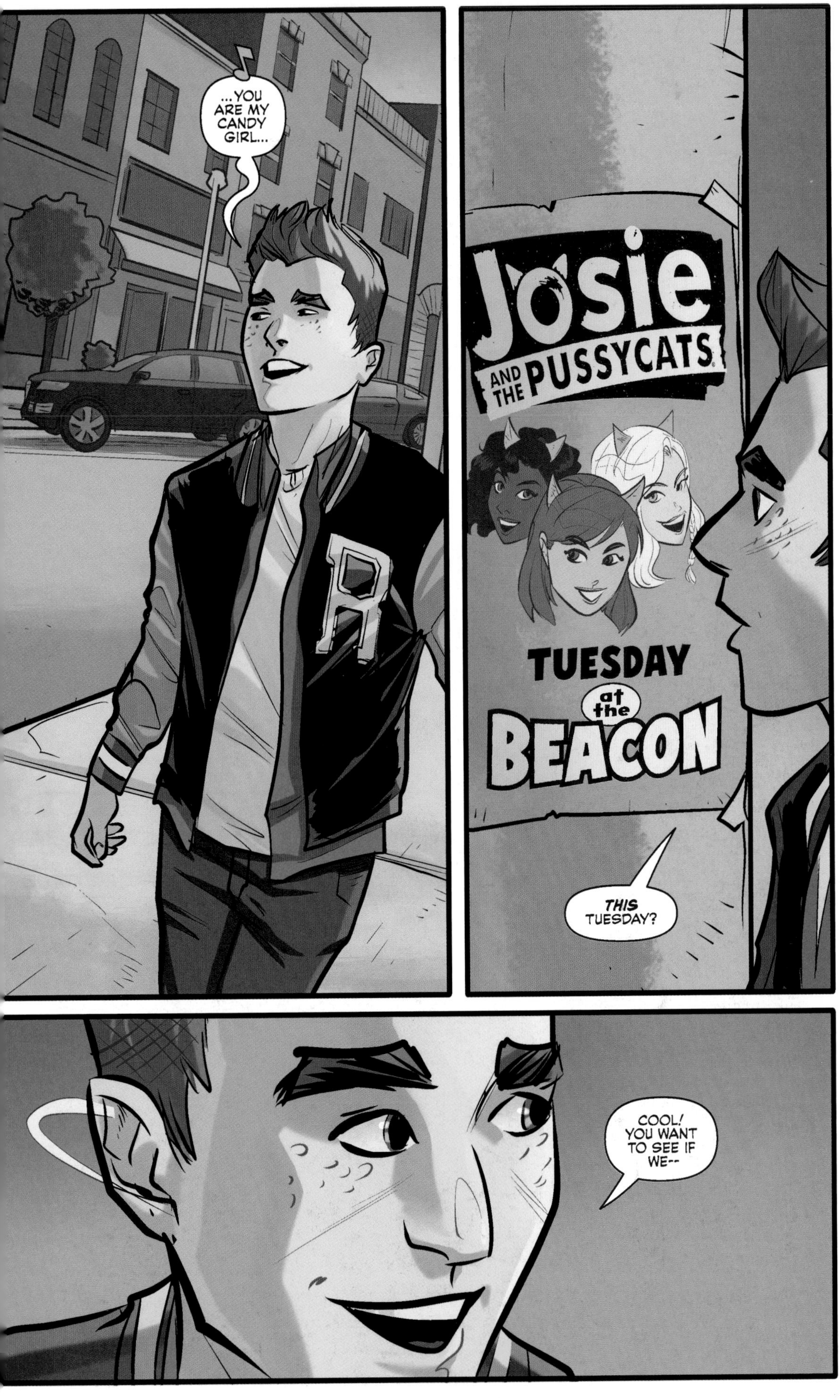
...YOU ARE MY CANDY GIRL...
JOSIE AND THE PUSSYCATS
TUESDAY at the BEACON
THIS TUESDAY?
COOL! YOU WANT TO SEE IF WE--

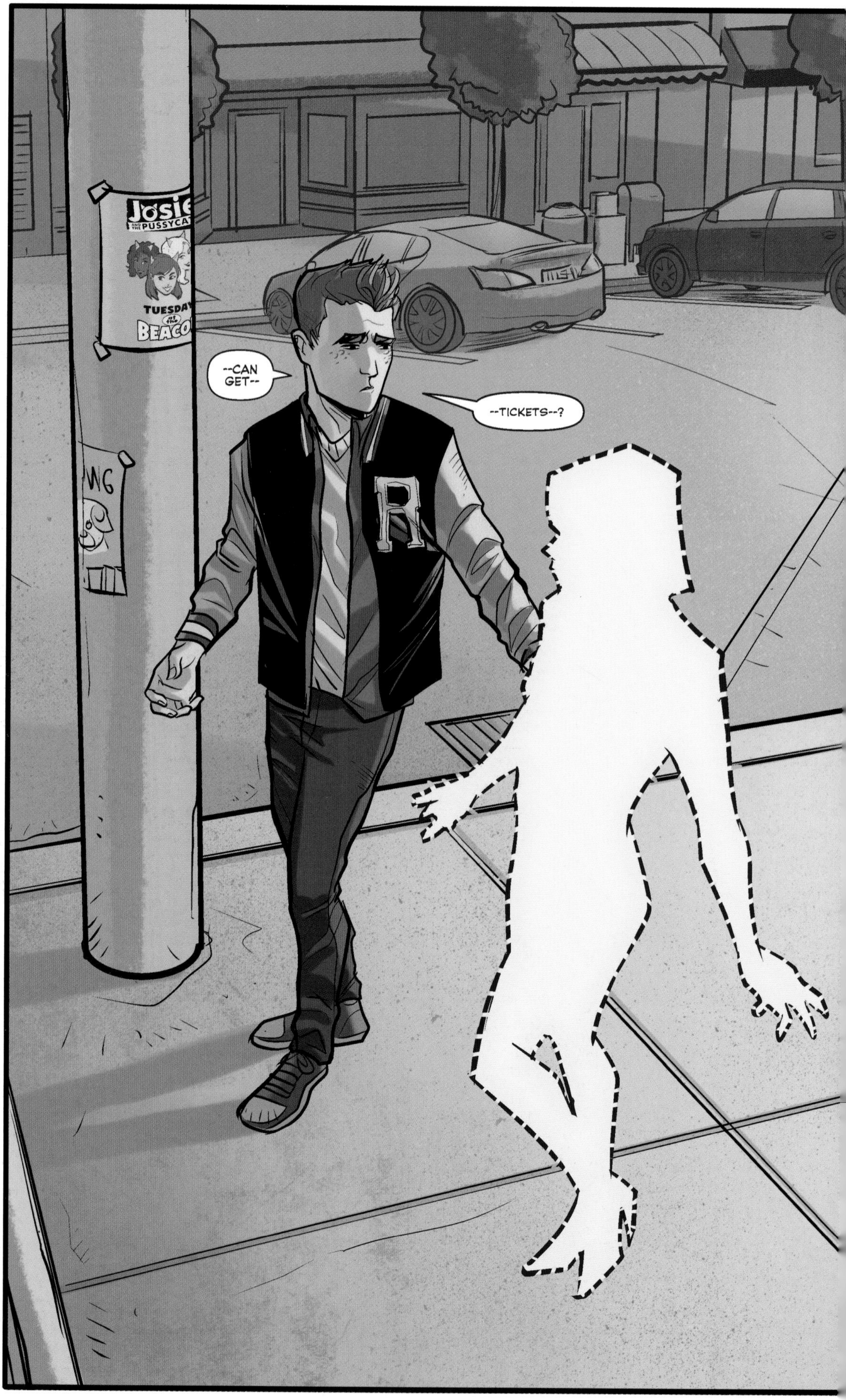
Josie
AND THE PUSSYCAT
TUESDAY
at the
BEACO
--CAN GET--
--TICKETS--?
R

# CHAPTER ONE: WORLDS APART

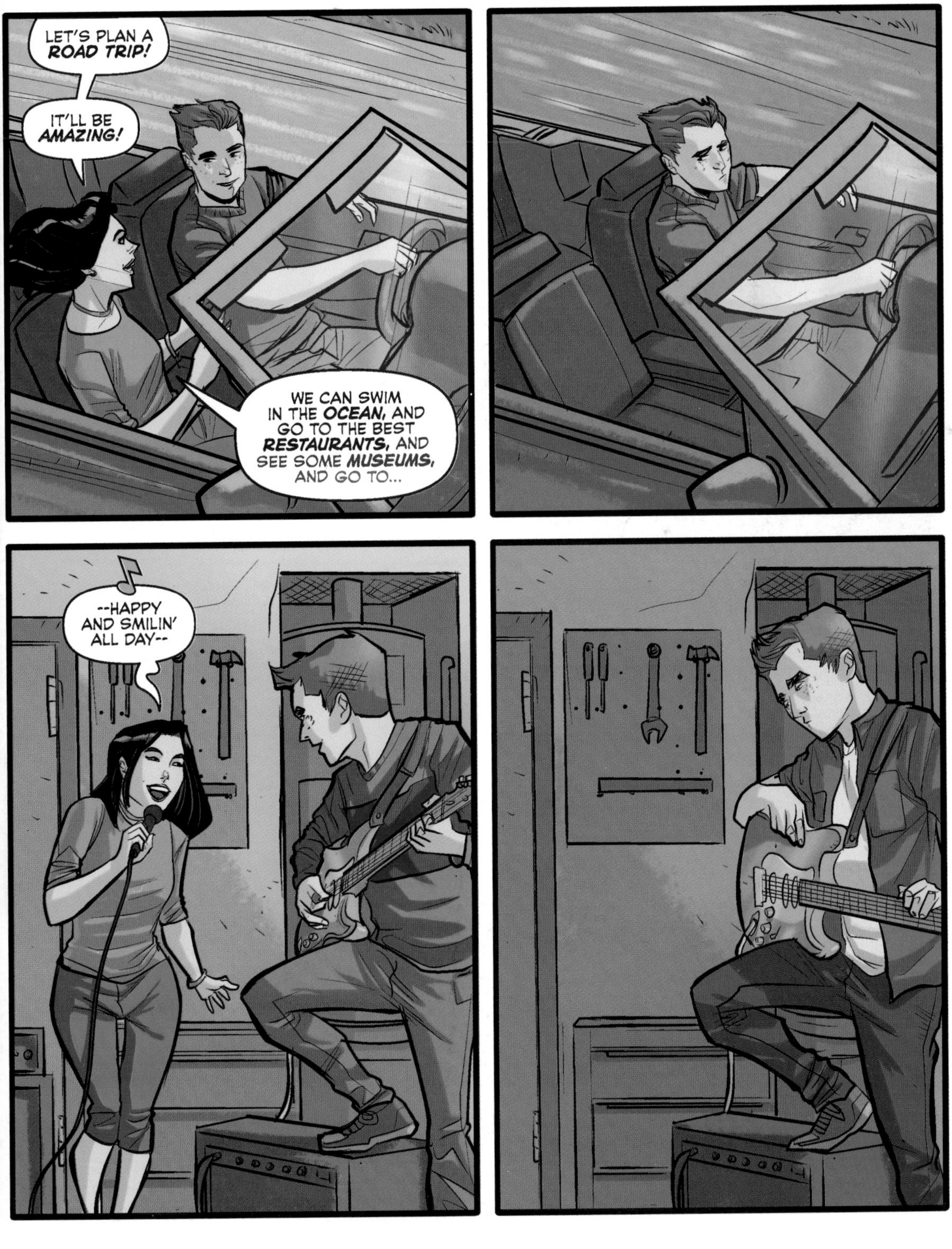
LET'S PLAN A ROAD TRIP!
IT'LL BE AMAZING!
WE CAN SWIM IN THE OCEAN, AND GO TO THE BEST RESTAURANTS, AND SEE SOME MUSEUMS, AND GO TO...
--HAPPY AND SMILIN' ALL DAY--

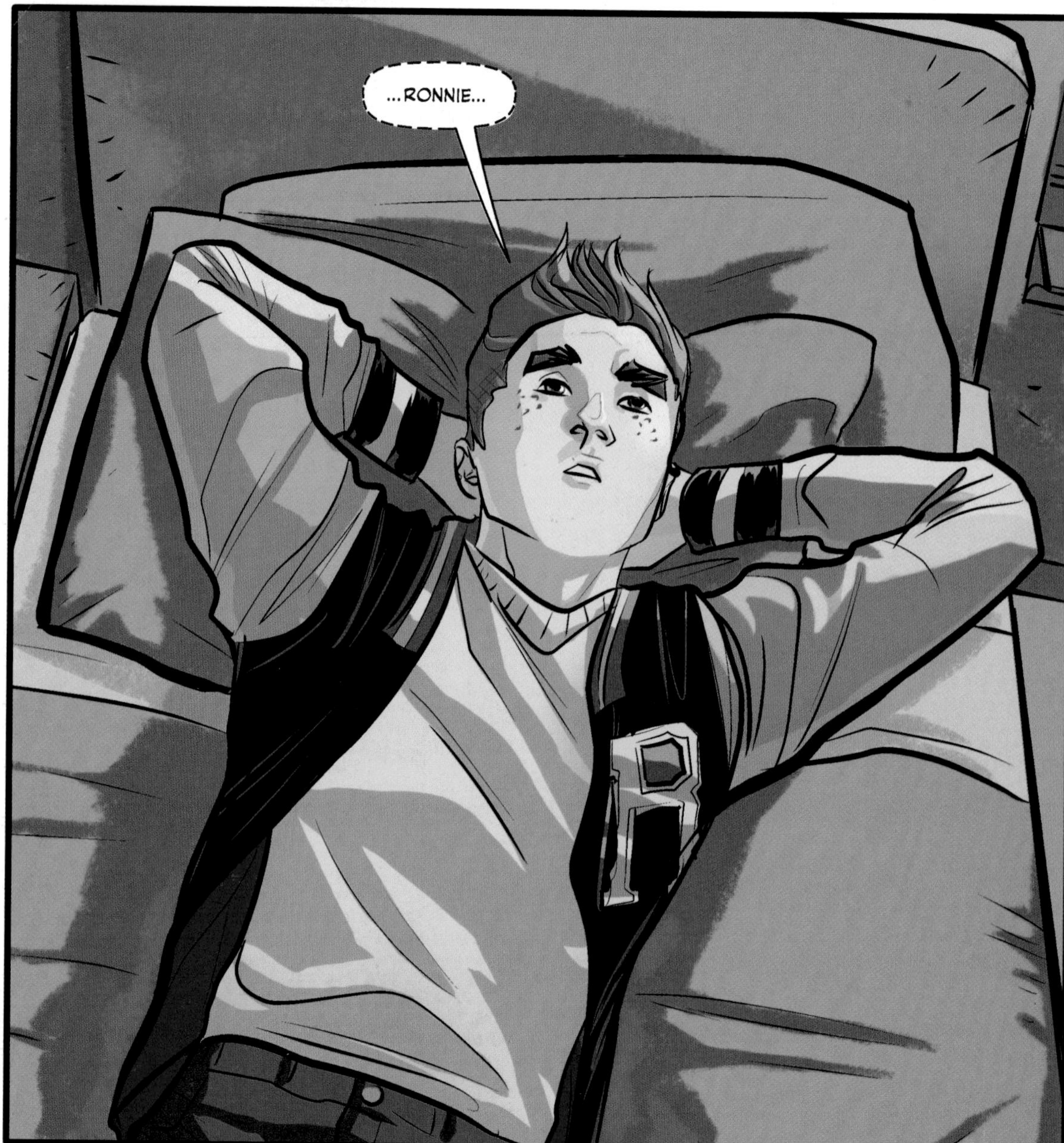
...RONNIE...

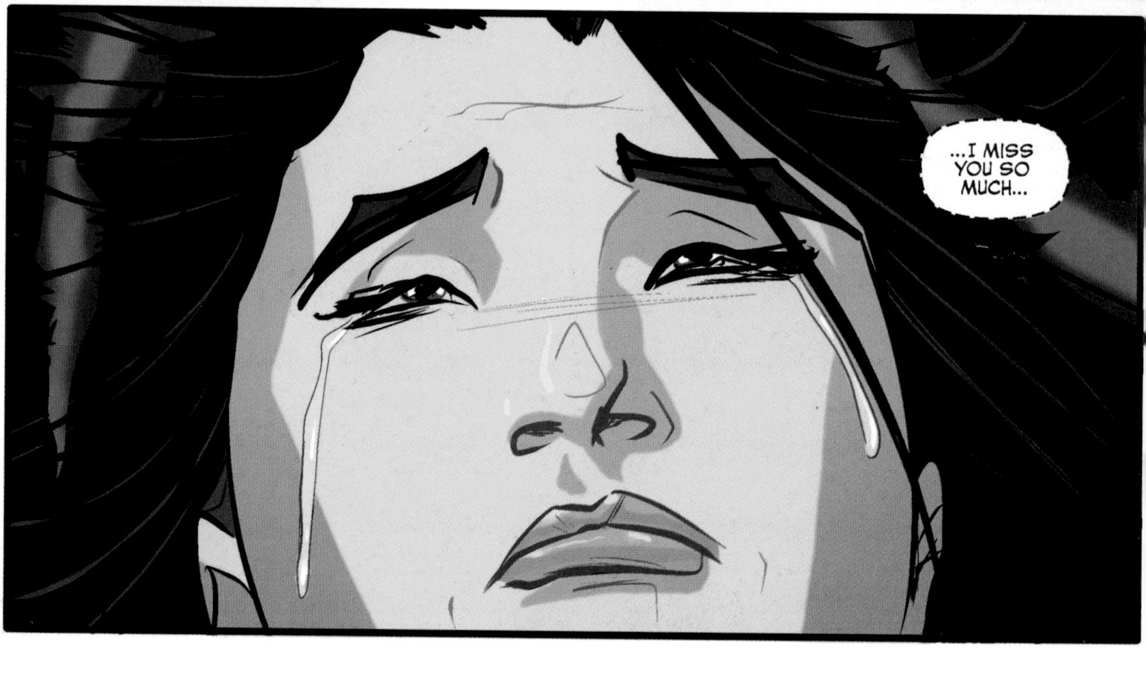
...I MISS YOU SO MUCH...

# CHAPTER TWO: SEEING Red

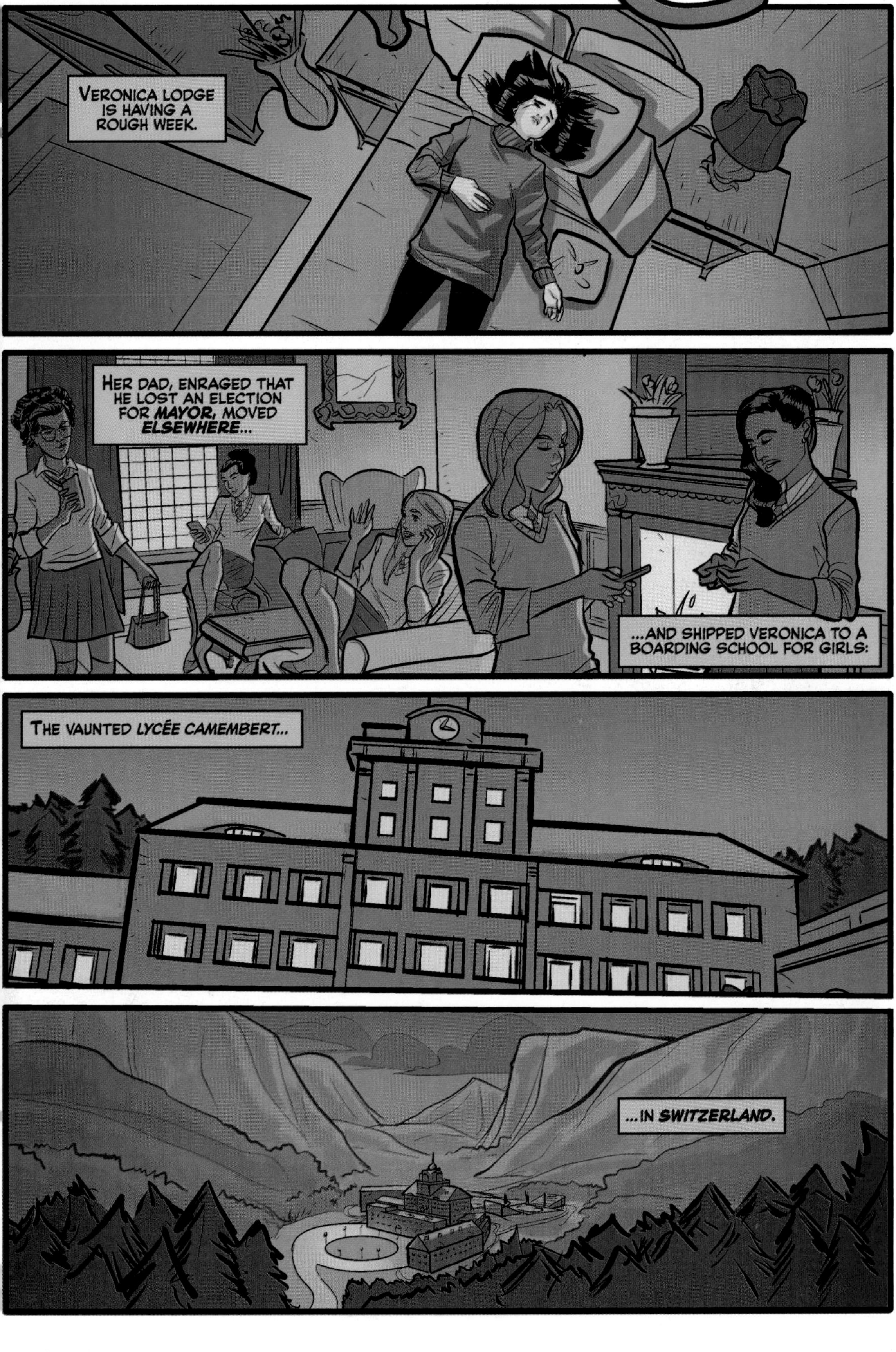
VERONICA LODGE IS HAVING A ROUGH WEEK.
HER DAD, ENRAGED THAT HE LOST AN ELECTION FOR *MAYOR*, MOVED *ELSEWHERE*...
...AND SHIPPED VERONICA TO A BOARDING SCHOOL FOR GIRLS:
THE VAUNTED *LYCÉE CAMEMBERT*...
...IN *SWITZERLAND.*

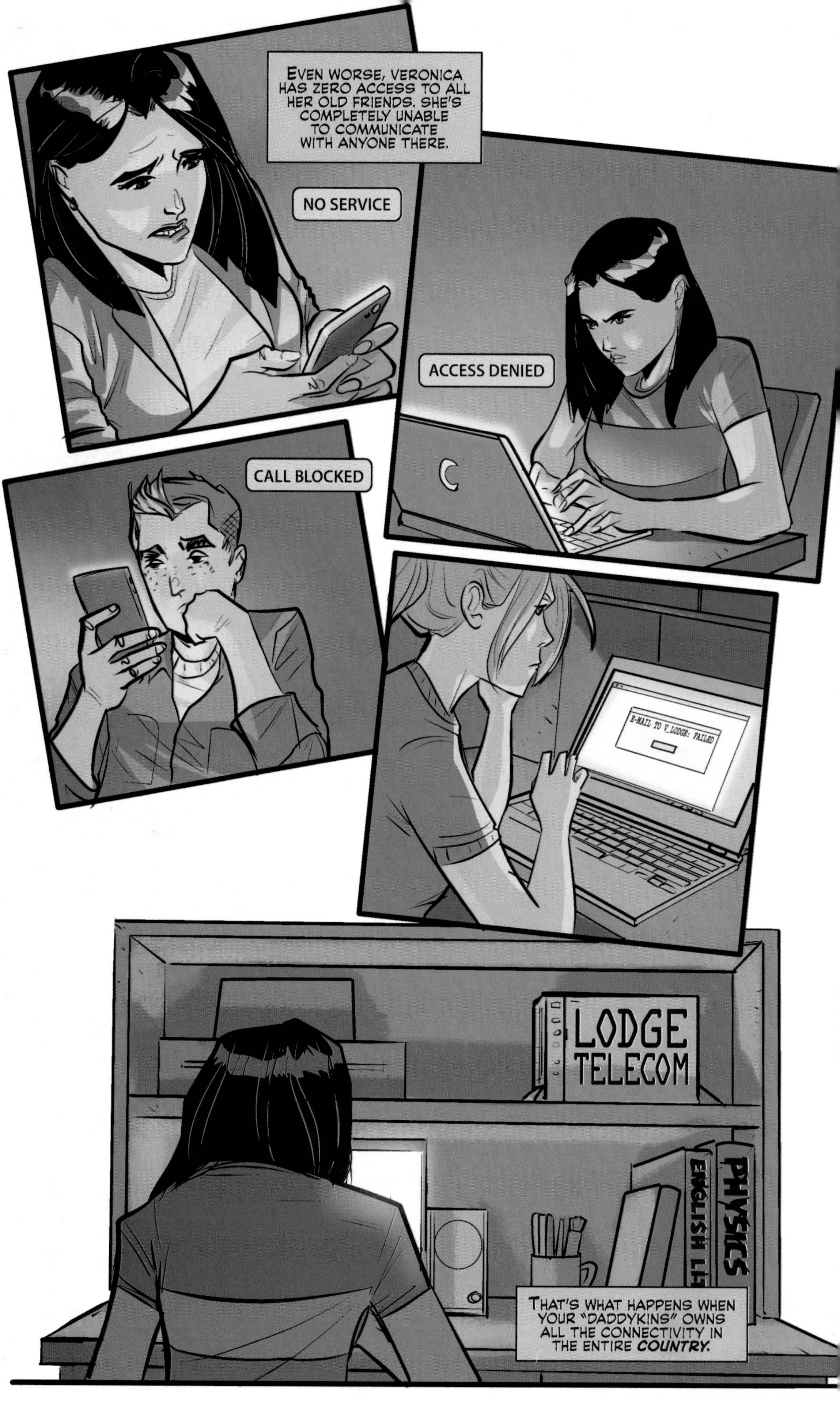

EVEN WORSE, VERONICA HAS ZERO ACCESS TO ALL HER OLD FRIENDS. SHE'S COMPLETELY UNABLE TO COMMUNICATE WITH ANYONE THERE.
NO SERVICE
ACCESS DENIED
CALL BLOCKED
E-MAIL TO V_LODGE: FAILED
LODGE TELECOM
ENGLISH LI
PHYSICS
THAT'S WHAT HAPPENS WHEN YOUR "DADDYKINS" OWNS ALL THE CONNECTIVITY IN THE ENTIRE COUNTRY.

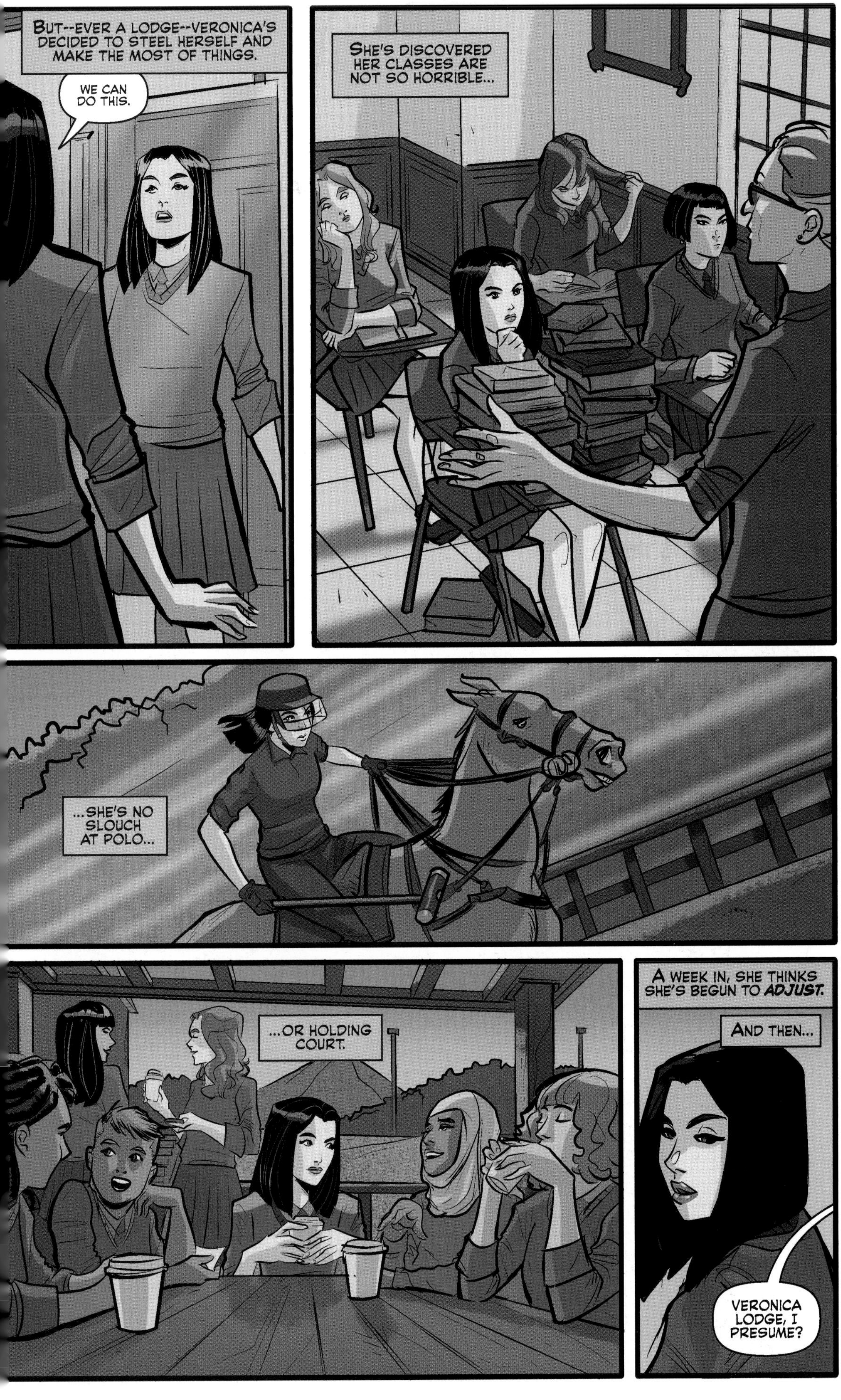

BUT--EVER A LODGE--VERONICA'S DECIDED TO STEEL HERSELF AND MAKE THE MOST OF THINGS.
WE CAN DO THIS.
SHE'S DISCOVERED HER CLASSES ARE NOT SO HORRIBLE...
...SHE'S NO SLOUCH AT POLO...
...OR HOLDING COURT.
A WEEK IN, SHE THINKS SHE'S BEGUN TO ***ADJUST.***
AND THEN...
VERONICA LODGE, I PRESUME?

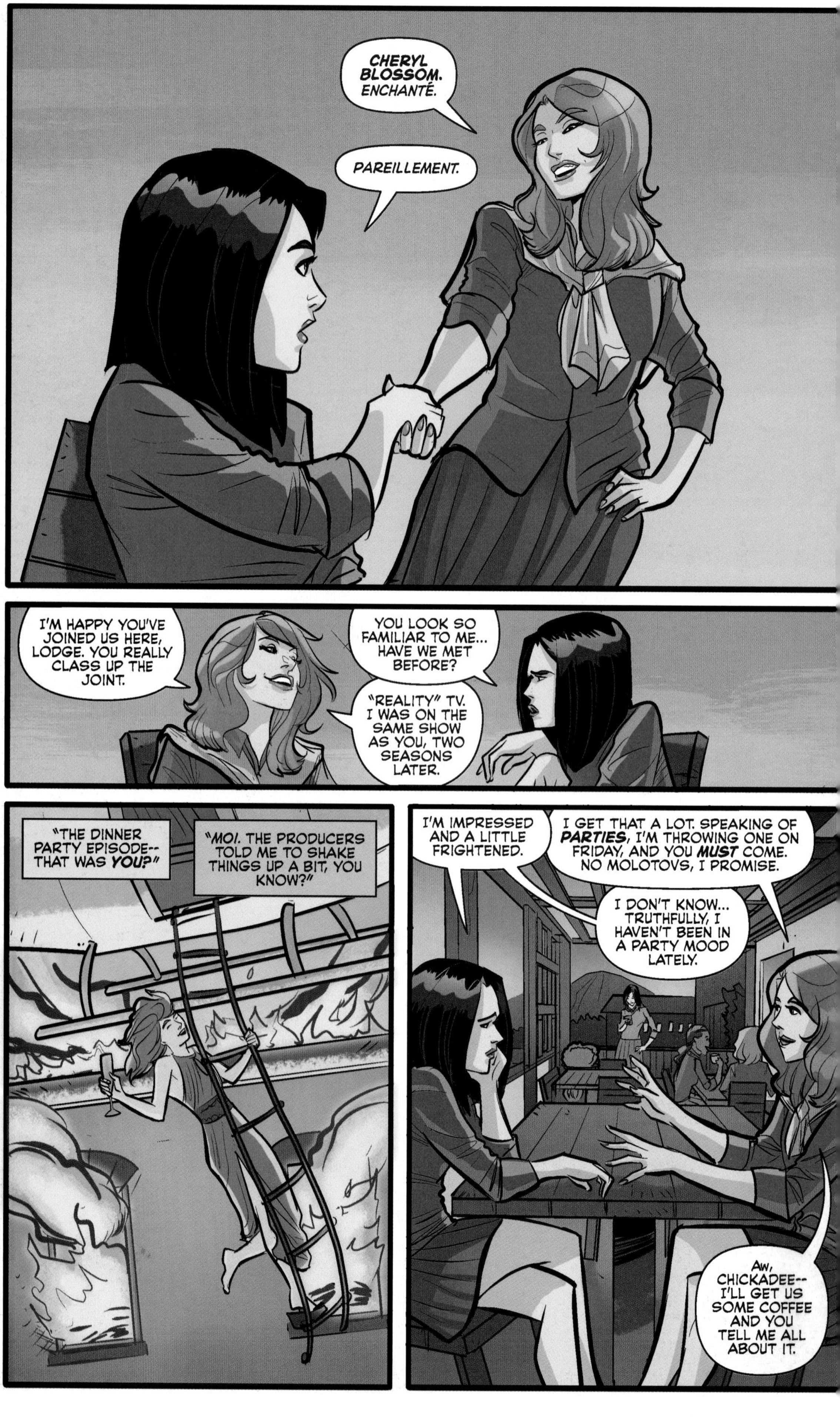
CHERYL BLOSSOM. ENCHANTÉ.
PAREILLEMENT.
I'M HAPPY YOU'VE JOINED US HERE, LODGE. YOU REALLY CLASS UP THE JOINT.
YOU LOOK SO FAMILIAR TO ME... HAVE WE MET BEFORE?
"REALITY" TV. I WAS ON THE SAME SHOW AS YOU, TWO SEASONS LATER.
"THE DINNER PARTY EPISODE--THAT WAS YOU?"
"MOI. THE PRODUCERS TOLD ME TO SHAKE THINGS UP A BIT, YOU KNOW?"
I'M IMPRESSED AND A LITTLE FRIGHTENED.
I GET THAT A LOT. SPEAKING OF PARTIES, I'M THROWING ONE ON FRIDAY, AND YOU MUST COME. NO MOLOTOVS, I PROMISE.
I DON'T KNOW... TRUTHFULLY, I HAVEN'T BEEN IN A PARTY MOOD LATELY.
AW, CHICKADEE--I'LL GET US SOME COFFEE AND YOU TELL ME ALL ABOUT IT.

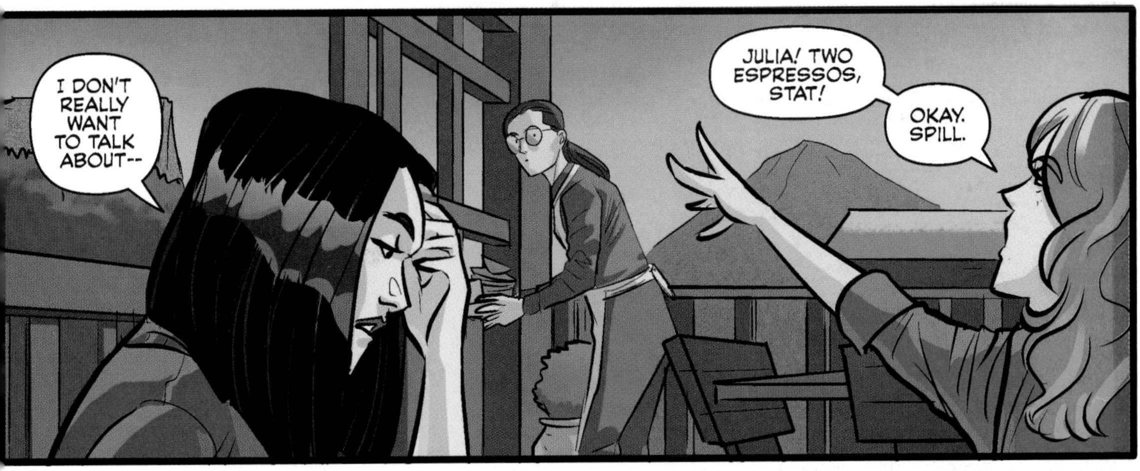
I DON'T REALLY WANT TO TALK ABOUT--
JULIA! TWO ESPRESSOS, STAT!
OKAY. SPILL.

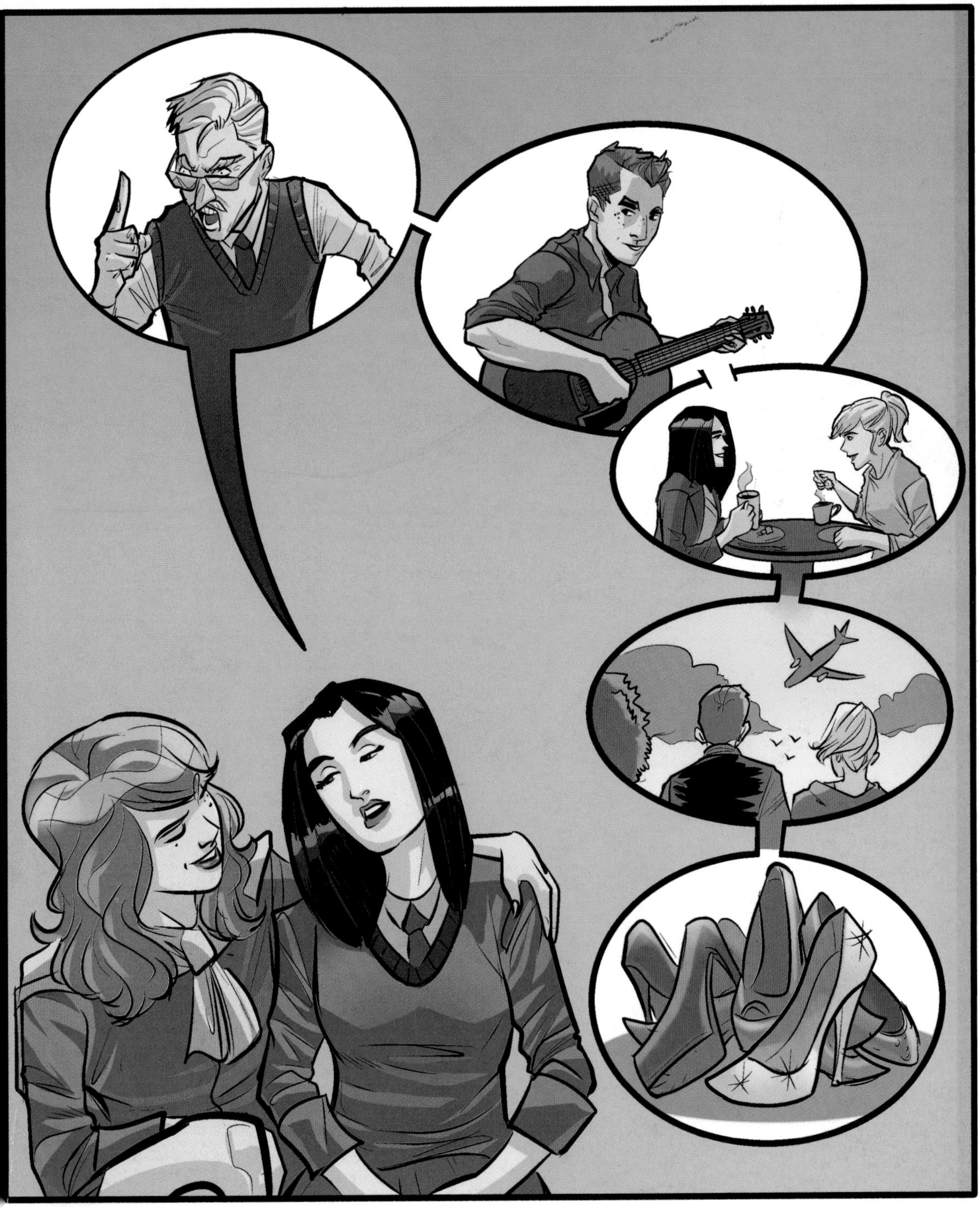

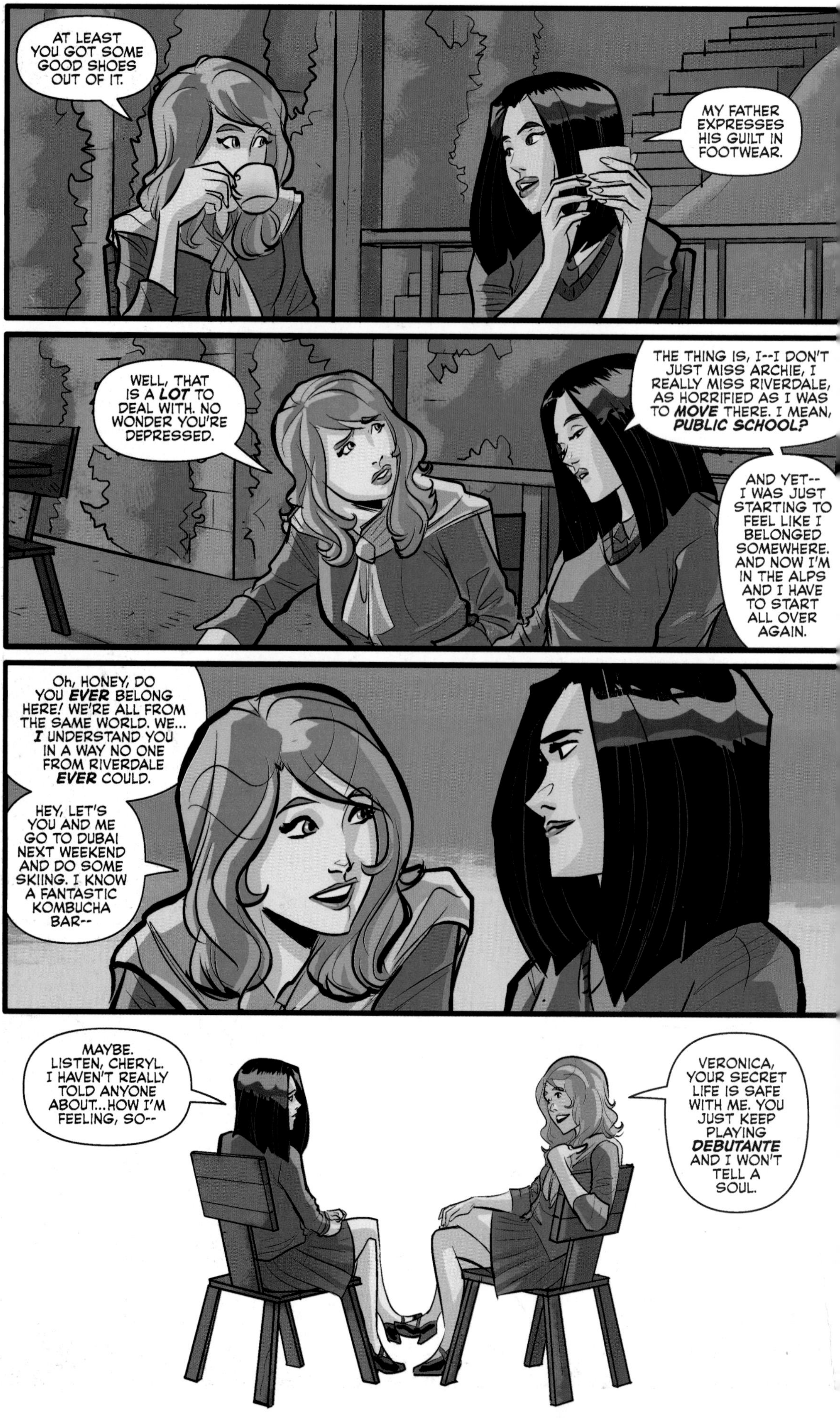
AT LEAST YOU GOT SOME GOOD SHOES OUT OF IT.
MY FATHER EXPRESSES HIS GUILT IN FOOTWEAR.
WELL, THAT IS A **LOT** TO DEAL WITH. NO WONDER YOU'RE DEPRESSED.
THE THING IS, I--I DON'T JUST MISS ARCHIE, I REALLY MISS RIVERDALE, AS HORRIFIED AS I WAS TO **MOVE** THERE. I MEAN, **PUBLIC SCHOOL?**
AND YET-- I WAS JUST STARTING TO FEEL LIKE I BELONGED SOMEWHERE. AND NOW I'M IN THE ALPS AND I HAVE TO START ALL OVER AGAIN.
Oh, HONEY, DO YOU **EVER** BELONG HERE! WE'RE ALL FROM THE SAME WORLD. WE... **I** UNDERSTAND YOU IN A WAY NO ONE FROM RIVERDALE **EVER** COULD.
HEY, LET'S YOU AND ME GO TO DUBAI NEXT WEEKEND AND DO SOME SKIING. I KNOW A FANTASTIC KOMBUCHA BAR--
MAYBE. LISTEN, CHERYL. I HAVEN'T REALLY TOLD ANYONE ABOUT...HOW I'M FEELING, SO--
VERONICA, YOUR SECRET LIFE IS SAFE WITH ME. YOU JUST KEEP PLAYING **DEBUTANTE** AND I WON'T TELL A SOUL.

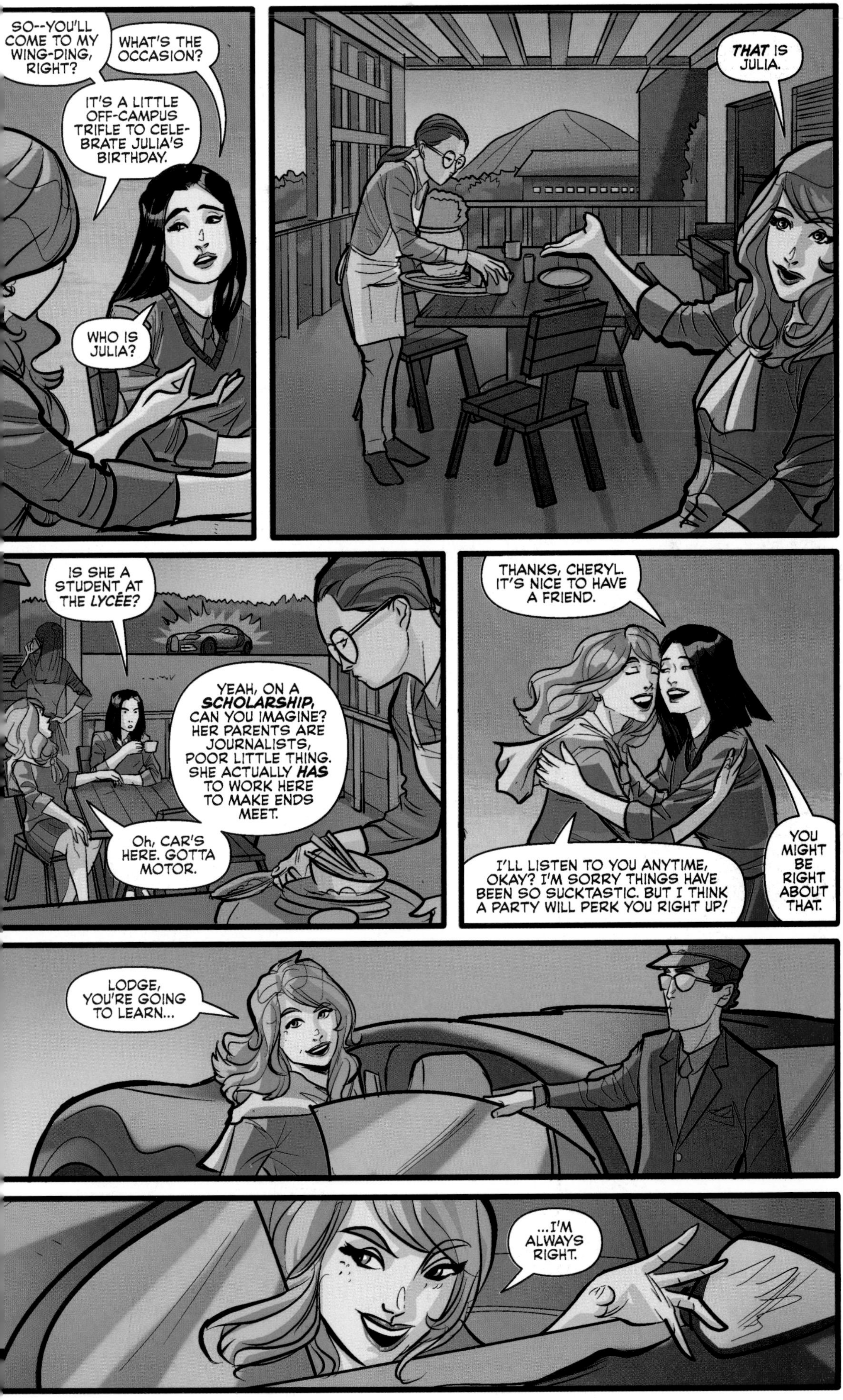
SO--YOU'LL COME TO MY WING-DING, RIGHT?
WHAT'S THE OCCASION?
IT'S A LITTLE OFF-CAMPUS TRIFLE TO CELE-BRATE JULIA'S BIRTHDAY.
WHO IS JULIA?
*THAT* IS JULIA.
IS SHE A STUDENT AT THE *LYCÉE*?
YEAH, ON A ***SCHOLARSHIP***, CAN YOU IMAGINE? HER PARENTS ARE JOURNALISTS, POOR LITTLE THING. SHE ACTUALLY ***HAS*** TO WORK HERE TO MAKE ENDS MEET.
Oh, CAR'S HERE. GOTTA MOTOR.
THANKS, CHERYL. IT'S NICE TO HAVE A FRIEND.
I'LL LISTEN TO YOU ANYTIME, OKAY? I'M SORRY THINGS HAVE BEEN SO SUCKTASTIC. BUT I THINK A PARTY WILL PERK YOU RIGHT UP!
YOU MIGHT BE RIGHT ABOUT THAT.
LODGE, YOU'RE GOING TO LEARN...
...I'M ALWAYS RIGHT.

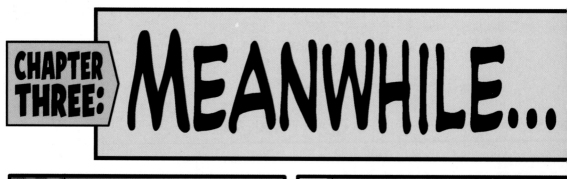

# CHAPTER THREE: MEANWHILE...

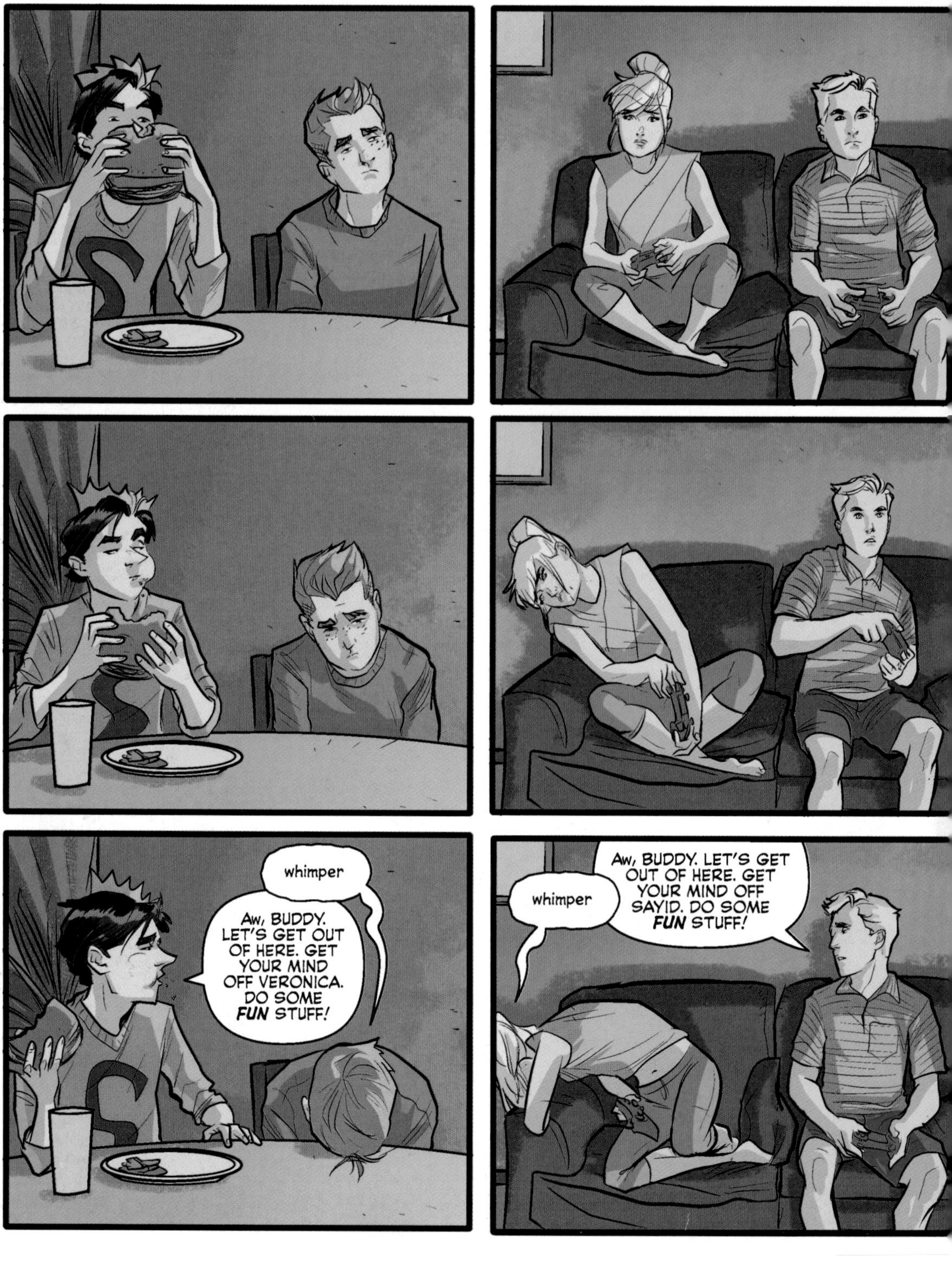

whimper
Aw, BUDDY. LET'S GET OUT OF HERE. GET YOUR MIND OFF VERONICA. DO SOME ***FUN*** STUFF!
whimper
Aw, BUDDY. LET'S GET OUT OF HERE. GET YOUR MIND OFF SAYID. DO SOME ***FUN*** STUFF!

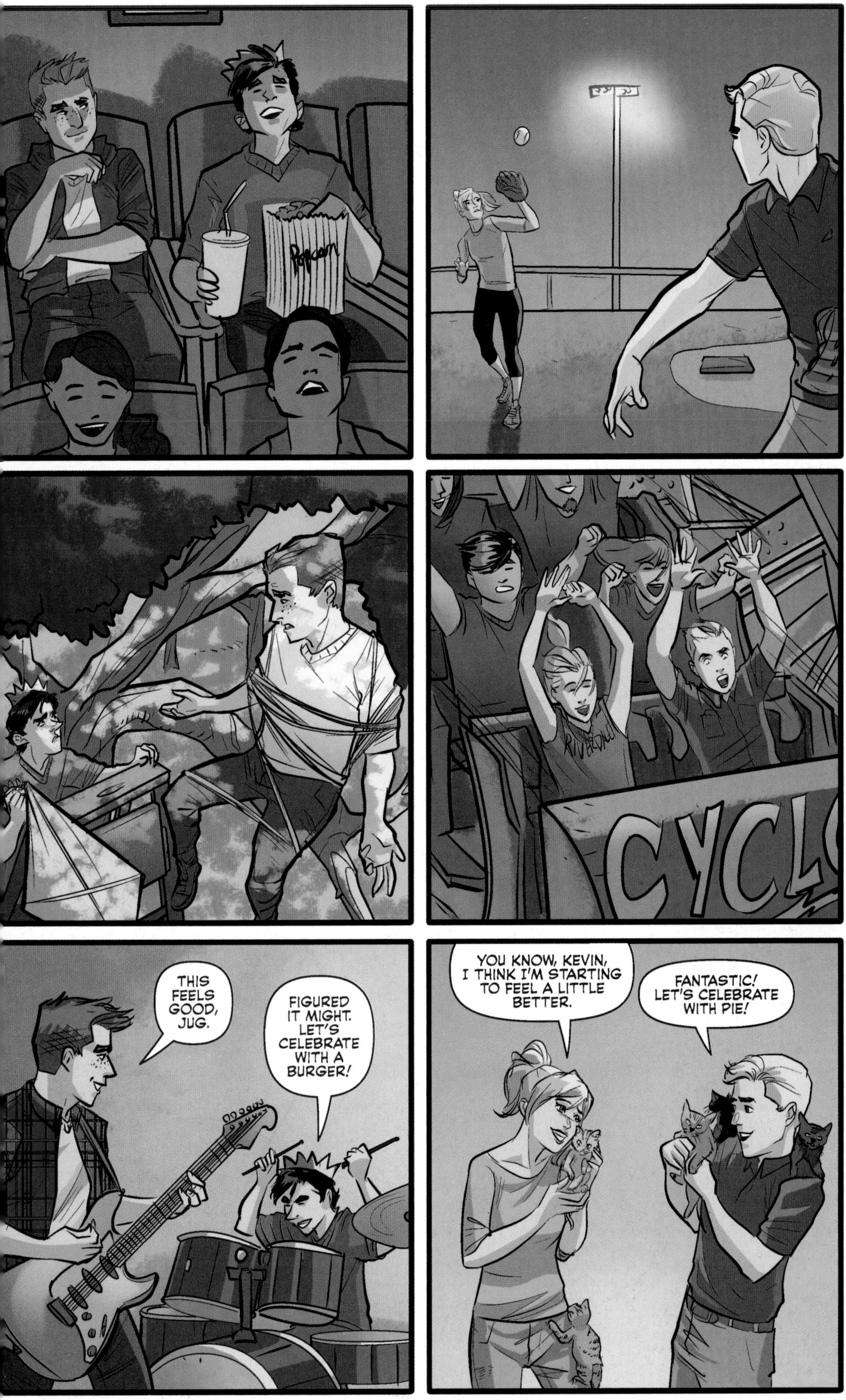
THIS FEELS GOOD, JUG.
FIGURED IT MIGHT. LET'S CELEBRATE WITH A BURGER!
YOU KNOW, KEVIN, I THINK I'M STARTING TO FEEL A LITTLE BETTER.
FANTASTIC! LET'S CELEBRATE WITH PIE!

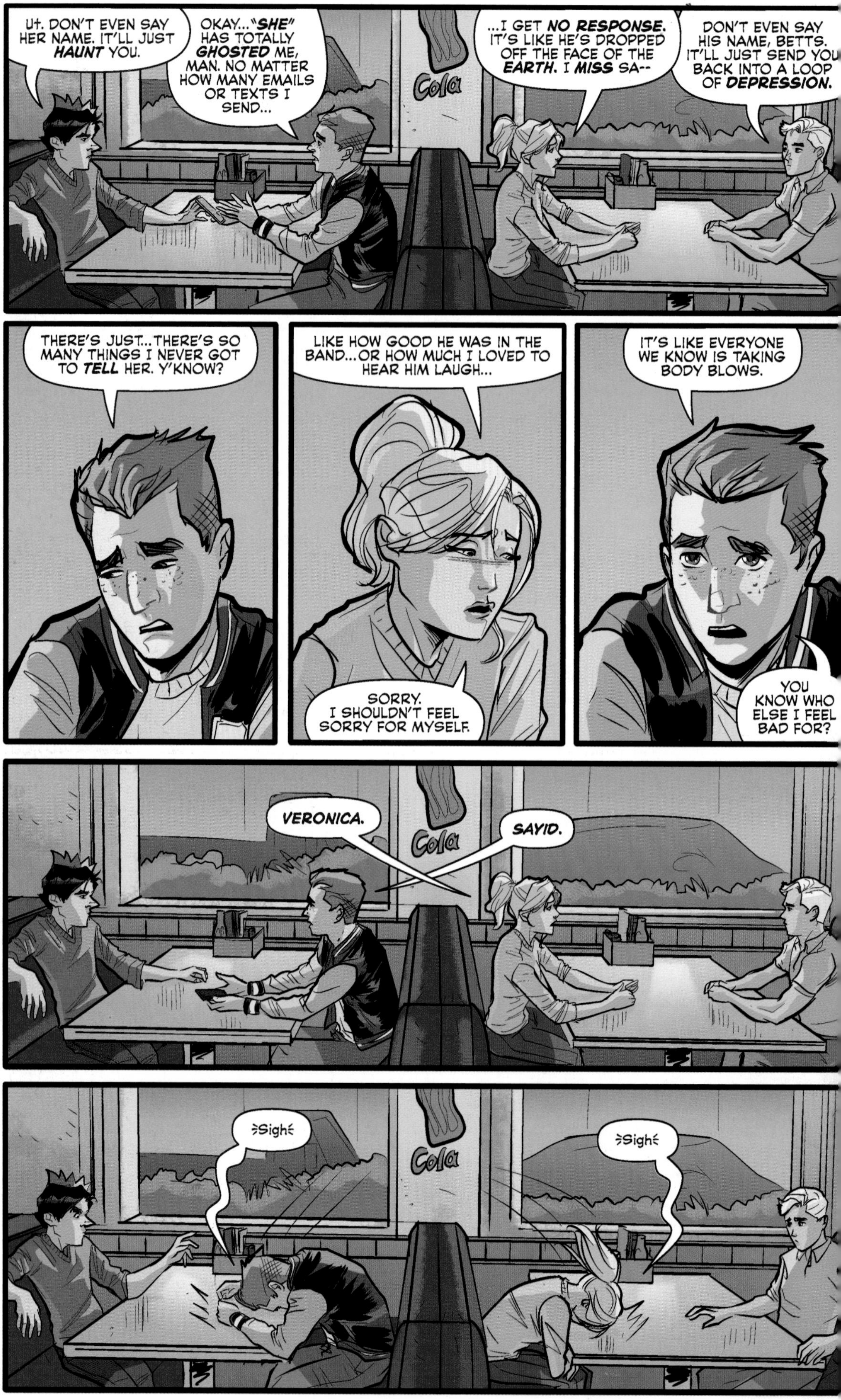
Ut. DON'T EVEN SAY HER NAME. IT'LL JUST HAUNT YOU.
OKAY... "SHE" HAS TOTALLY GHOSTED ME, MAN. NO MATTER HOW MANY EMAILS OR TEXTS I SEND...
...I GET NO RESPONSE. IT'S LIKE HE'S DROPPED OFF THE FACE OF THE EARTH. I MISS SA--
DON'T EVEN SAY HIS NAME, BETTS. IT'LL JUST SEND YOU BACK INTO A LOOP OF DEPRESSION.
THERE'S JUST...THERE'S SO MANY THINGS I NEVER GOT TO TELL HER. Y'KNOW?
LIKE HOW GOOD HE WAS IN THE BAND...OR HOW MUCH I LOVED TO HEAR HIM LAUGH...
SORRY. I SHOULDN'T FEEL SORRY FOR MYSELF.
IT'S LIKE EVERYONE WE KNOW IS TAKING BODY BLOWS.
YOU KNOW WHO ELSE I FEEL BAD FOR?
Cola
VERONICA.
SAYID.
Cola
Sigh
Sigh
Cola

# CHAPTER FOUR: Surprise Party

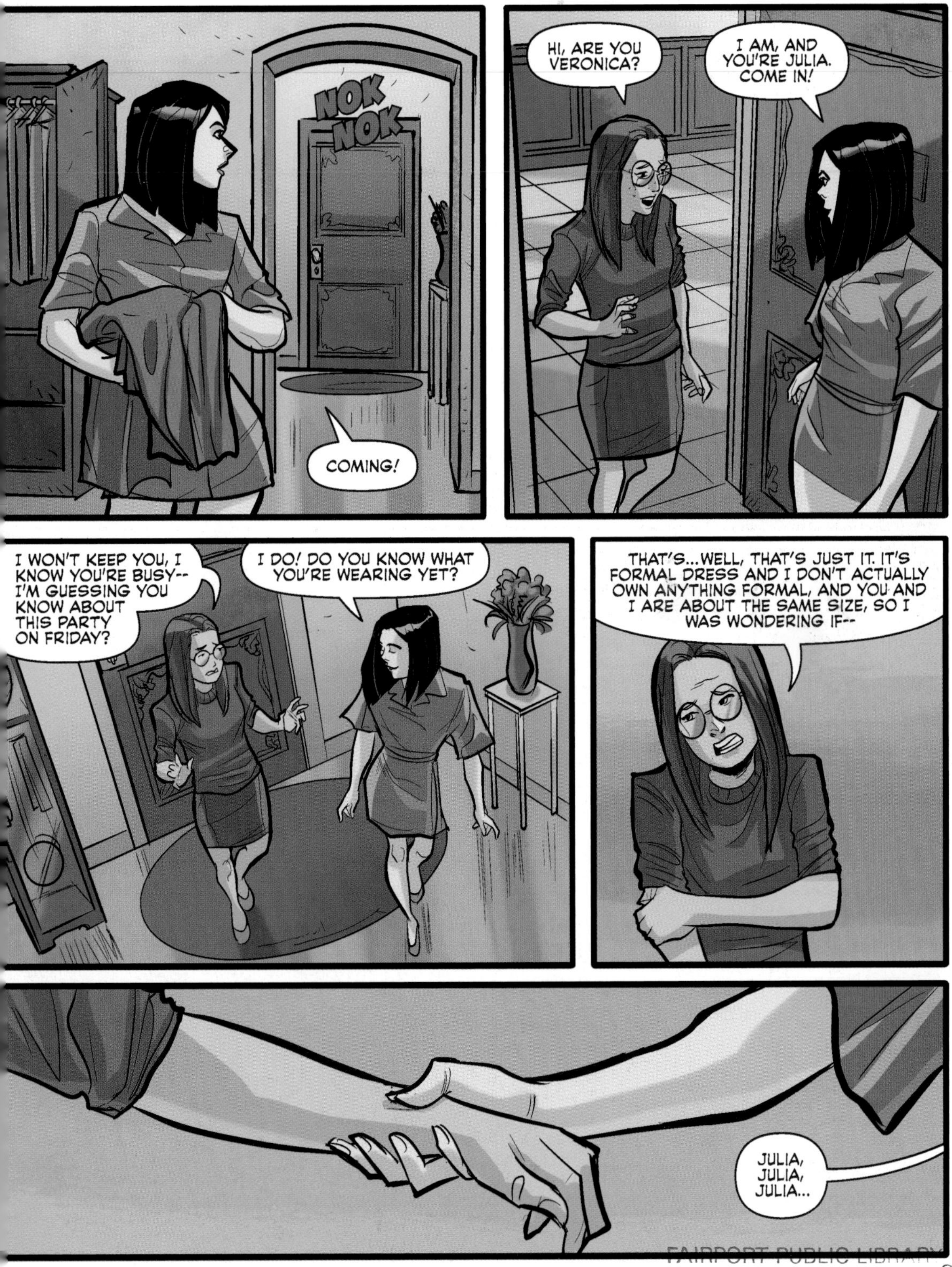
NOK NOK
COMING!
HI, ARE YOU VERONICA?
I AM, AND YOU'RE JULIA. COME IN!
I WON'T KEEP YOU, I KNOW YOU'RE BUSY-- I'M GUESSING YOU KNOW ABOUT THIS PARTY ON FRIDAY?
I DO! DO YOU KNOW WHAT YOU'RE WEARING YET?
THAT'S...WELL, THAT'S JUST IT. IT'S FORMAL DRESS AND I DON'T ACTUALLY OWN ANYTHING FORMAL, AND YOU AND I ARE ABOUT THE SAME SIZE, SO I WAS WONDERING IF--
JULIA, JULIA, JULIA...

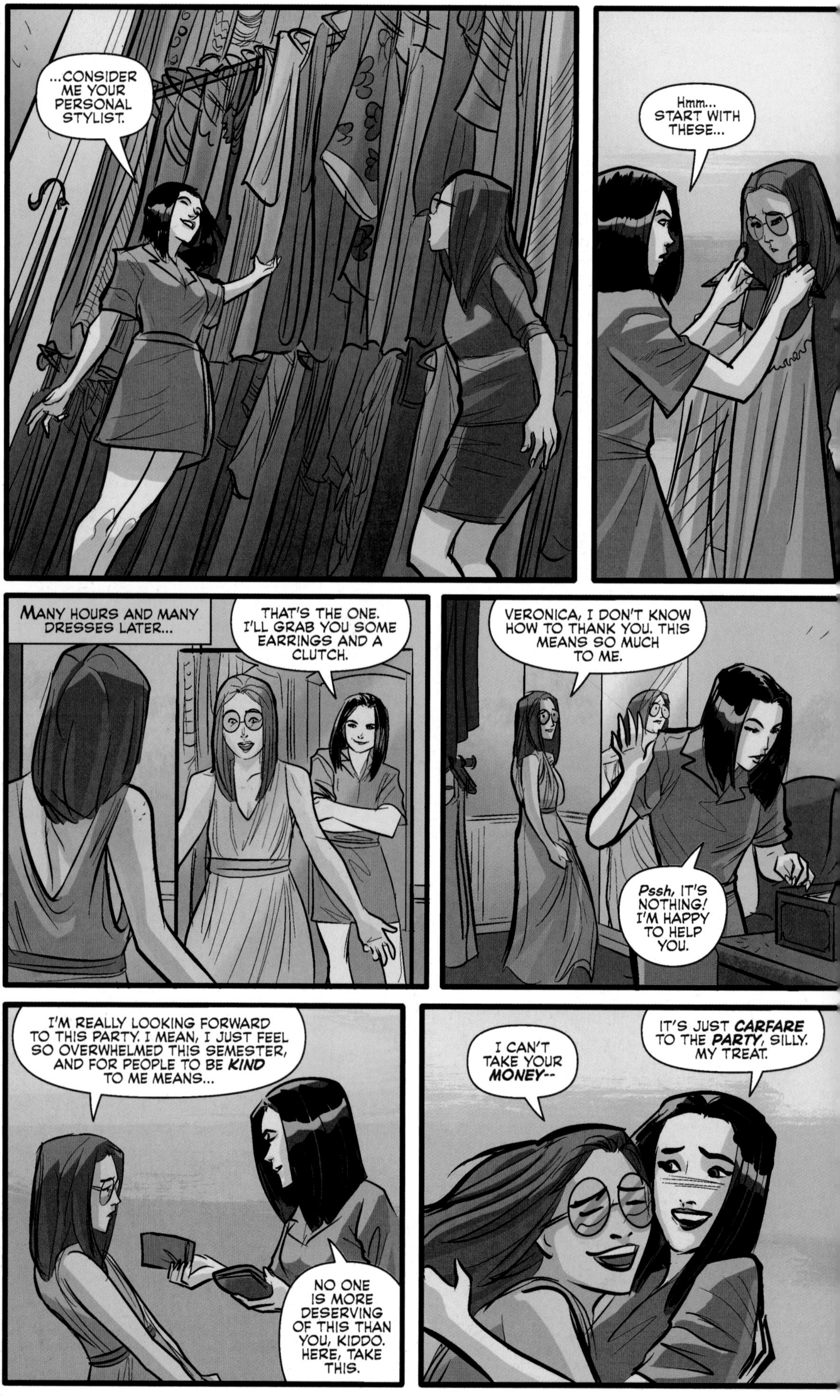
...CONSIDER ME YOUR PERSONAL STYLIST.
Hmm... START WITH THESE...
MANY HOURS AND MANY DRESSES LATER...
THAT'S THE ONE. I'LL GRAB YOU SOME EARRINGS AND A CLUTCH.
VERONICA, I DON'T KNOW HOW TO THANK YOU. THIS MEANS SO MUCH TO ME.
Pssh, IT'S NOTHING! I'M HAPPY TO HELP YOU.
I'M REALLY LOOKING FORWARD TO THIS PARTY. I MEAN, I JUST FEEL SO OVERWHELMED THIS SEMESTER, AND FOR PEOPLE TO BE KIND TO ME MEANS...
NO ONE IS MORE DESERVING OF THIS THAN YOU, KIDDO. HERE, TAKE THIS.
I CAN'T TAKE YOUR MONEY--
IT'S JUST CARFARE TO THE PARTY, SILLY. MY TREAT.

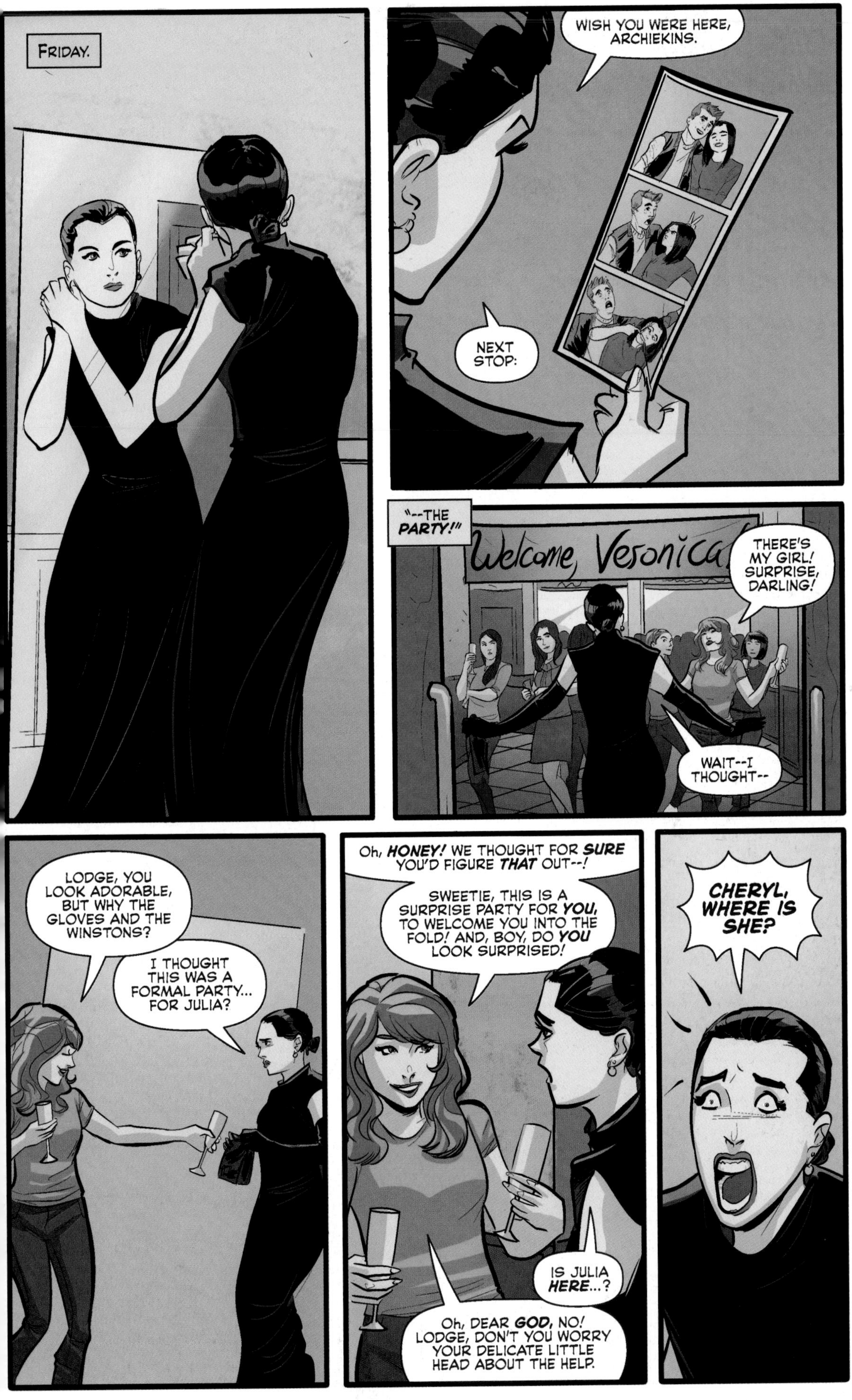
FRIDAY.
WISH YOU WERE HERE, ARCHIEKINS.
NEXT STOP:
"--THE PARTY!"
Welcome, Veronica!
THERE'S MY GIRL! SURPRISE, DARLING!
WAIT--I THOUGHT--
LODGE, YOU LOOK ADORABLE, BUT WHY THE GLOVES AND THE WINSTONS?
I THOUGHT THIS WAS A FORMAL PARTY... FOR JULIA?
Oh, HONEY! WE THOUGHT FOR SURE YOU'D FIGURE THAT OUT--!
SWEETIE, THIS IS A SURPRISE PARTY FOR YOU, TO WELCOME YOU INTO THE FOLD! AND, BOY, DO YOU LOOK SURPRISED!
IS JULIA HERE...?
Oh, DEAR GOD, NO! LODGE, DON'T YOU WORRY YOUR DELICATE LITTLE HEAD ABOUT THE HELP.
CHERYL, WHERE IS SHE?

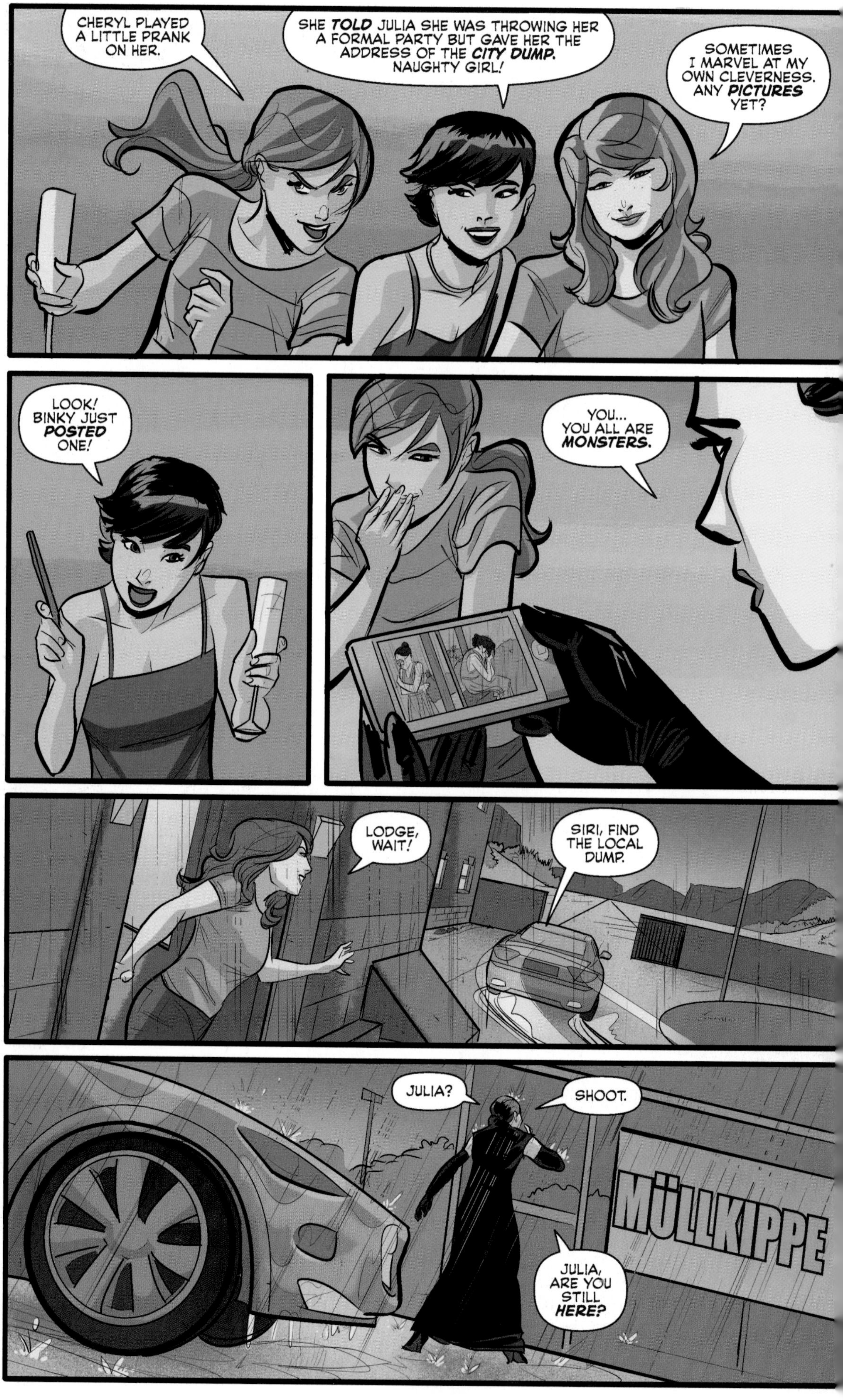
CHERYL PLAYED A LITTLE PRANK ON HER.
SHE TOLD JULIA SHE WAS THROWING HER A FORMAL PARTY BUT GAVE HER THE ADDRESS OF THE CITY DUMP. NAUGHTY GIRL!
SOMETIMES I MARVEL AT MY OWN CLEVERNESS. ANY PICTURES YET?
LOOK! BINKY JUST POSTED ONE!
YOU... YOU ALL ARE MONSTERS.
LODGE, WAIT!
SIRI, FIND THE LOCAL DUMP.
JULIA?
SHOOT.
MÜLLKIPPE
JULIA, ARE YOU STILL HERE?

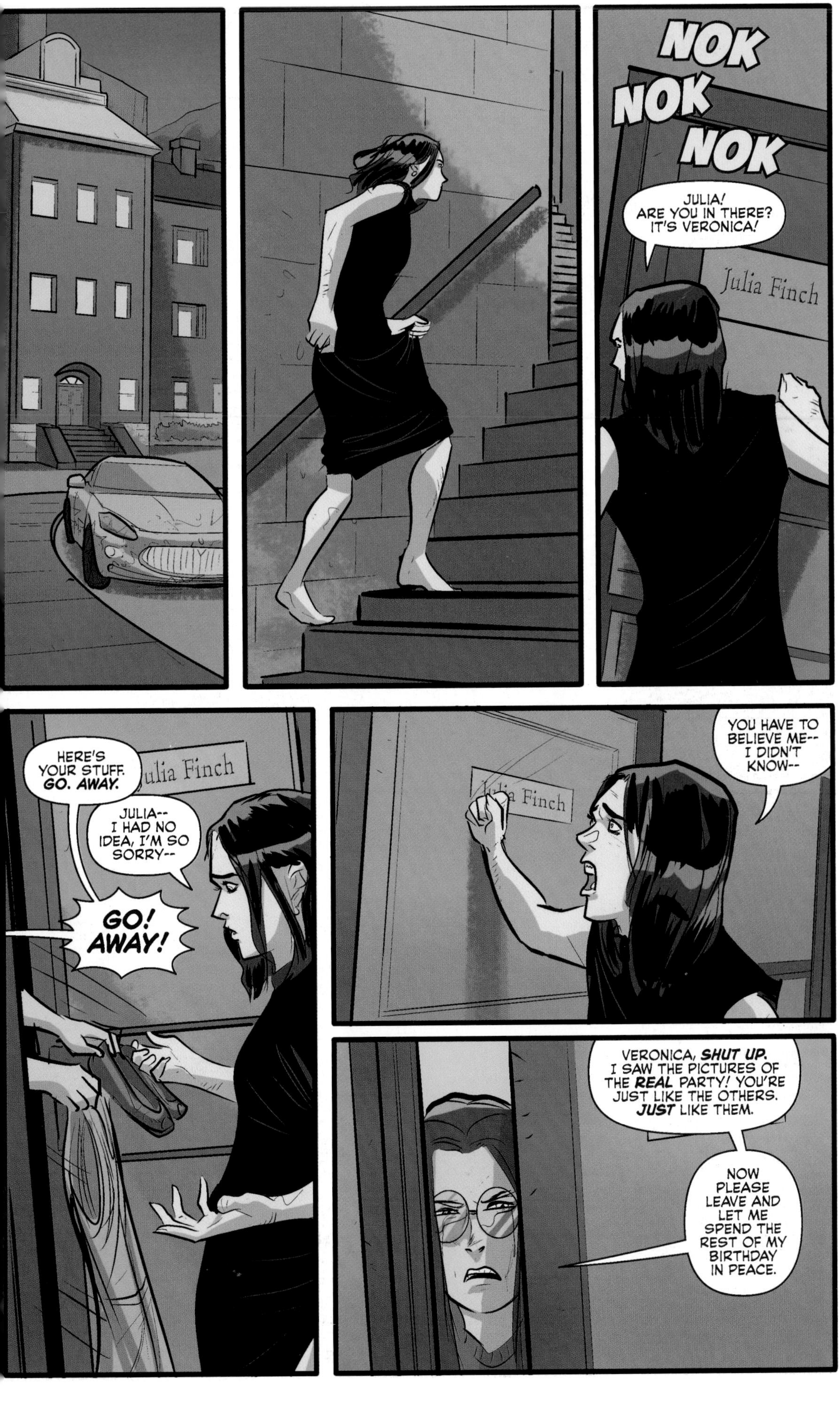
NOK
NOK
NOK
JULIA! ARE YOU IN THERE? IT'S VERONICA!
Julia Finch
Julia Finch
HERE'S YOUR STUFF. **GO. AWAY.**
JULIA-- I HAD NO IDEA, I'M SO SORRY--
**GO! AWAY!**
YOU HAVE TO BELIEVE ME-- I DIDN'T KNOW--
Julia Finch
VERONICA, **SHUT UP.** I SAW THE PICTURES OF THE **REAL** PARTY! YOU'RE JUST LIKE THE OTHERS. **JUST** LIKE THEM.
NOW PLEASE LEAVE AND LET ME SPEND THE REST OF MY BIRTHDAY IN PEACE.

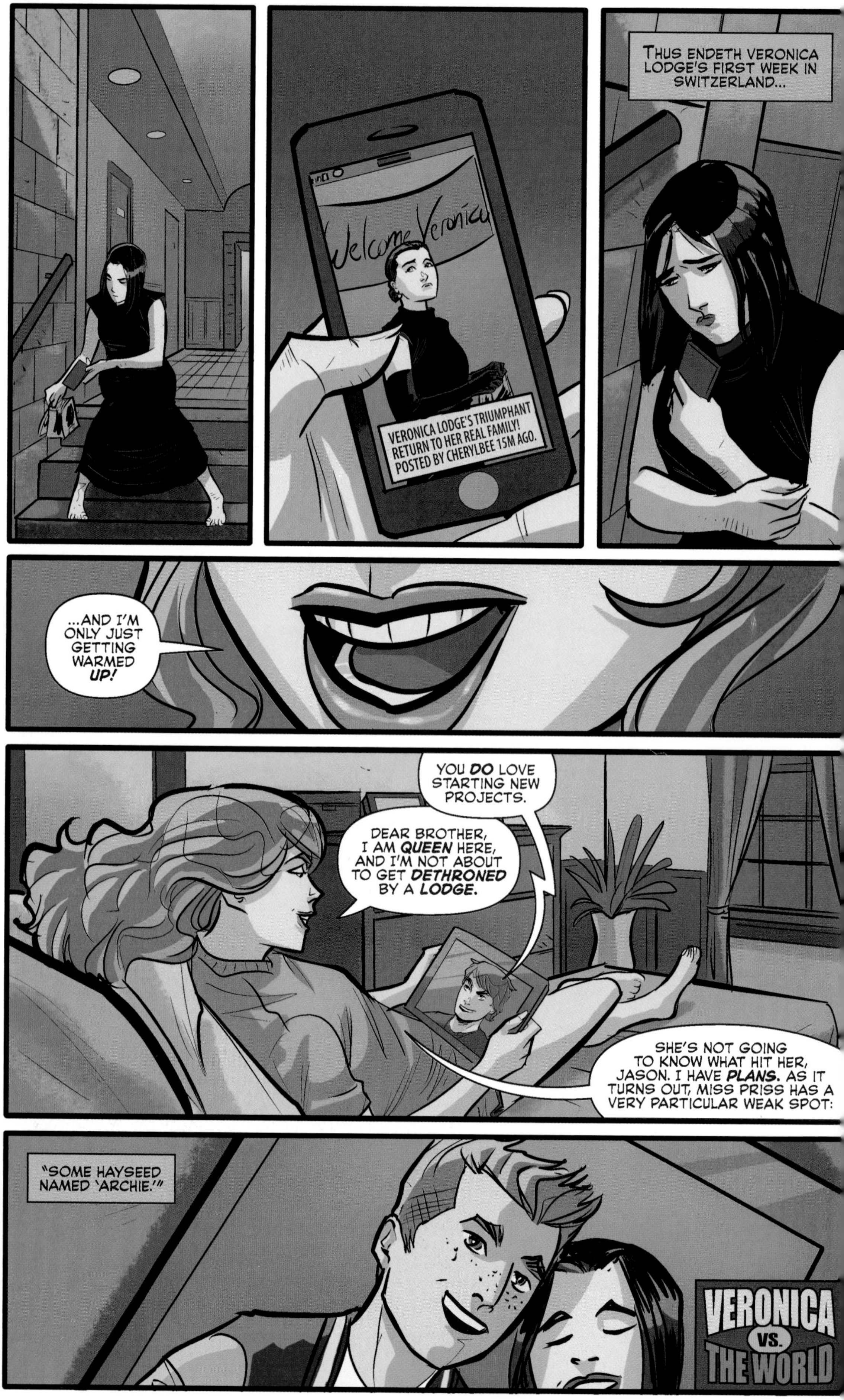

Welcome Veronica
VERONICA LODGE'S TRIUMPHANT RETURN TO HER REAL FAMILY! POSTED BY CHERYLBEE 15M AGO.
THUS ENDETH VERONICA LODGE'S FIRST WEEK IN SWITZERLAND...
...AND I'M ONLY JUST GETTING WARMED UP!
YOU DO LOVE STARTING NEW PROJECTS.
DEAR BROTHER, I AM QUEEN HERE, AND I'M NOT ABOUT TO GET DETHRONED BY A LODGE.
SHE'S NOT GOING TO KNOW WHAT HIT HER, JASON. I HAVE PLANS. AS IT TURNS OUT, MISS PRISS HAS A VERY PARTICULAR WEAK SPOT:
"SOME HAYSEED NAMED 'ARCHIE.'"
VERONICA VS. THE WORLD

TO BE CONTINUED...

# ISSUE FOURTEEN

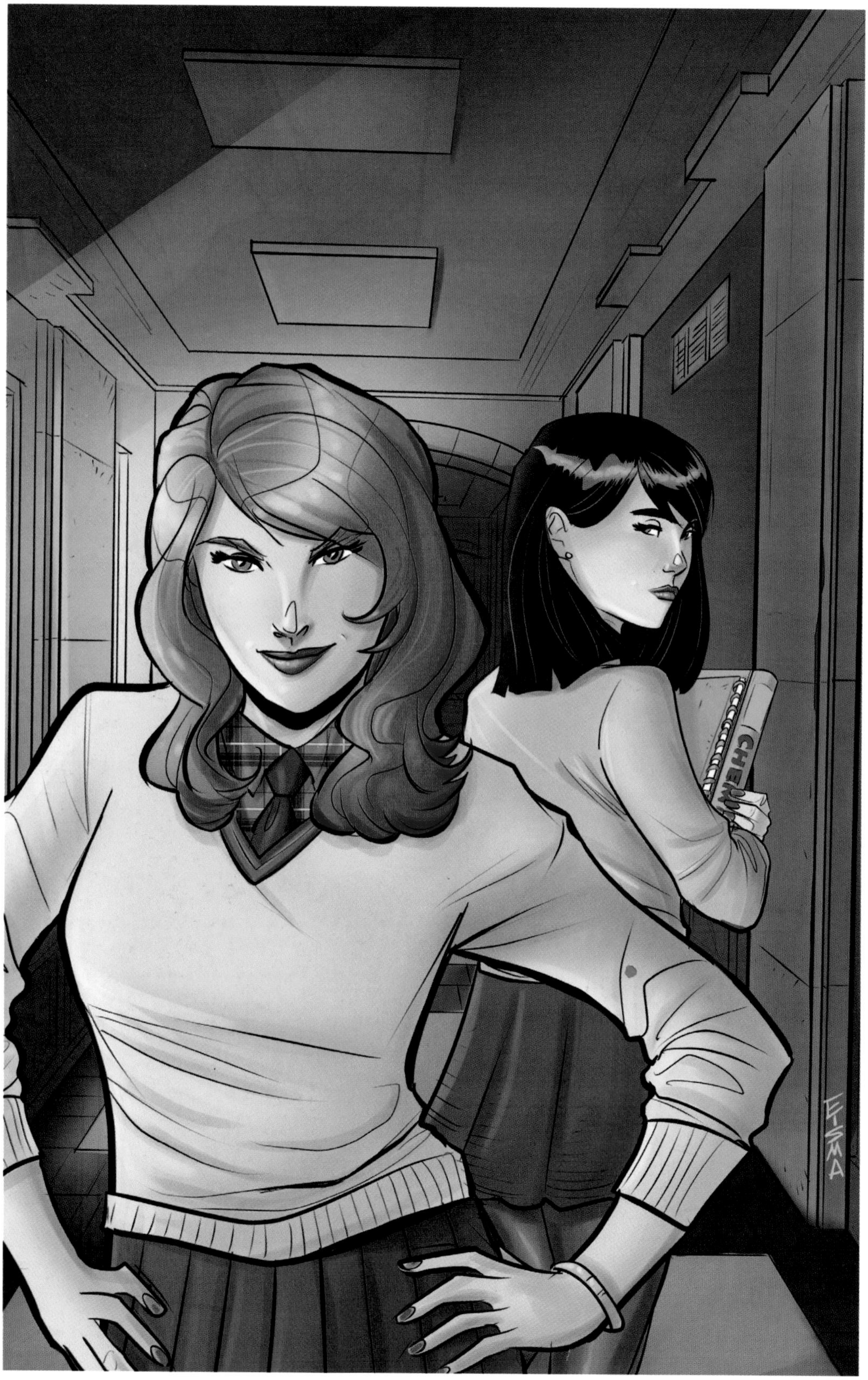

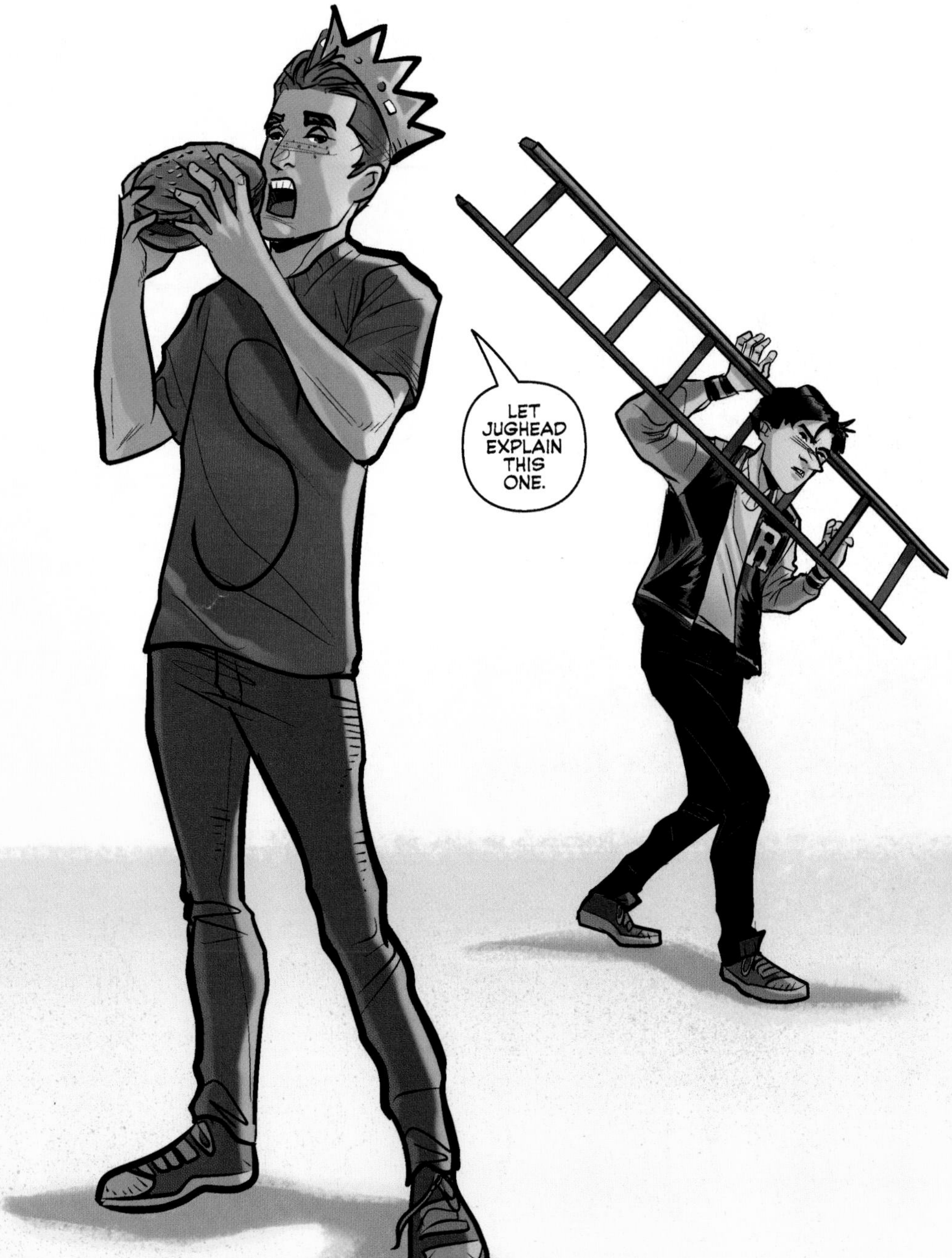
LET JUGHEAD EXPLAIN THIS ONE.

# CHAPTER ONE: The PAVEMENT KING

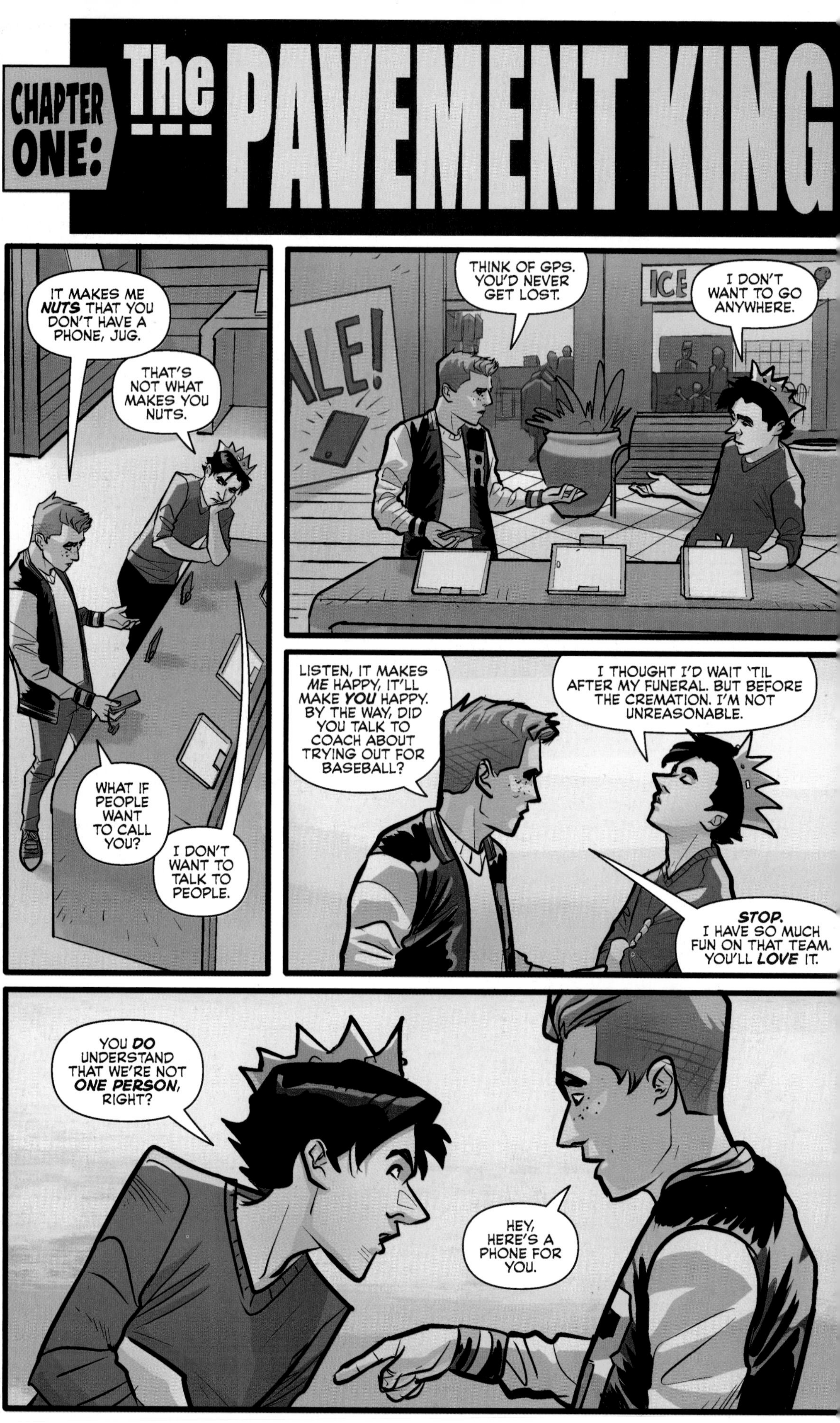
IT MAKES ME NUTS THAT YOU DON'T HAVE A PHONE, JUG.
THAT'S NOT WHAT MAKES YOU NUTS.
WHAT IF PEOPLE WANT TO CALL YOU?
I DON'T WANT TO TALK TO PEOPLE.
ALE!
THINK OF GPS. YOU'D NEVER GET LOST.
ICE
I DON'T WANT TO GO ANYWHERE.
LISTEN, IT MAKES ME HAPPY, IT'LL MAKE YOU HAPPY. BY THE WAY, DID YOU TALK TO COACH ABOUT TRYING OUT FOR BASEBALL?
I THOUGHT I'D WAIT 'TIL AFTER MY FUNERAL. BUT BEFORE THE CREMATION. I'M NOT UNREASONABLE.
STOP. I HAVE SO MUCH FUN ON THAT TEAM. YOU'LL LOVE IT.
YOU DO UNDERSTAND THAT WE'RE NOT ONE PERSON, RIGHT?
HEY, HERE'S A PHONE FOR YOU.

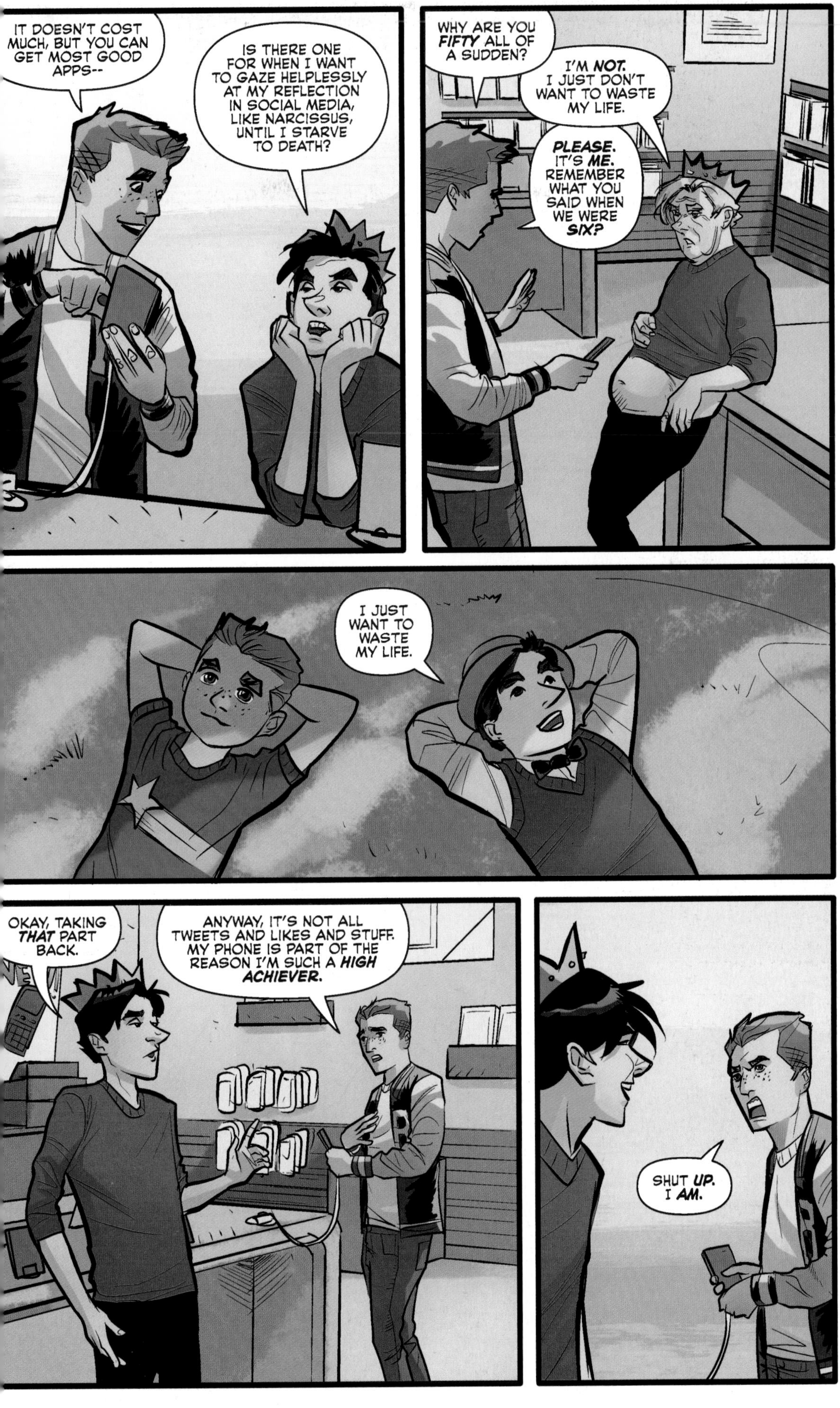
IT DOESN'T COST MUCH, BUT YOU CAN GET MOST GOOD APPS--
IS THERE ONE FOR WHEN I WANT TO GAZE HELPLESSLY AT MY REFLECTION IN SOCIAL MEDIA, LIKE NARCISSUS, UNTIL I STARVE TO DEATH?
WHY ARE YOU *FIFTY* ALL OF A SUDDEN?
I'M *NOT.* I JUST DON'T WANT TO WASTE MY LIFE.
*PLEASE.* IT'S *ME.* REMEMBER WHAT YOU SAID WHEN WE WERE *SIX?*
I JUST WANT TO WASTE MY LIFE.
OKAY, TAKING *THAT* PART BACK.
ANYWAY, IT'S NOT ALL TWEETS AND LIKES AND STUFF. MY PHONE IS PART OF THE REASON I'M SUCH A *HIGH ACHIEVER.*
SHUT *UP.* I *AM.*

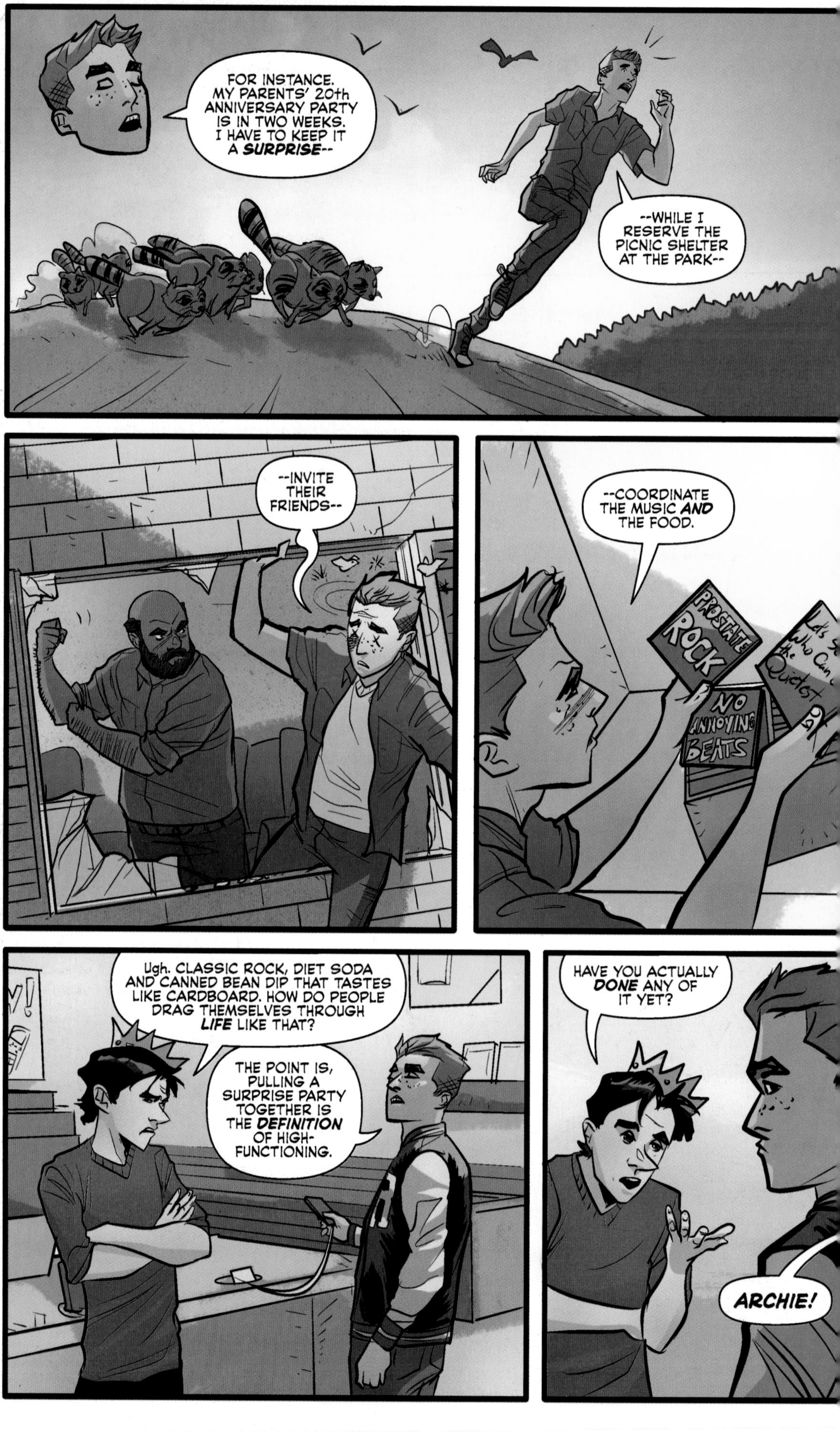
FOR INSTANCE. MY PARENTS' 20th ANNIVERSARY PARTY IS IN TWO WEEKS. I HAVE TO KEEP IT A **SURPRISE**--
--WHILE I RESERVE THE PICNIC SHELTER AT THE PARK--
--INVITE THEIR FRIENDS--
--COORDINATE THE MUSIC **AND** THE FOOD.
PROSTATE ROCK
NO ANNOYING BEATS
Ugh. CLASSIC ROCK, DIET SODA AND CANNED BEAN DIP THAT TASTES LIKE CARDBOARD. HOW DO PEOPLE DRAG THEMSELVES THROUGH **LIFE** LIKE THAT?
THE POINT IS, PULLING A SURPRISE PARTY TOGETHER IS THE **DEFINITION** OF HIGH-FUNCTIONING.
HAVE YOU ACTUALLY **DONE** ANY OF IT YET?
**ARCHIE!**

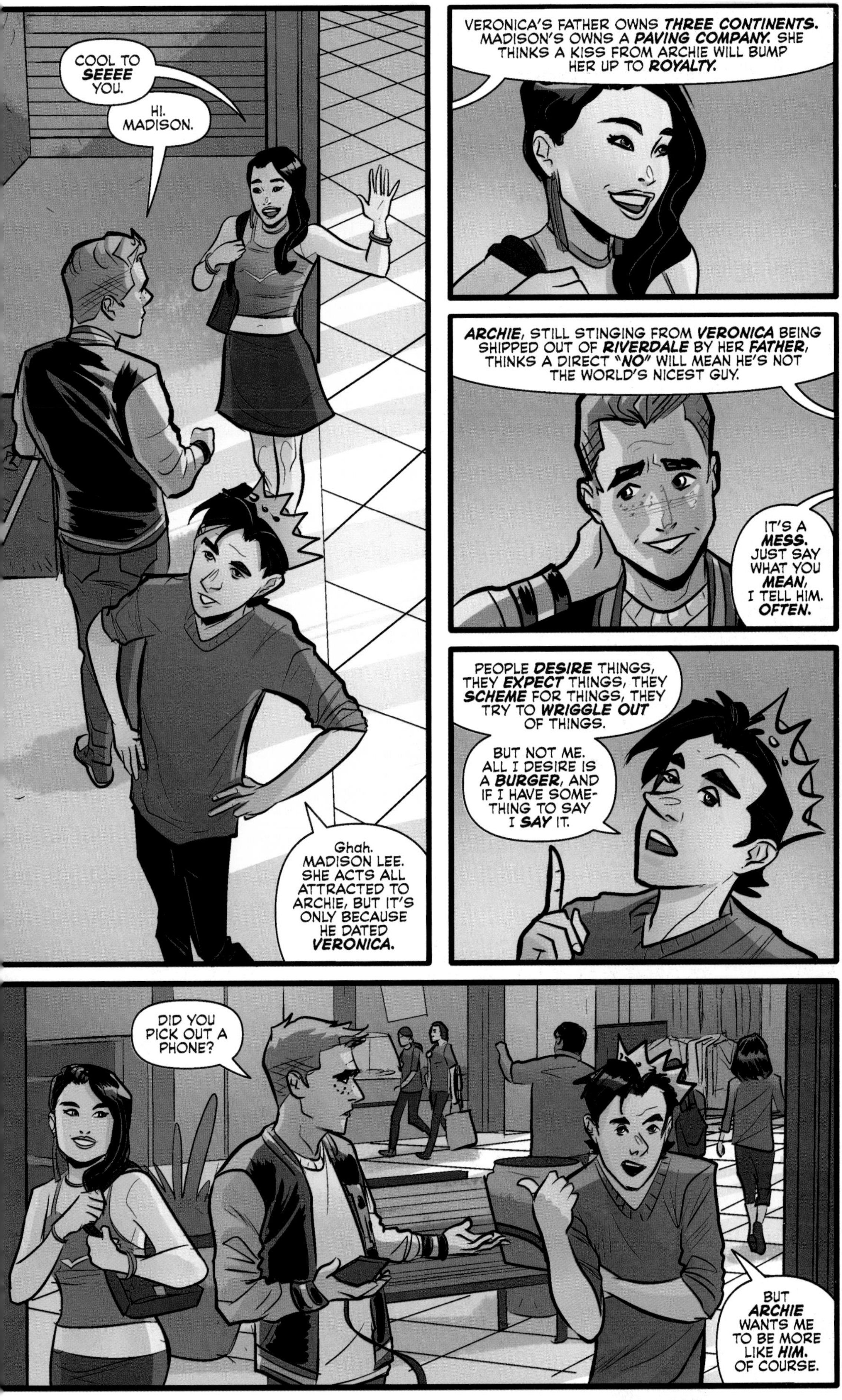

COOL TO SEEEE YOU.
HI. MADISON.
Ghah. MADISON LEE. SHE ACTS ALL ATTRACTED TO ARCHIE, BUT IT'S ONLY BECAUSE HE DATED VERONICA.
VERONICA'S FATHER OWNS THREE CONTINENTS. MADISON'S OWNS A PAVING COMPANY. SHE THINKS A KISS FROM ARCHIE WILL BUMP HER UP TO ROYALTY.
ARCHIE, STILL STINGING FROM VERONICA BEING SHIPPED OUT OF RIVERDALE BY HER FATHER, THINKS A DIRECT "NO" WILL MEAN HE'S NOT THE WORLD'S NICEST GUY.
IT'S A MESS. JUST SAY WHAT YOU MEAN, I TELL HIM. OFTEN.
PEOPLE DESIRE THINGS, THEY EXPECT THINGS, THEY SCHEME FOR THINGS, THEY TRY TO WRIGGLE OUT OF THINGS.
BUT NOT ME. ALL I DESIRE IS A BURGER, AND IF I HAVE SOMETHING TO SAY I SAY IT.
DID YOU PICK OUT A PHONE?
BUT ARCHIE WANTS ME TO BE MORE LIKE HIM. OF COURSE.

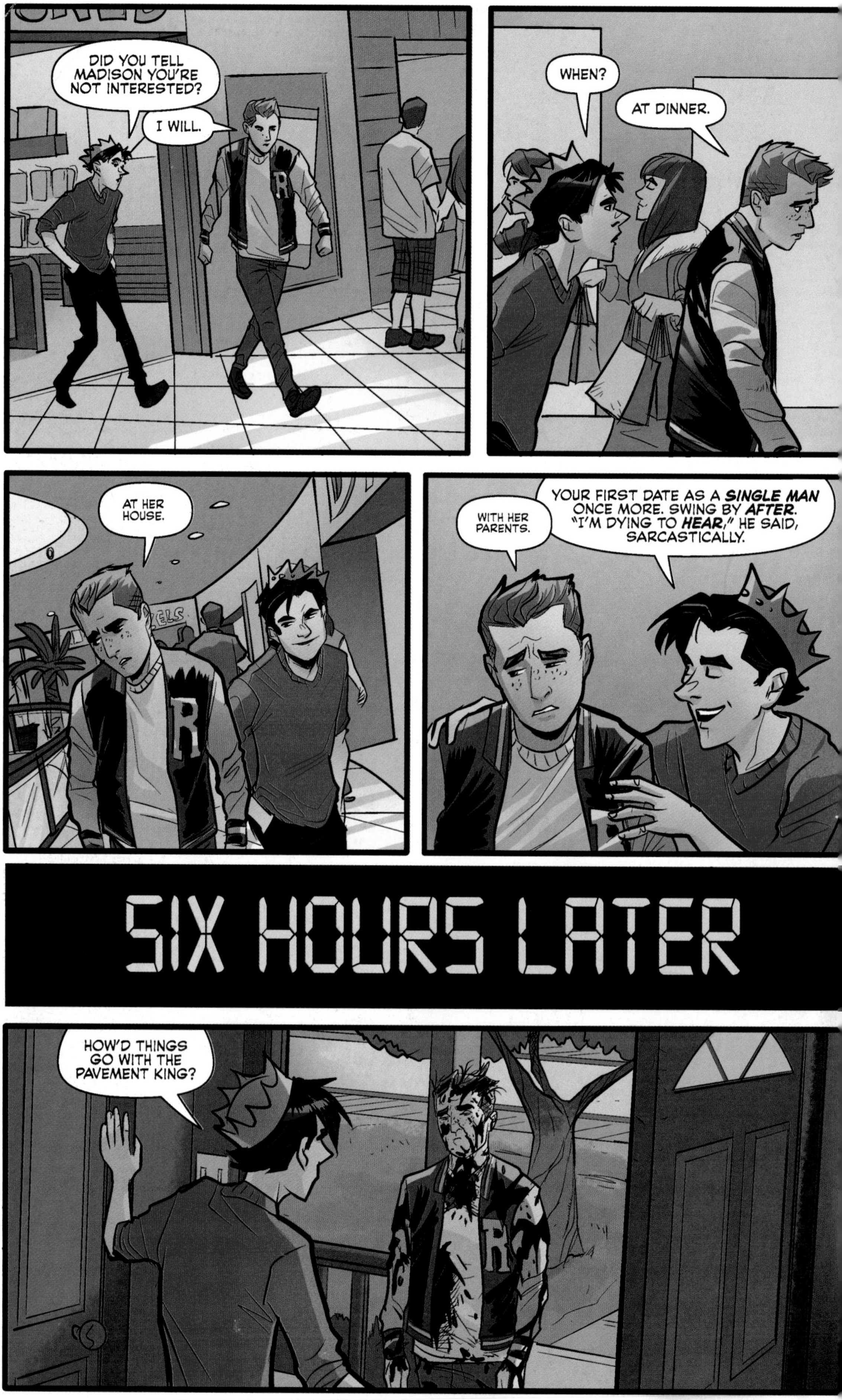
DID YOU TELL MADISON YOU'RE NOT INTERESTED?
I WILL.
WHEN?
AT DINNER.
AT HER HOUSE.
WITH HER PARENTS.
YOUR FIRST DATE AS A SINGLE MAN ONCE MORE. SWING BY AFTER. "I'M DYING TO HEAR," HE SAID, SARCASTICALLY.
SIX HOURS LATER
HOW'D THINGS GO WITH THE PAVEMENT KING?

# CHAPTER TWO: SURPRISE!

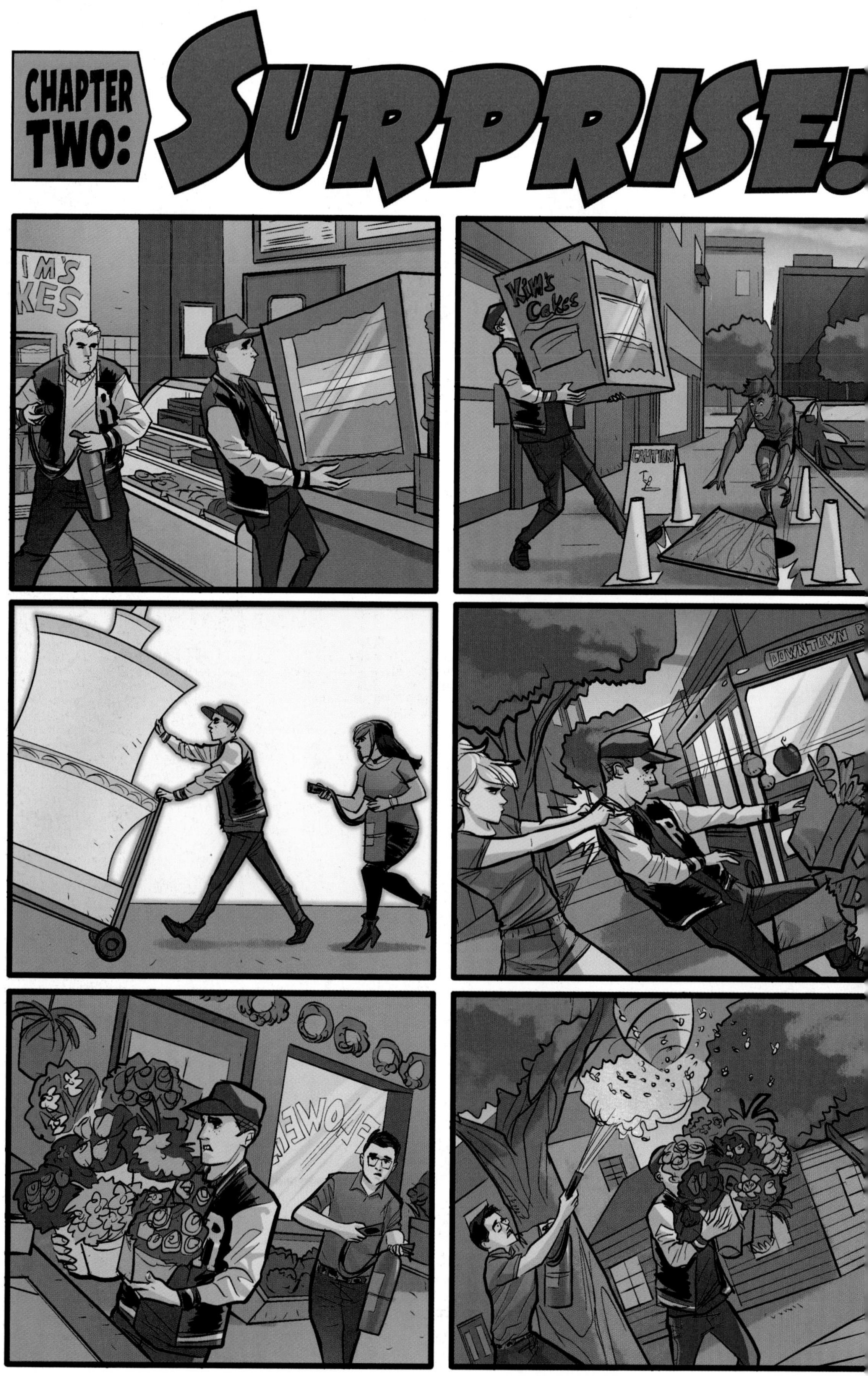

Kim's Cakes
CAUTION
DOWNTOWN

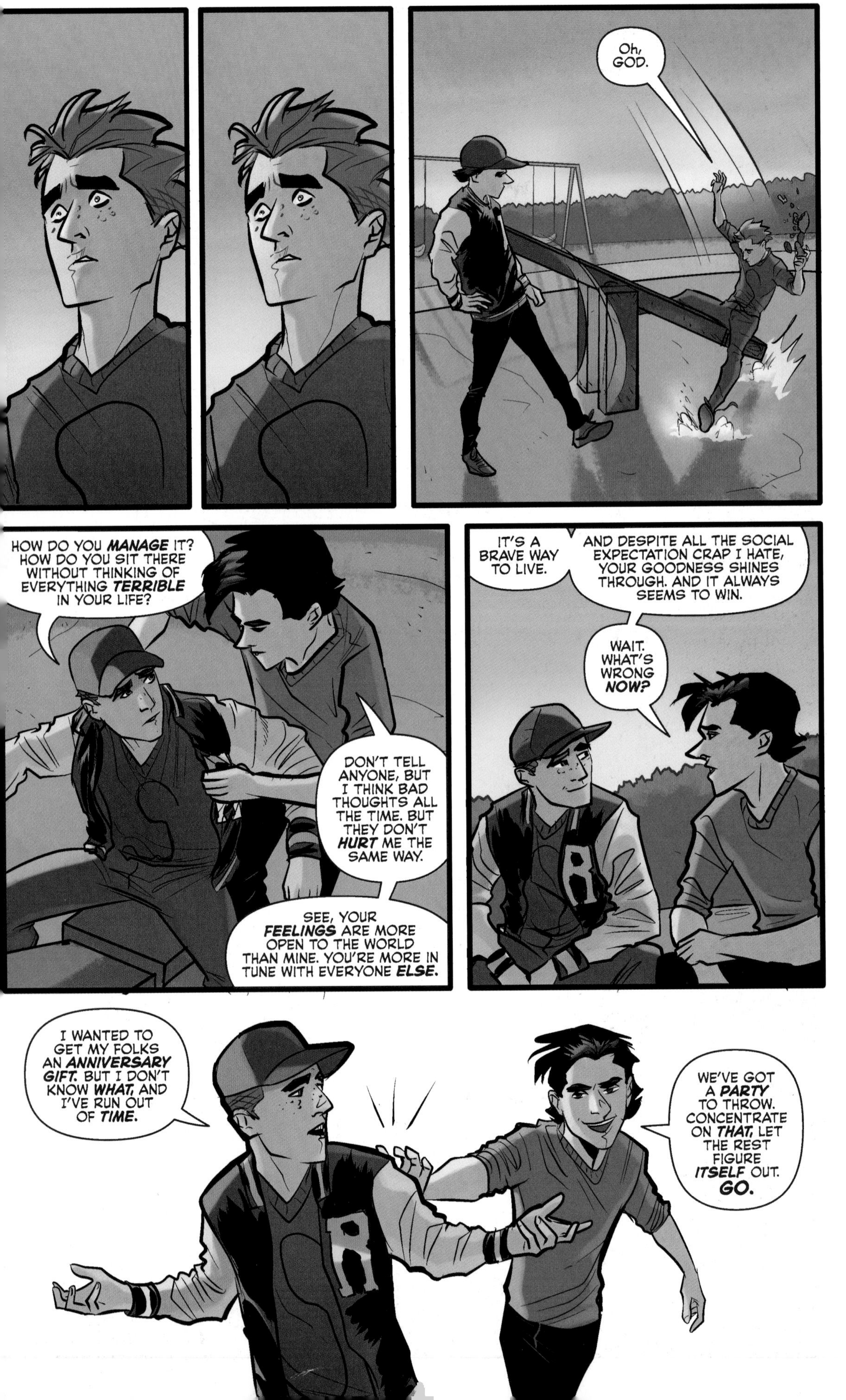
Oh, GOD.
HOW DO YOU MANAGE IT? HOW DO YOU SIT THERE WITHOUT THINKING OF EVERYTHING TERRIBLE IN YOUR LIFE?
DON'T TELL ANYONE, BUT I THINK BAD THOUGHTS ALL THE TIME. BUT THEY DON'T HURT ME THE SAME WAY.
SEE, YOUR FEELINGS ARE MORE OPEN TO THE WORLD THAN MINE. YOU'RE MORE IN TUNE WITH EVERYONE ELSE.
IT'S A BRAVE WAY TO LIVE.
AND DESPITE ALL THE SOCIAL EXPECTATION CRAP I HATE, YOUR GOODNESS SHINES THROUGH. AND IT ALWAYS SEEMS TO WIN.
WAIT. WHAT'S WRONG NOW?
I WANTED TO GET MY FOLKS AN ANNIVERSARY GIFT. BUT I DON'T KNOW WHAT, AND I'VE RUN OUT OF TIME.
WE'VE GOT A PARTY TO THROW. CONCENTRATE ON THAT, LET THE REST FIGURE ITSELF OUT. GO.

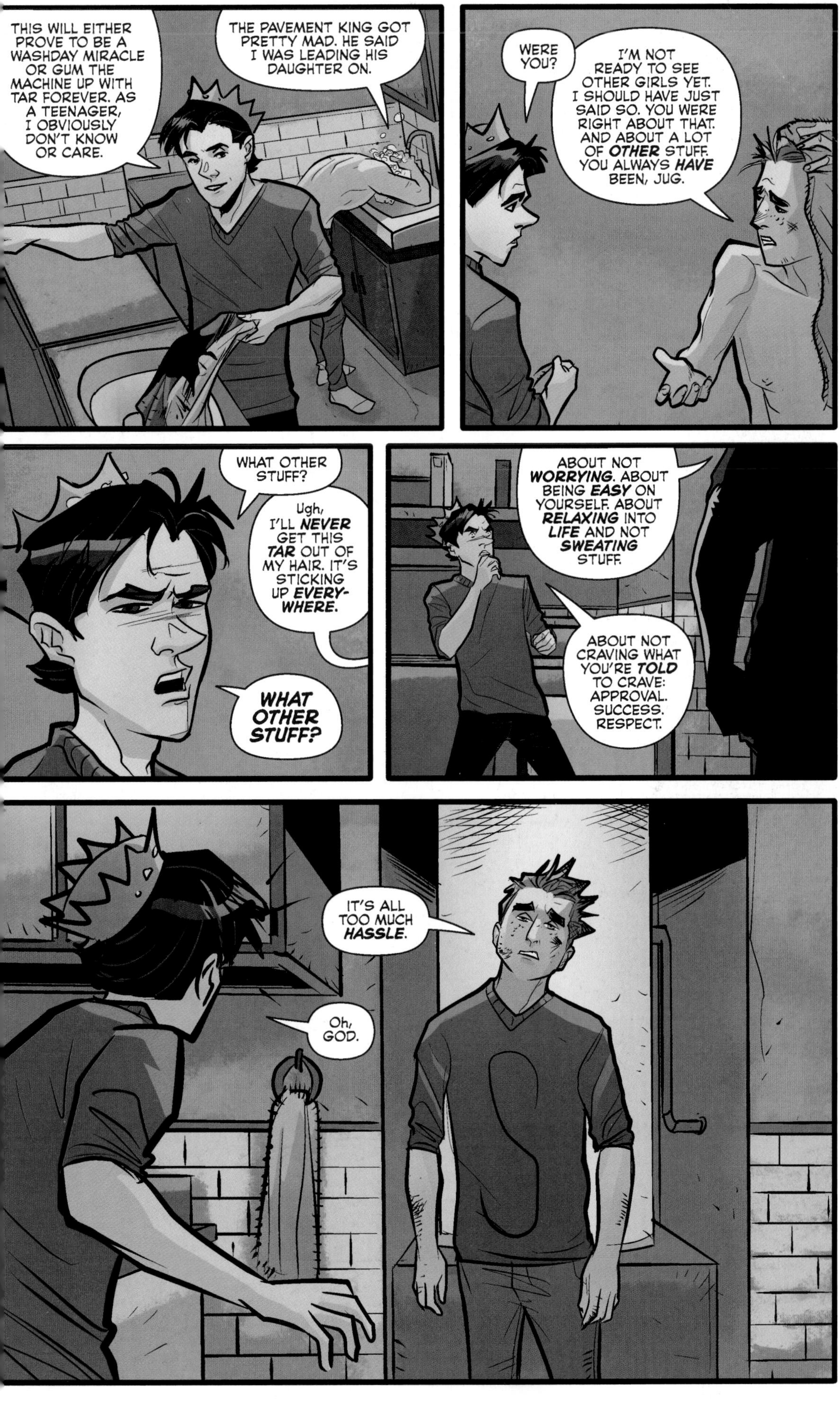

THIS WILL EITHER PROVE TO BE A WASHDAY MIRACLE OR GUM THE MACHINE UP WITH TAR FOREVER. AS A TEENAGER, I OBVIOUSLY DON'T KNOW OR CARE.
THE PAVEMENT KING GOT PRETTY MAD. HE SAID I WAS LEADING HIS DAUGHTER ON.
WERE YOU?
I'M NOT READY TO SEE OTHER GIRLS YET. I SHOULD HAVE JUST SAID SO. YOU WERE RIGHT ABOUT THAT. AND ABOUT A LOT OF OTHER STUFF. YOU ALWAYS HAVE BEEN, JUG.
WHAT OTHER STUFF?
Ugh, I'LL NEVER GET THIS TAR OUT OF MY HAIR. IT'S STICKING UP EVERY-WHERE.
WHAT OTHER STUFF?
ABOUT NOT WORRYING. ABOUT BEING EASY ON YOURSELF. ABOUT RELAXING INTO LIFE AND NOT SWEATING STUFF.
ABOUT NOT CRAVING WHAT YOU'RE TOLD TO CRAVE: APPROVAL. SUCCESS. RESPECT.
IT'S ALL TOO MUCH HASSLE.
Oh, GOD.

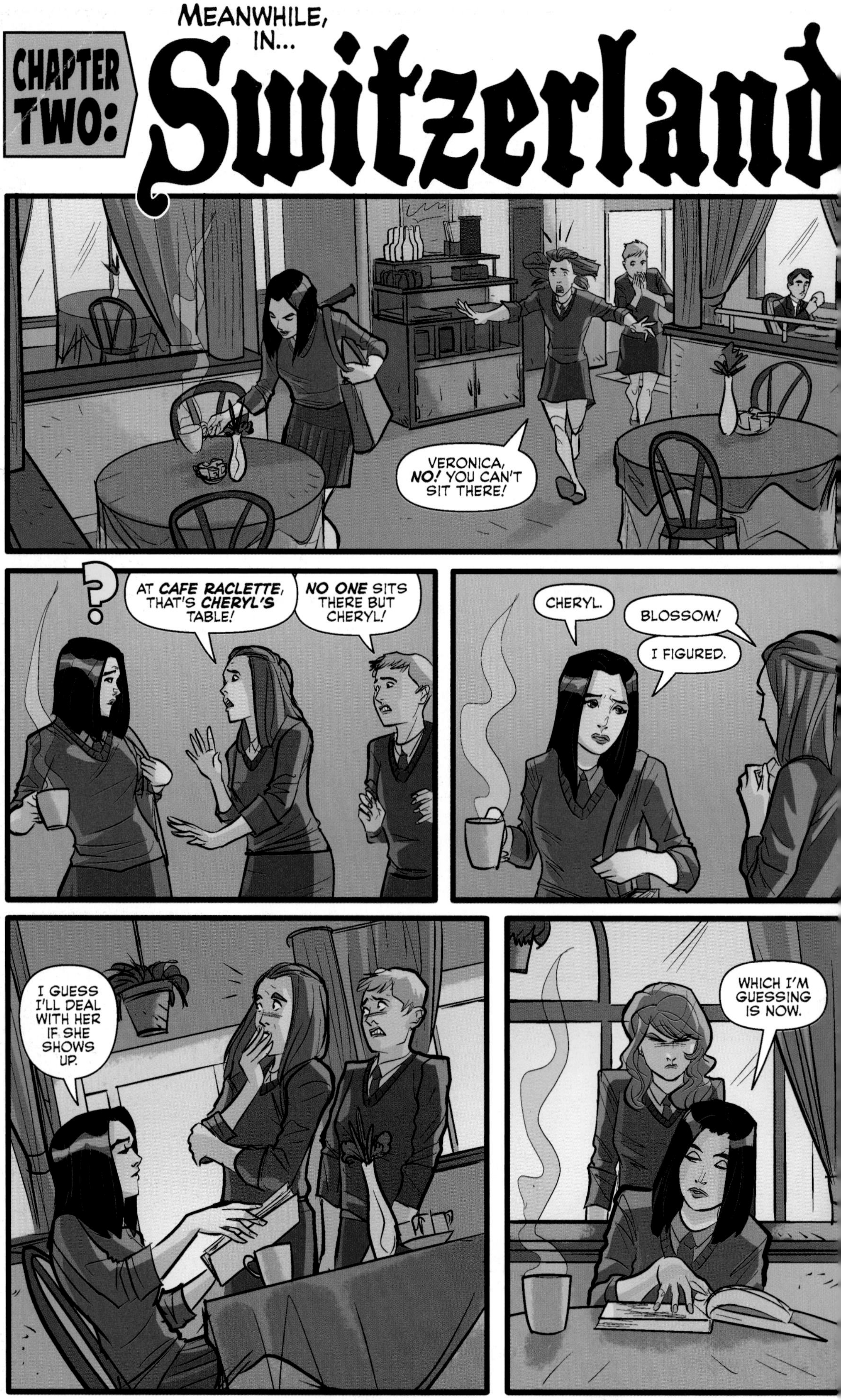
MEANWHILE, IN...
CHAPTER TWO:
Switzerland
VERONICA, NO! YOU CAN'T SIT THERE!
?
AT CAFE RACLETTE, THAT'S CHERYL'S TABLE!
NO ONE SITS THERE BUT CHERYL!
CHERYL.
BLOSSOM!
I FIGURED.
I GUESS I'LL DEAL WITH HER IF SHE SHOWS UP.
WHICH I'M GUESSING IS NOW.

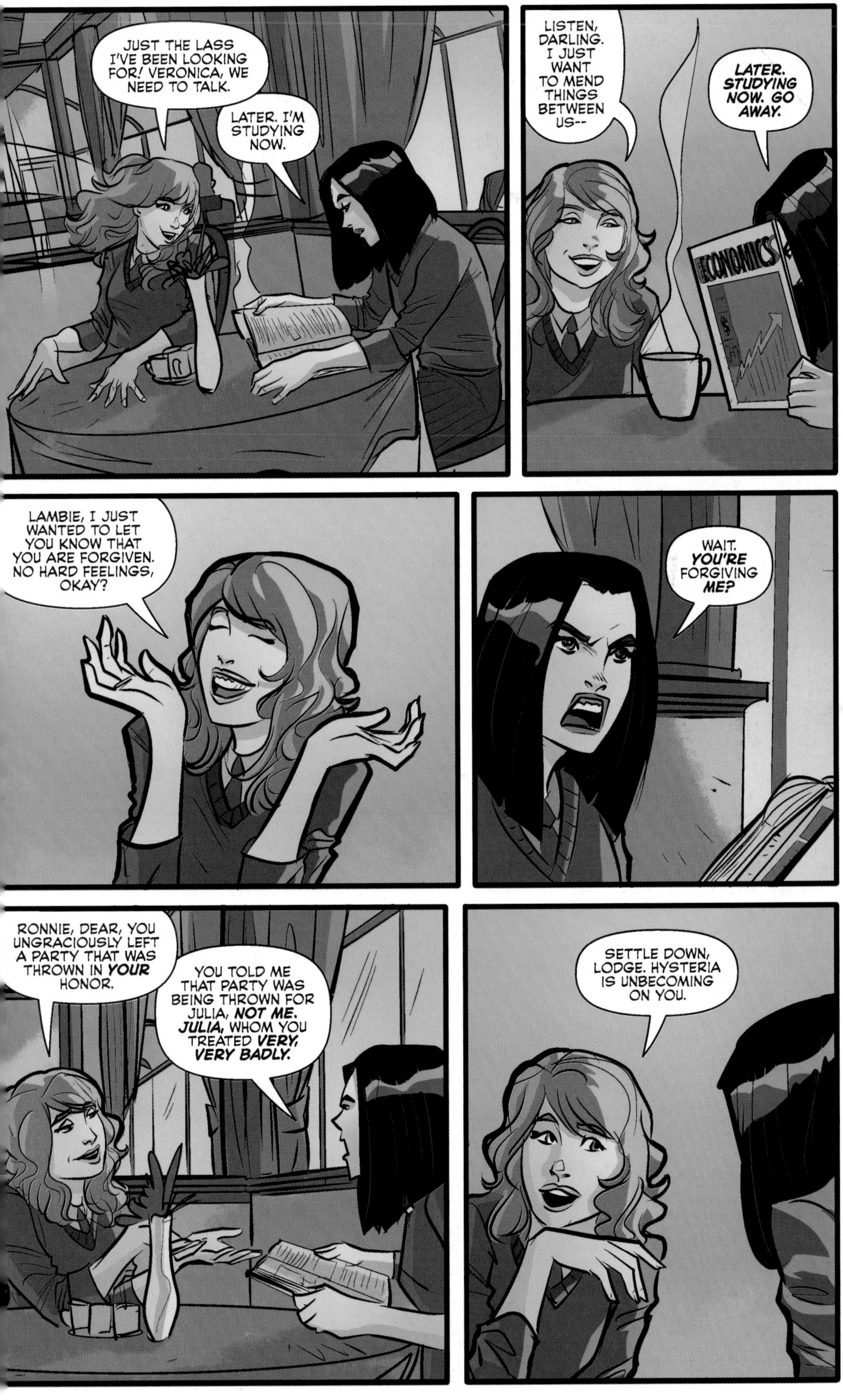
JUST THE LASS I'VE BEEN LOOKING FOR! VERONICA, WE NEED TO TALK.
LATER. I'M STUDYING NOW.
LISTEN, DARLING. I JUST WANT TO MEND THINGS BETWEEN US--
LATER. STUDYING NOW. GO AWAY.
ECONOMICS
LAMBIE, I JUST WANTED TO LET YOU KNOW THAT YOU ARE FORGIVEN. NO HARD FEELINGS, OKAY?
WAIT. YOU'RE FORGIVING ME?
RONNIE, DEAR, YOU UNGRACIOUSLY LEFT A PARTY THAT WAS THROWN IN YOUR HONOR.
YOU TOLD ME THAT PARTY WAS BEING THROWN FOR JULIA, NOT ME. JULIA, WHOM YOU TREATED VERY, VERY BADLY.
SETTLE DOWN, LODGE. HYSTERIA IS UNBECOMING ON YOU.

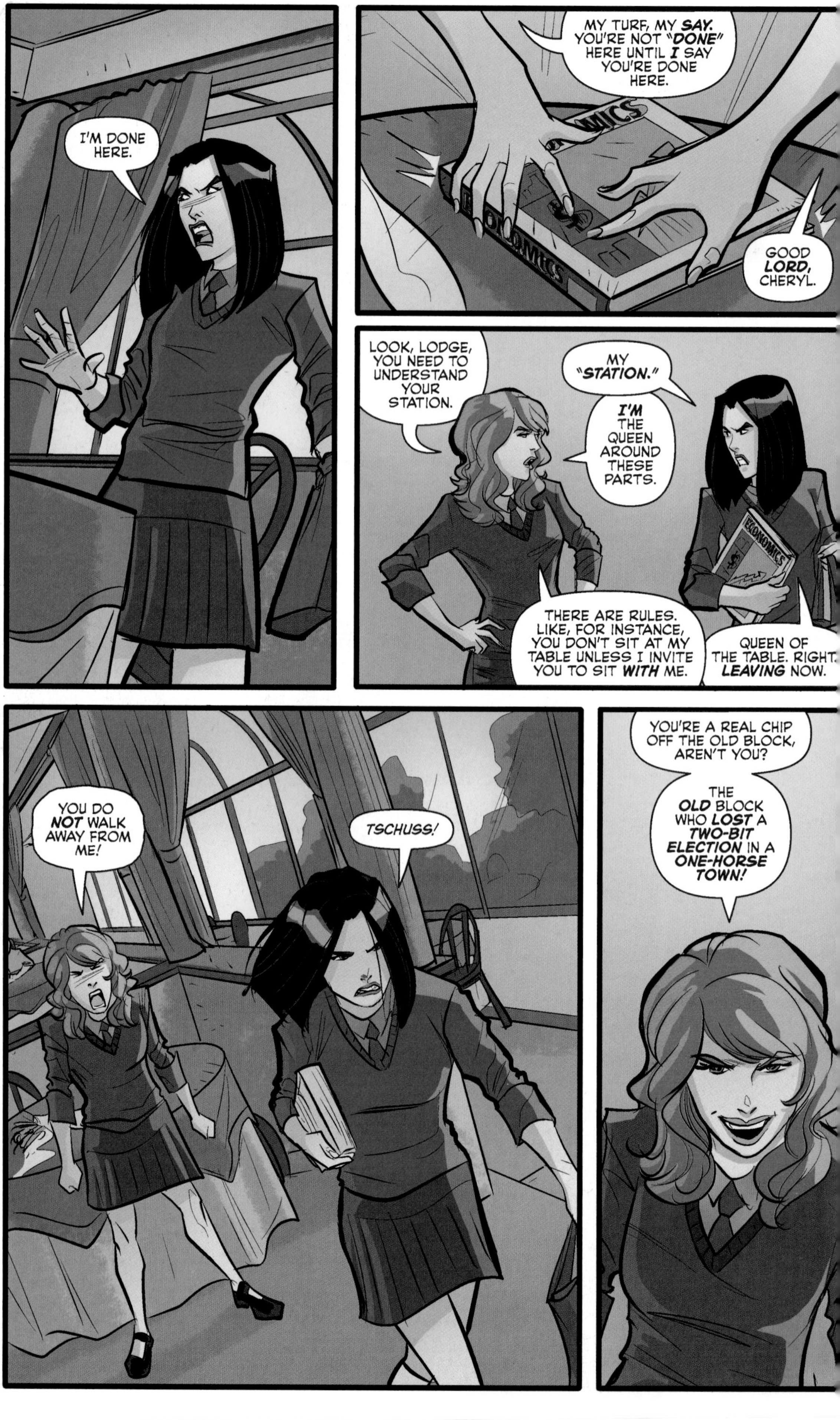

I'M DONE HERE.
MY TURF, MY SAY. YOU'RE NOT "DONE" HERE UNTIL I SAY YOU'RE DONE HERE.
ECONOMICS
GOOD LORD, CHERYL.
LOOK, LODGE, YOU NEED TO UNDERSTAND YOUR STATION.
MY "STATION."
I'M THE QUEEN AROUND THESE PARTS.
ECONOMICS
THERE ARE RULES. LIKE, FOR INSTANCE, YOU DON'T SIT AT MY TABLE UNLESS I INVITE YOU TO SIT WITH ME.
QUEEN OF THE TABLE. RIGHT. LEAVING NOW.
YOU DO NOT WALK AWAY FROM ME!
TSCHUSS!
YOU'RE A REAL CHIP OFF THE OLD BLOCK, AREN'T YOU?
THE OLD BLOCK WHO LOST A TWO-BIT ELECTION IN A ONE-HORSE TOWN!

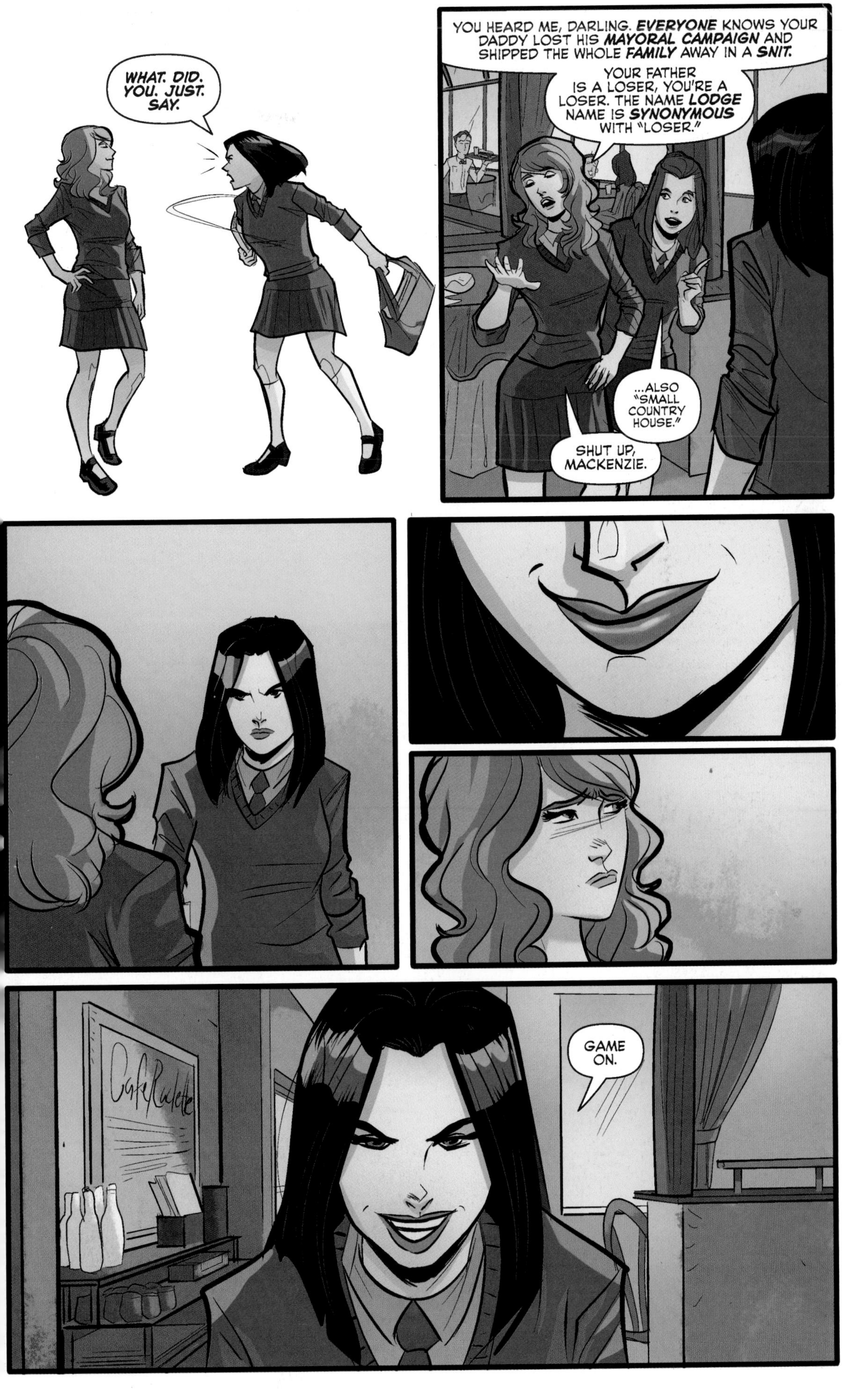
WHAT. DID. YOU. JUST. SAY.
YOU HEARD ME, DARLING. EVERYONE KNOWS YOUR DADDY LOST HIS MAYORAL CAMPAIGN AND SHIPPED THE WHOLE FAMILY AWAY IN A SNIT.
YOUR FATHER IS A LOSER, YOU'RE A LOSER. THE NAME LODGE NAME IS SYNONYMOUS WITH "LOSER."
...ALSO "SMALL COUNTRY HOUSE."
SHUT UP, MACKENZIE.
Cafe Roulette
GAME ON.

# CHAPTER THREE: INVASIVE IS FINE

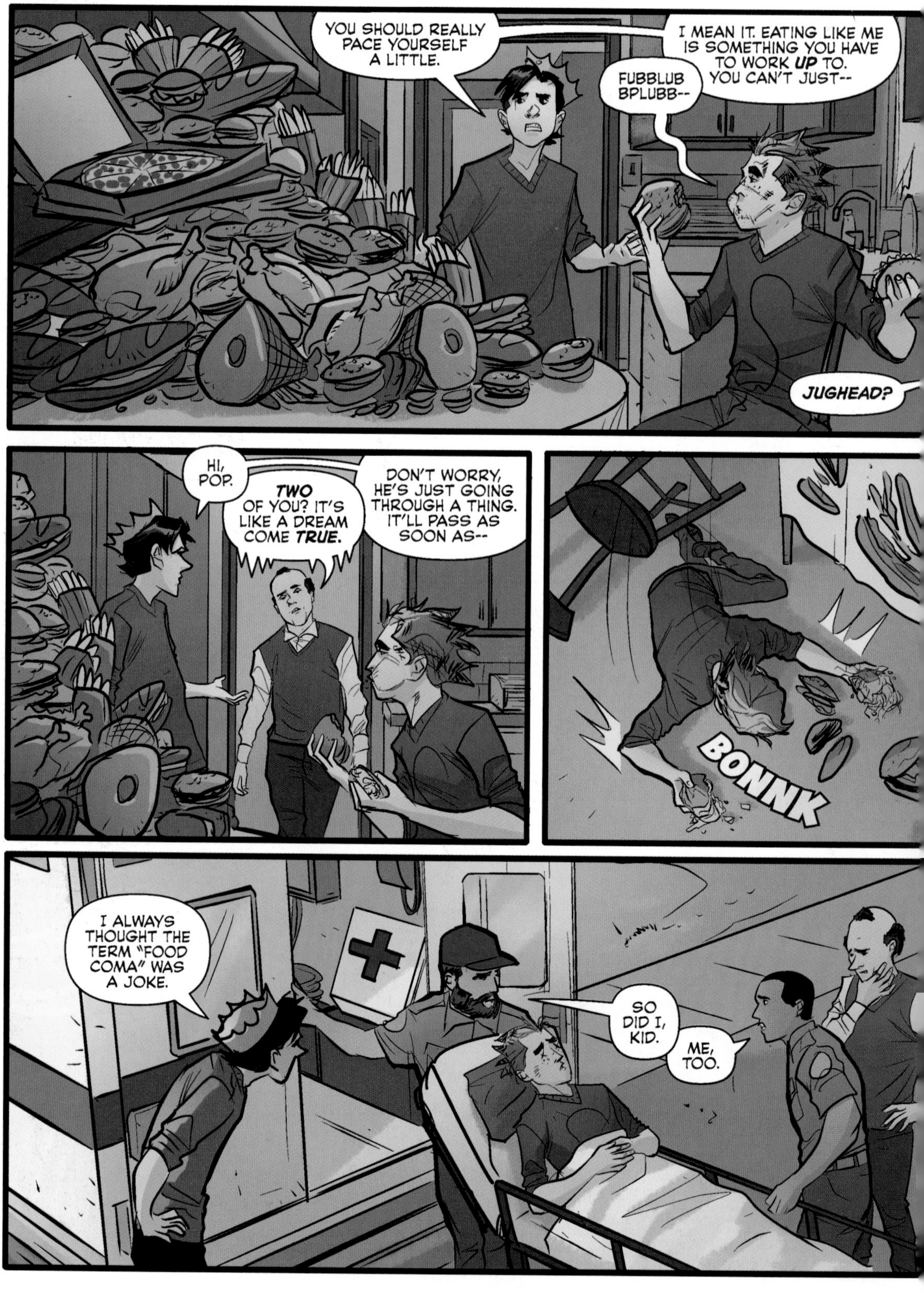

YOU SHOULD REALLY PACE YOURSELF A LITTLE.
I MEAN IT. EATING LIKE ME IS SOMETHING YOU HAVE TO WORK *UP* TO. YOU CAN'T JUST--
FUBBLUB BPLUBB--
JUGHEAD?
HI, POP.
*TWO* OF YOU? IT'S LIKE A DREAM COME *TRUE*.
DON'T WORRY, HE'S JUST GOING THROUGH A THING. IT'LL PASS AS SOON AS--
BONNK
I ALWAYS THOUGHT THE TERM "FOOD COMA" WAS A JOKE.
SO DID I, KID.
ME, TOO.

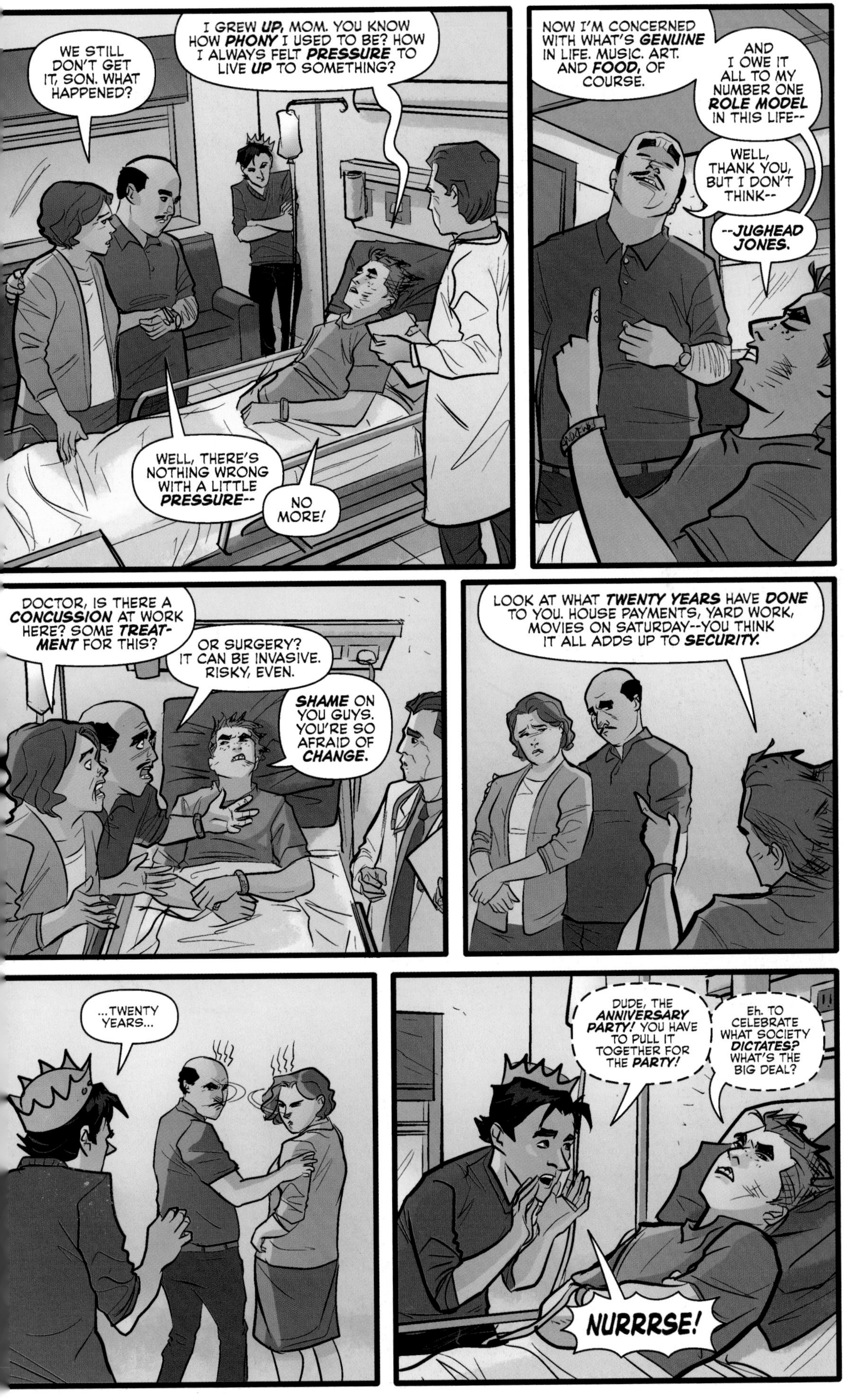
WE STILL DON'T GET IT, SON. WHAT HAPPENED?
I GREW UP, MOM. YOU KNOW HOW PHONY I USED TO BE? HOW I ALWAYS FELT PRESSURE TO LIVE UP TO SOMETHING?
WELL, THERE'S NOTHING WRONG WITH A LITTLE PRESSURE--
NO MORE!
NOW I'M CONCERNED WITH WHAT'S GENUINE IN LIFE. MUSIC. ART. AND FOOD, OF COURSE.
AND I OWE IT ALL TO MY NUMBER ONE ROLE MODEL IN THIS LIFE--
WELL, THANK YOU, BUT I DON'T THINK--
--JUGHEAD JONES.
DOCTOR, IS THERE A CONCUSSION AT WORK HERE? SOME TREATMENT FOR THIS?
OR SURGERY? IT CAN BE INVASIVE. RISKY, EVEN.
SHAME ON YOU GUYS. YOU'RE SO AFRAID OF CHANGE.
LOOK AT WHAT TWENTY YEARS HAVE DONE TO YOU. HOUSE PAYMENTS, YARD WORK, MOVIES ON SATURDAY--YOU THINK IT ALL ADDS UP TO SECURITY.
...TWENTY YEARS...
DUDE, THE ANNIVERSARY PARTY! YOU HAVE TO PULL IT TOGETHER FOR THE PARTY!
Eh. TO CELEBRATE WHAT SOCIETY DICTATES? WHAT'S THE BIG DEAL?
NURRRSE!

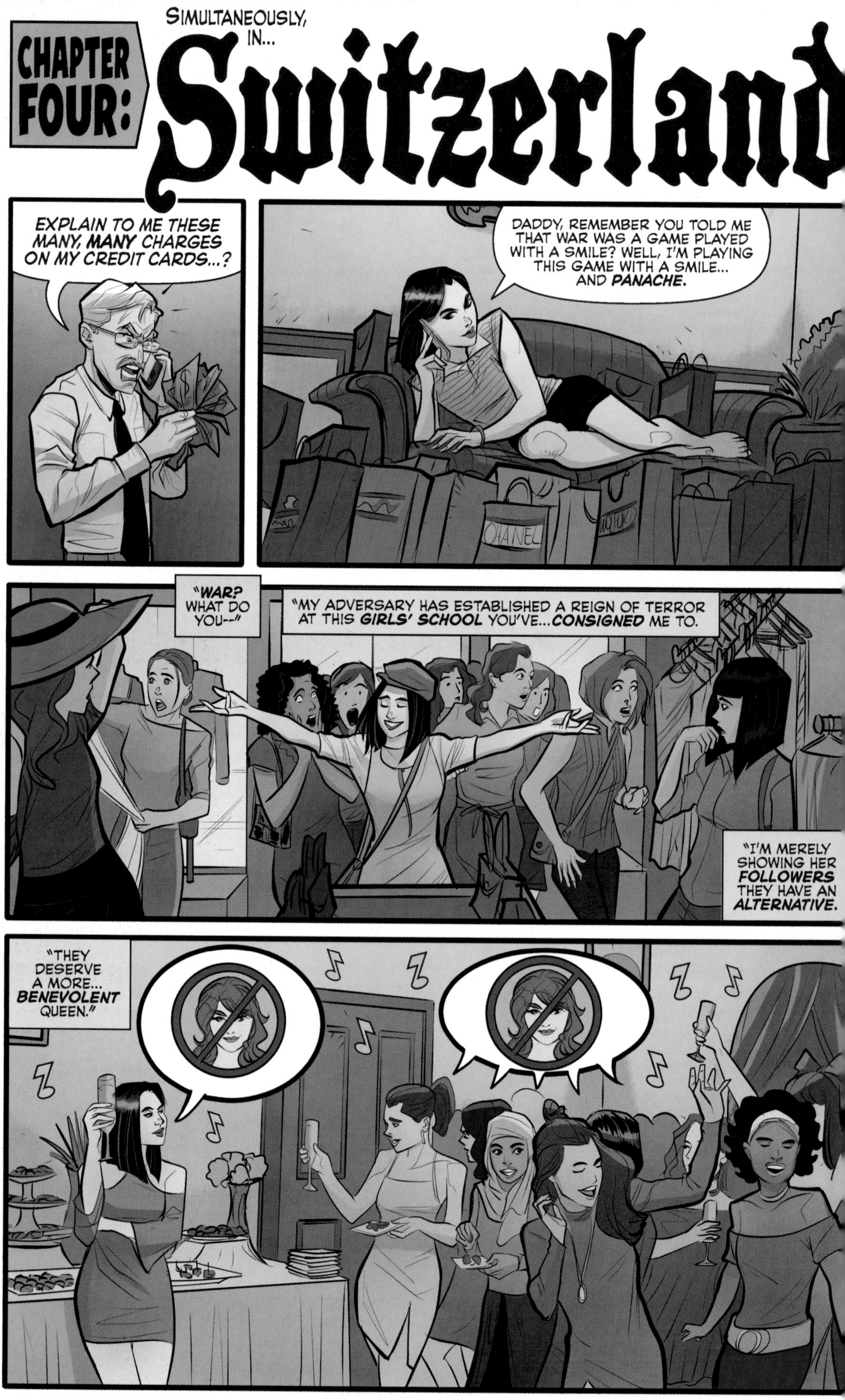
CHAPTER FOUR:
SIMULTANEOUSLY, IN...
Switzerland
EXPLAIN TO ME THESE MANY, MANY CHARGES ON MY CREDIT CARDS...?
DADDY, REMEMBER YOU TOLD ME THAT WAR WAS A GAME PLAYED WITH A SMILE? WELL, I'M PLAYING THIS GAME WITH A SMILE... AND PANACHE.
CHANEL
"WAR? WHAT DO YOU--"
"MY ADVERSARY HAS ESTABLISHED A REIGN OF TERROR AT THIS GIRLS' SCHOOL YOU'VE...CONSIGNED ME TO.
"I'M MERELY SHOWING HER FOLLOWERS THEY HAVE AN ALTERNATIVE.
"THEY DESERVE A MORE... BENEVOLENT QUEEN."

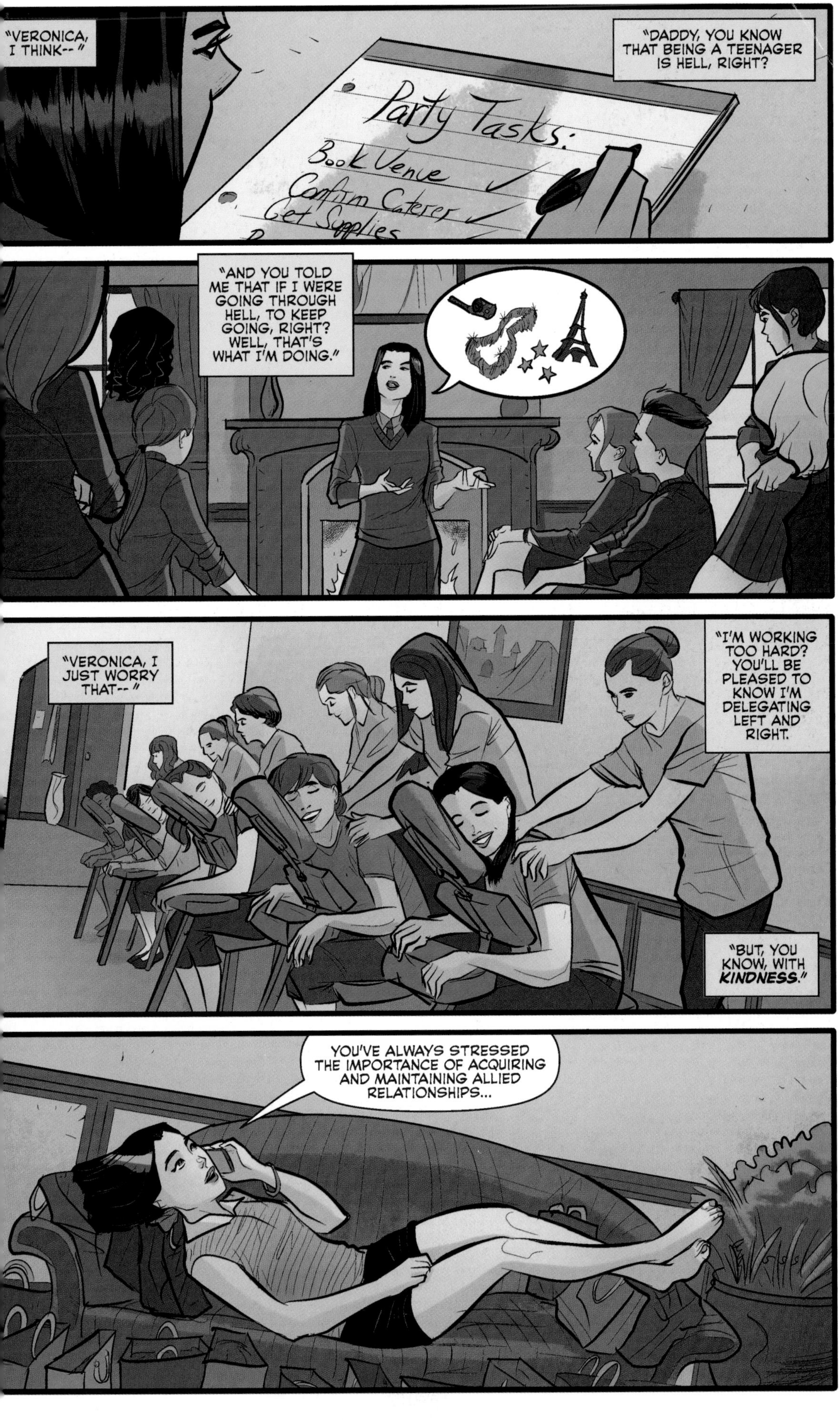

"VERONICA, I THINK--"
Party Tasks:
Book Venue
Confirm Caterer
Get Supplies
"DADDY, YOU KNOW THAT BEING A TEENAGER IS HELL, RIGHT?
"AND YOU TOLD ME THAT IF I WERE GOING THROUGH HELL, TO KEEP GOING, RIGHT? WELL, THAT'S WHAT I'M DOING."
"VERONICA, I JUST WORRY THAT--"
"I'M WORKING TOO HARD? YOU'LL BE PLEASED TO KNOW I'M DELEGATING LEFT AND RIGHT.
"BUT, YOU KNOW, WITH KINDNESS."
YOU'VE ALWAYS STRESSED THE IMPORTANCE OF ACQUIRING AND MAINTAINING ALLIED RELATIONSHIPS...

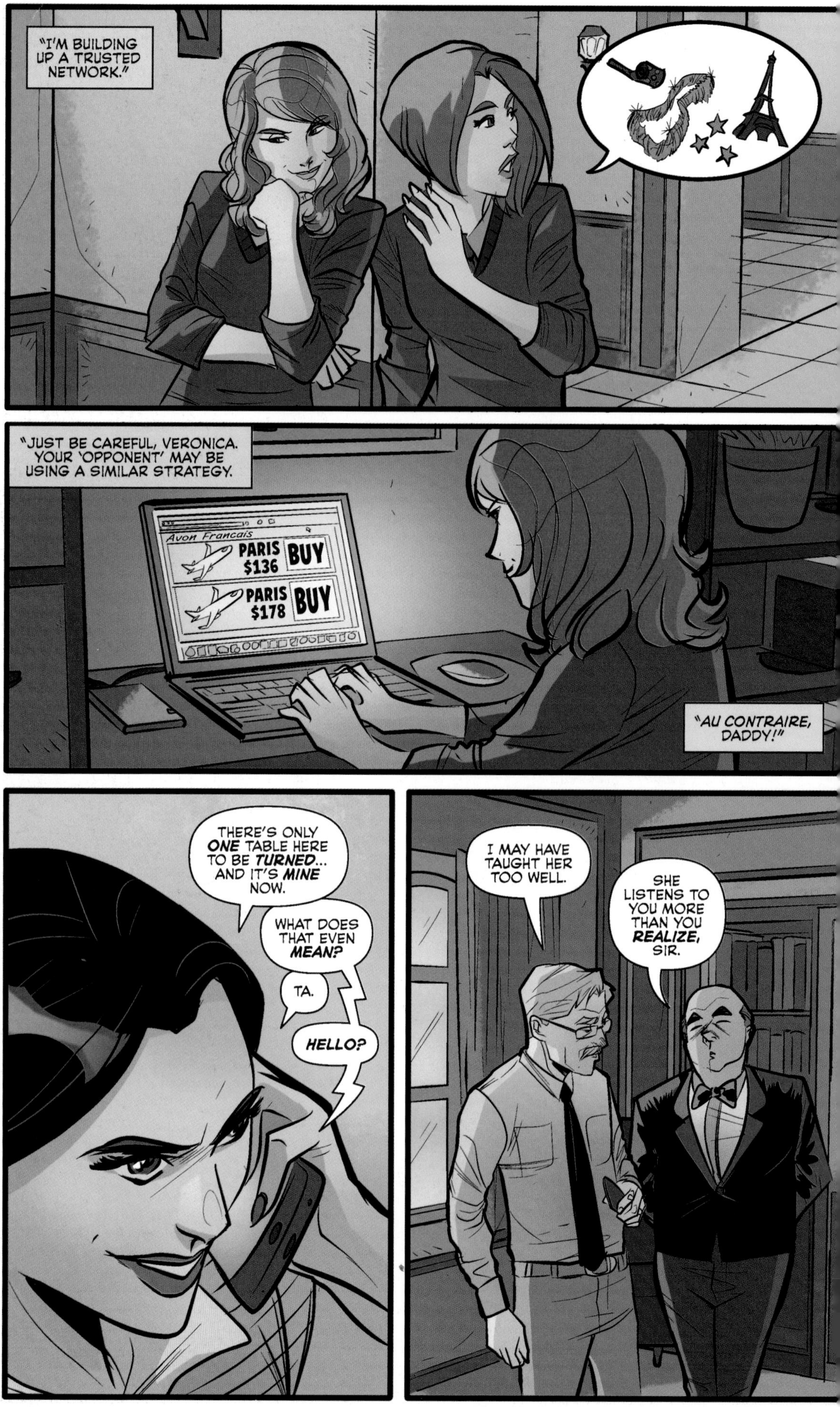
"I'M BUILDING UP A TRUSTED NETWORK."
"JUST BE CAREFUL, VERONICA. YOUR 'OPPONENT' MAY BE USING A SIMILAR STRATEGY.
Avon Francais
PARIS $136 BUY
PARIS $178 BUY
"AU CONTRAIRE, DADDY!"
THERE'S ONLY ONE TABLE HERE TO BE TURNED... AND IT'S MINE NOW.
WHAT DOES THAT EVEN MEAN?
TA.
HELLO?
I MAY HAVE TAUGHT HER TOO WELL.
SHE LISTENS TO YOU MORE THAN YOU REALIZE, SIR.

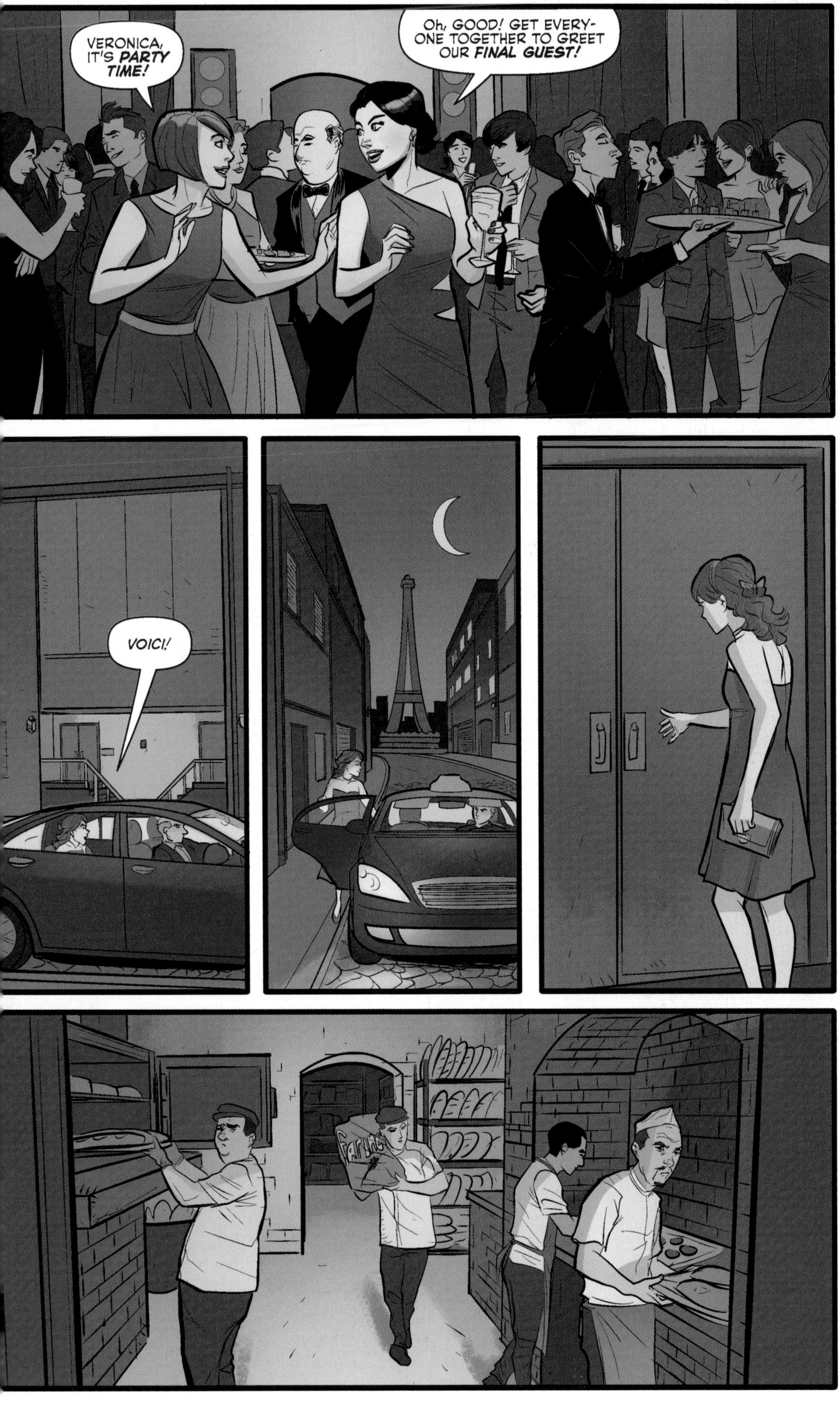
VERONICA, IT'S **PARTY TIME!**
Oh, GOOD! GET EVERY-ONE TOGETHER TO GREET OUR **FINAL GUEST!**
*VOICI!*

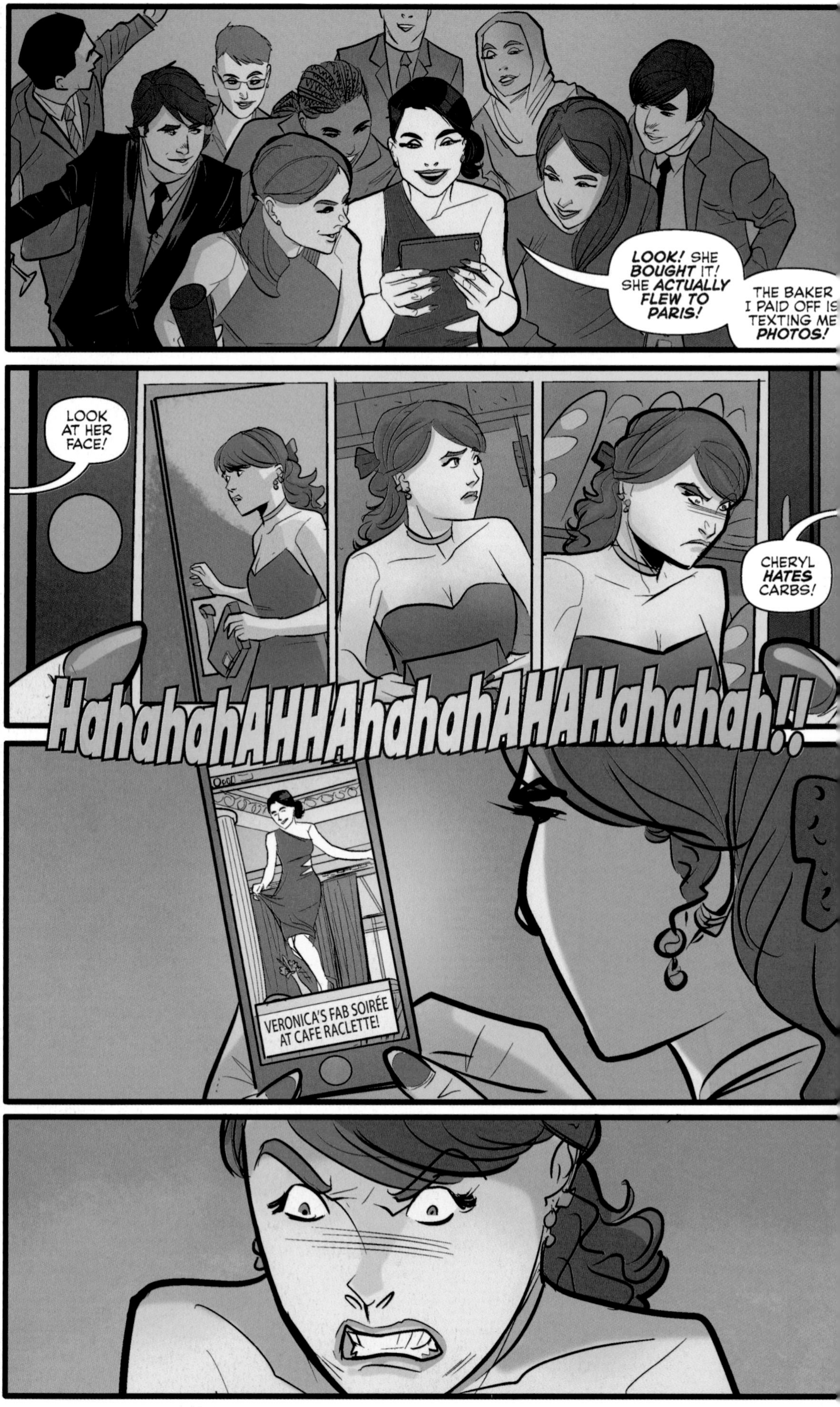

LOOK! SHE BOUGHT IT! SHE ACTUALLY FLEW TO PARIS!
THE BAKER I PAID OFF IS TEXTING ME PHOTOS!
LOOK AT HER FACE!
CHERYL HATES CARBS!
HahahahAHHAhahahAHAHahahah!!
VERONICA'S FAB SOIRÉE AT CAFE RACLETTE!

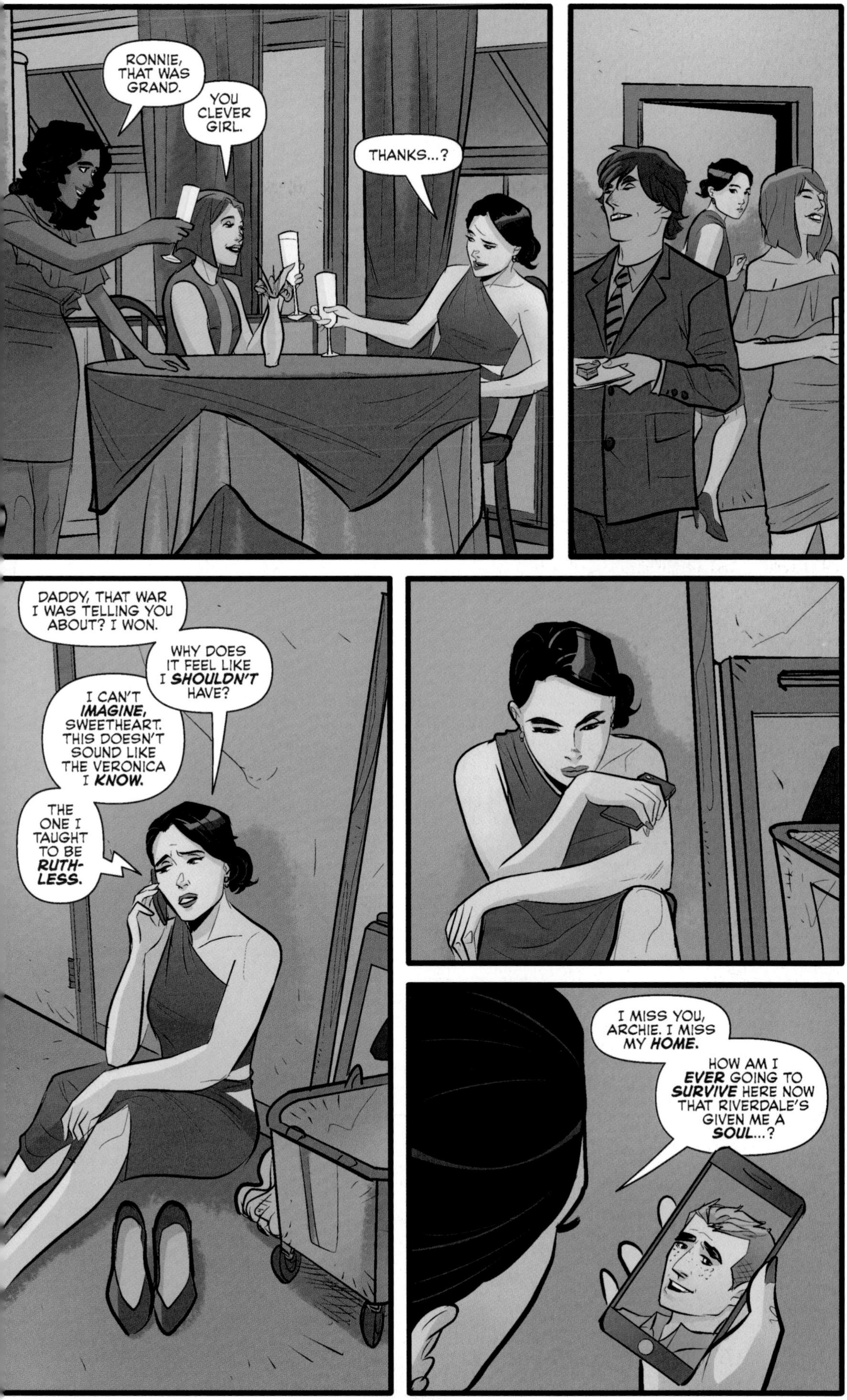
RONNIE, THAT WAS GRAND.
YOU CLEVER GIRL.
THANKS...?
DADDY, THAT WAR I WAS TELLING YOU ABOUT? I WON.
WHY DOES IT FEEL LIKE I SHOULDN'T HAVE?
I CAN'T IMAGINE, SWEETHEART. THIS DOESN'T SOUND LIKE THE VERONICA I KNOW.
THE ONE I TAUGHT TO BE RUTHLESS.
I MISS YOU, ARCHIE. I MISS MY HOME.
HOW AM I EVER GOING TO SURVIVE HERE NOW THAT RIVERDALE'S GIVEN ME A SOUL...?

# CHAPTER FIVE: VICTORY...?

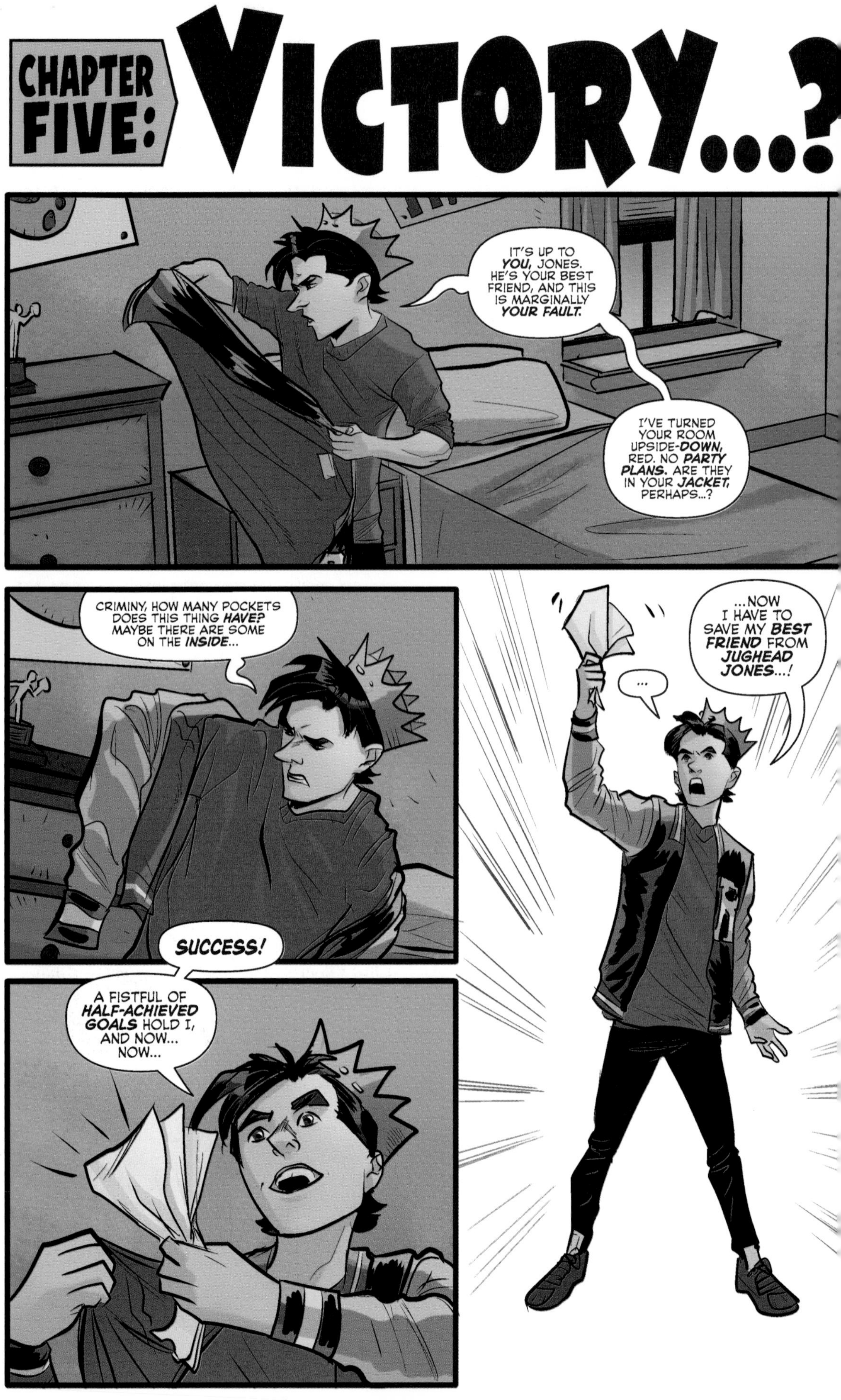
IT'S UP TO YOU, JONES. HE'S YOUR BEST FRIEND, AND THIS IS MARGINALLY YOUR FAULT.
I'VE TURNED YOUR ROOM UPSIDE-DOWN, RED. NO PARTY PLANS. ARE THEY IN YOUR JACKET, PERHAPS...?
CRIMINY, HOW MANY POCKETS DOES THIS THING HAVE? MAYBE THERE ARE SOME ON THE INSIDE...
SUCCESS!
A FISTFUL OF HALF-ACHIEVED GOALS HOLD I, AND NOW... NOW...
...
...NOW I HAVE TO SAVE MY BEST FRIEND FROM JUGHEAD JONES...!

TO BE CONTINUED...

# ISSUE FIFTEEN

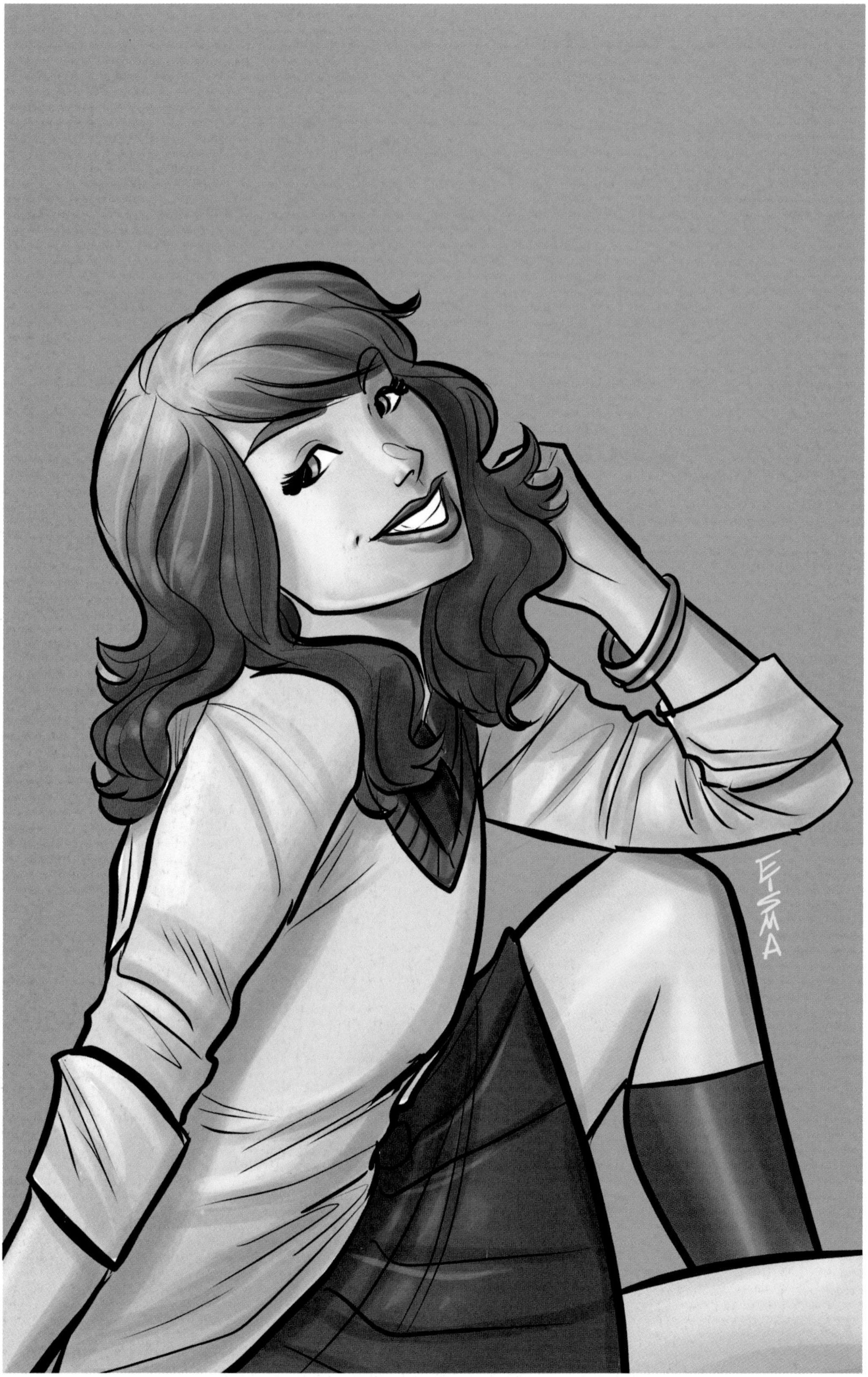
EISMA

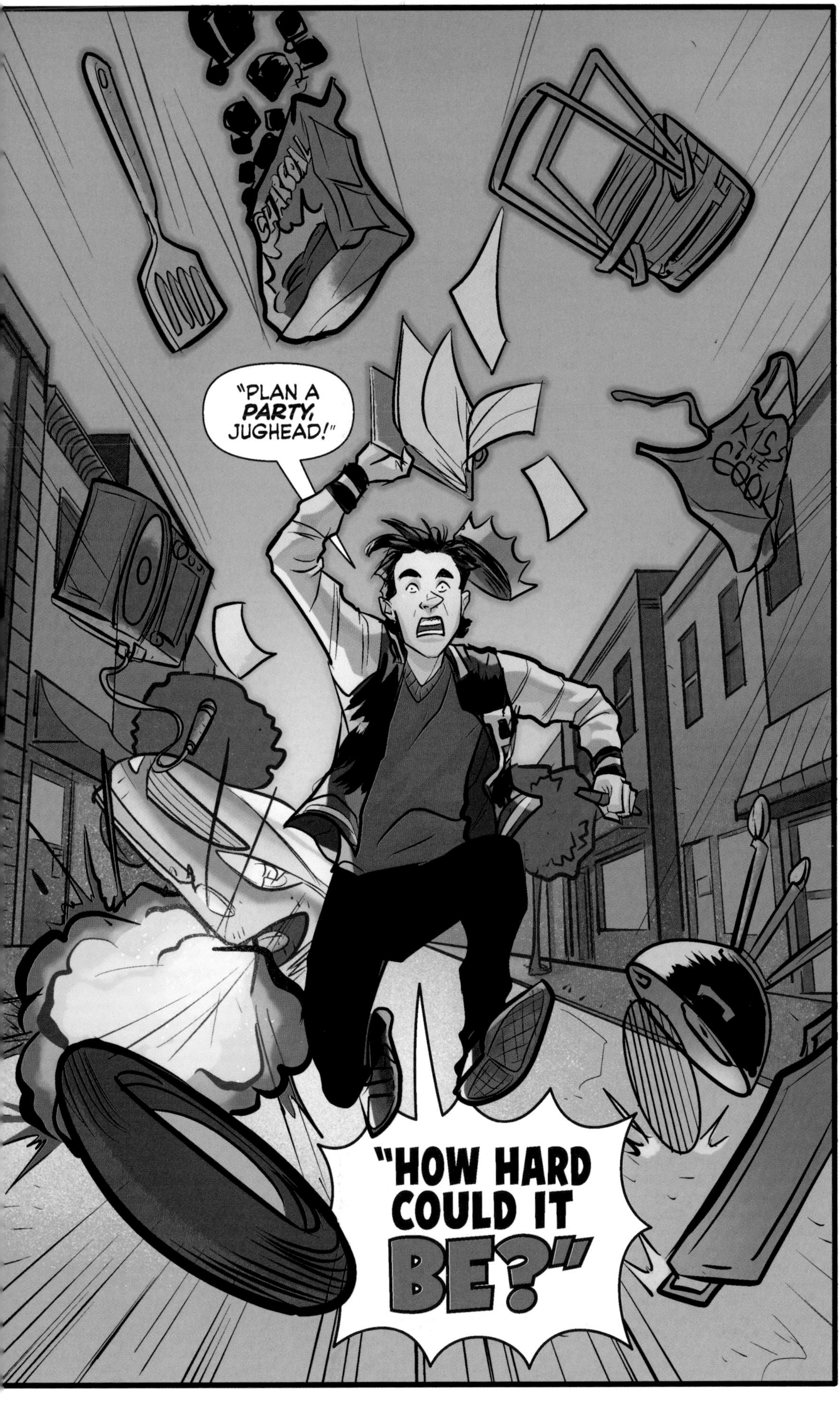
CHARCOAL
"PLAN A PARTY, JUGHEAD!"
KISS THE COOK
"HOW HARD COULD IT BE?"

# CHAPTER ONE: Don't Be ABSURD.

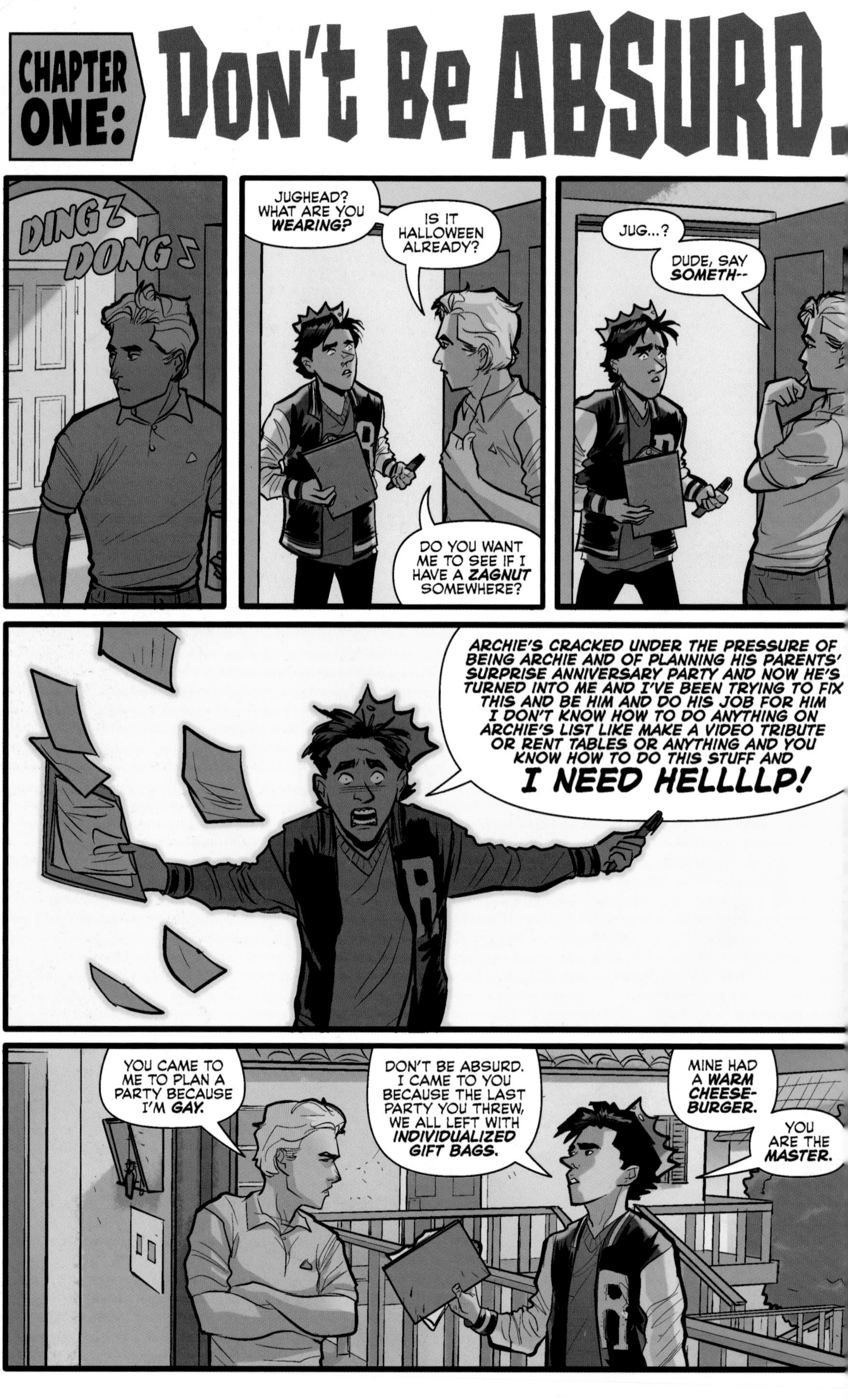

DING DONG
JUGHEAD? WHAT ARE YOU WEARING?
IS IT HALLOWEEN ALREADY?
DO YOU WANT ME TO SEE IF I HAVE A ZAGNUT SOMEWHERE?
JUG...?
DUDE, SAY SOMETH--
ARCHIE'S CRACKED UNDER THE PRESSURE OF BEING ARCHIE AND OF PLANNING HIS PARENTS' SURPRISE ANNIVERSARY PARTY AND NOW HE'S TURNED INTO ME AND I'VE BEEN TRYING TO FIX THIS AND BE HIM AND DO HIS JOB FOR HIM I DON'T KNOW HOW TO DO ANYTHING ON ARCHIE'S LIST LIKE MAKE A VIDEO TRIBUTE OR RENT TABLES OR ANYTHING AND YOU KNOW HOW TO DO THIS STUFF AND I NEED HELLLLP!
YOU CAME TO ME TO PLAN A PARTY BECAUSE I'M GAY.
DON'T BE ABSURD. I CAME TO YOU BECAUSE THE LAST PARTY YOU THREW, WE ALL LEFT WITH INDIVIDUALIZED GIFT BAGS.
MINE HAD A WARM CHEESE-BURGER.
YOU ARE THE MASTER.

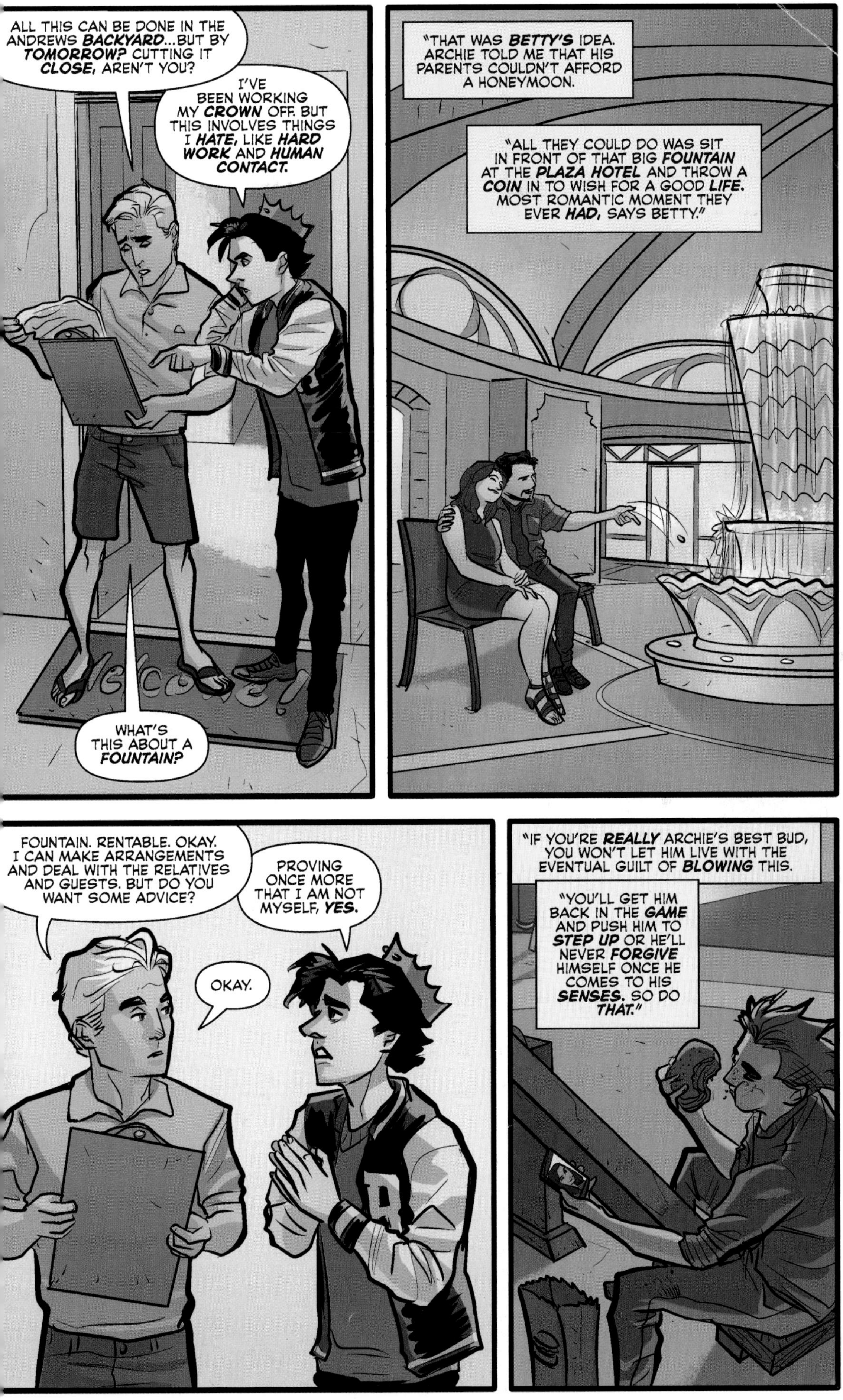
ALL THIS CAN BE DONE IN THE ANDREWS BACKYARD...BUT BY TOMORROW? CUTTING IT CLOSE, AREN'T YOU?
I'VE BEEN WORKING MY CROWN OFF. BUT THIS INVOLVES THINGS I HATE, LIKE HARD WORK AND HUMAN CONTACT.
WHAT'S THIS ABOUT A FOUNTAIN?
"THAT WAS BETTY'S IDEA. ARCHIE TOLD ME THAT HIS PARENTS COULDN'T AFFORD A HONEYMOON.
"ALL THEY COULD DO WAS SIT IN FRONT OF THAT BIG FOUNTAIN AT THE PLAZA HOTEL AND THROW A COIN IN TO WISH FOR A GOOD LIFE. MOST ROMANTIC MOMENT THEY EVER HAD, SAYS BETTY."
FOUNTAIN. RENTABLE. OKAY. I CAN MAKE ARRANGEMENTS AND DEAL WITH THE RELATIVES AND GUESTS. BUT DO YOU WANT SOME ADVICE?
PROVING ONCE MORE THAT I AM NOT MYSELF, YES.
OKAY.
"IF YOU'RE REALLY ARCHIE'S BEST BUD, YOU WON'T LET HIM LIVE WITH THE EVENTUAL GUILT OF BLOWING THIS.
"YOU'LL GET HIM BACK IN THE GAME AND PUSH HIM TO STEP UP OR HE'LL NEVER FORGIVE HIMSELF ONCE HE COMES TO HIS SENSES. SO DO THAT."

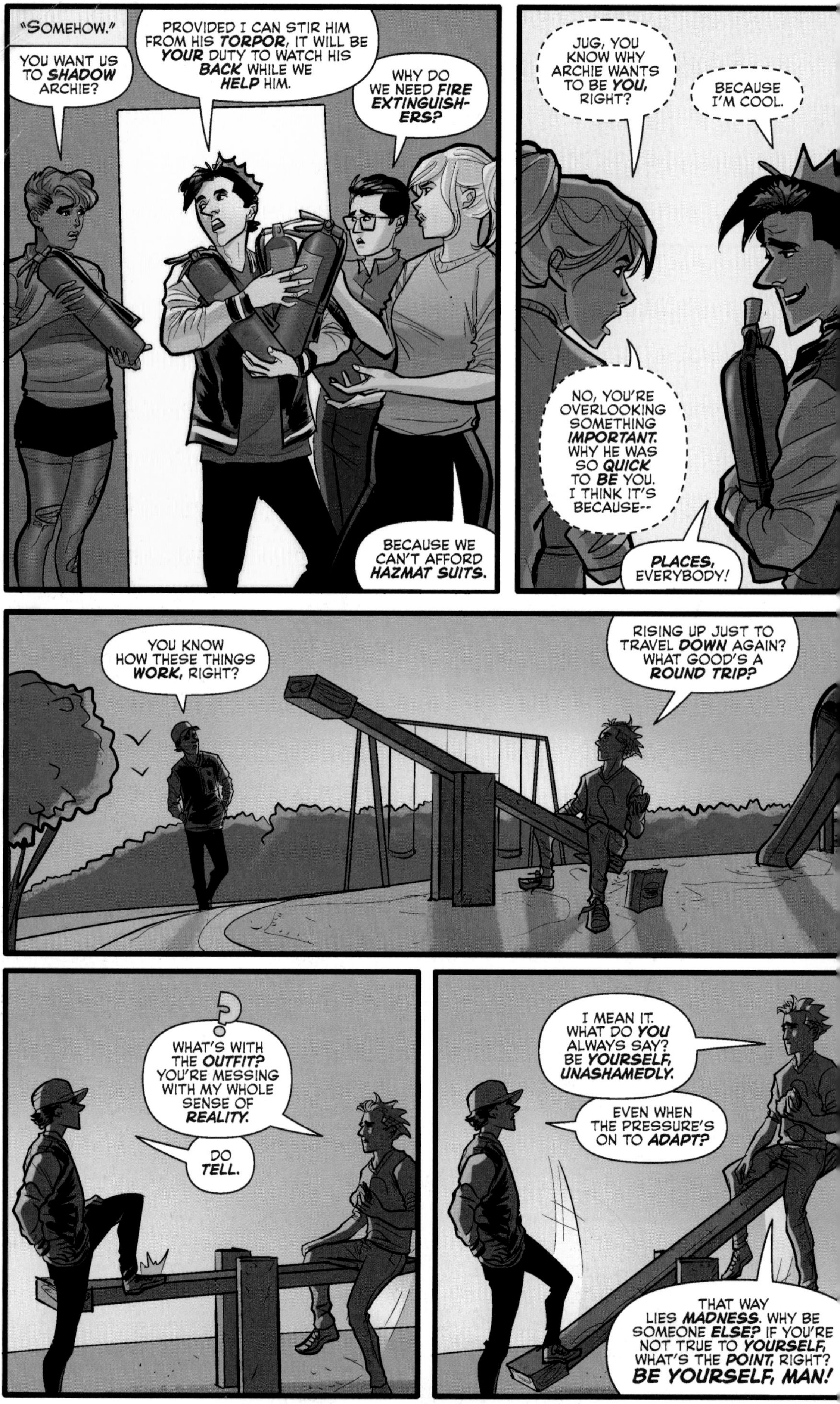
"SOMEHOW."
YOU WANT US TO SHADOW ARCHIE?
PROVIDED I CAN STIR HIM FROM HIS TORPOR, IT WILL BE YOUR DUTY TO WATCH HIS BACK WHILE WE HELP HIM.
WHY DO WE NEED FIRE EXTINGUISHERS?
BECAUSE WE CAN'T AFFORD HAZMAT SUITS.
JUG, YOU KNOW WHY ARCHIE WANTS TO BE YOU, RIGHT?
BECAUSE I'M COOL.
NO, YOU'RE OVERLOOKING SOMETHING IMPORTANT. WHY HE WAS SO QUICK TO BE YOU. I THINK IT'S BECAUSE--
PLACES, EVERYBODY!
YOU KNOW HOW THESE THINGS WORK, RIGHT?
RISING UP JUST TO TRAVEL DOWN AGAIN? WHAT GOOD'S A ROUND TRIP?
?
WHAT'S WITH THE OUTFIT? YOU'RE MESSING WITH MY WHOLE SENSE OF REALITY.
DO TELL.
I MEAN IT. WHAT DO YOU ALWAYS SAY? BE YOURSELF, UNASHAMEDLY.
EVEN WHEN THE PRESSURE'S ON TO ADAPT?
THAT WAY LIES MADNESS. WHY BE SOMEONE ELSE? IF YOU'RE NOT TRUE TO YOURSELF, WHAT'S THE POINT, RIGHT? BE YOURSELF, MAN!

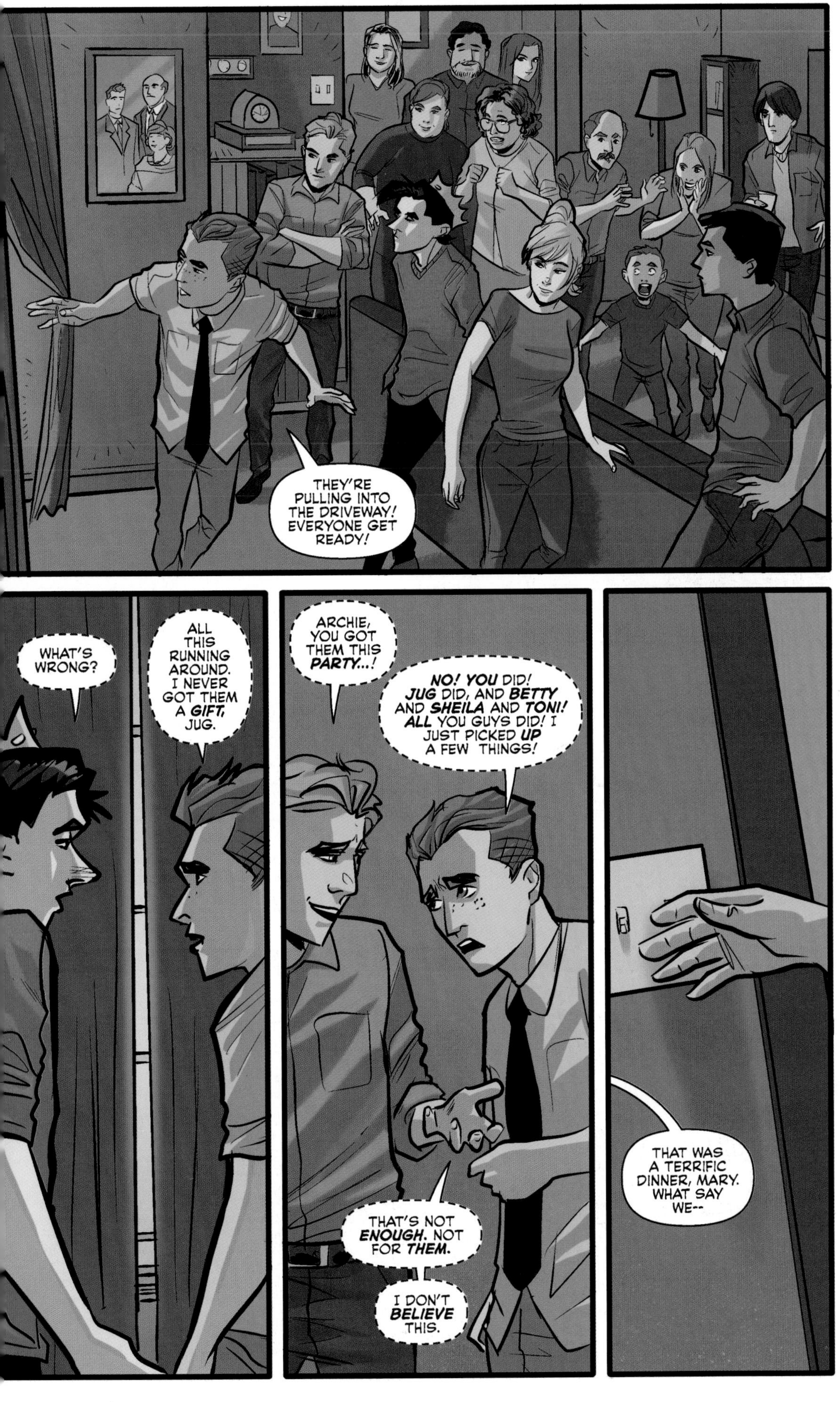
THEY'RE PULLING INTO THE DRIVEWAY! EVERYONE GET READY!
WHAT'S WRONG?
ALL THIS RUNNING AROUND. I NEVER GOT THEM A GIFT, JUG.
ARCHIE, YOU GOT THEM THIS PARTY...!
NO! YOU DID! JUG DID, AND BETTY AND SHEILA AND TONI! ALL YOU GUYS DID! I JUST PICKED UP A FEW THINGS!
THAT'S NOT ENOUGH. NOT FOR THEM.
I DON'T BELIEVE THIS.
THAT WAS A TERRIFIC DINNER, MARY. WHAT SAY WE--

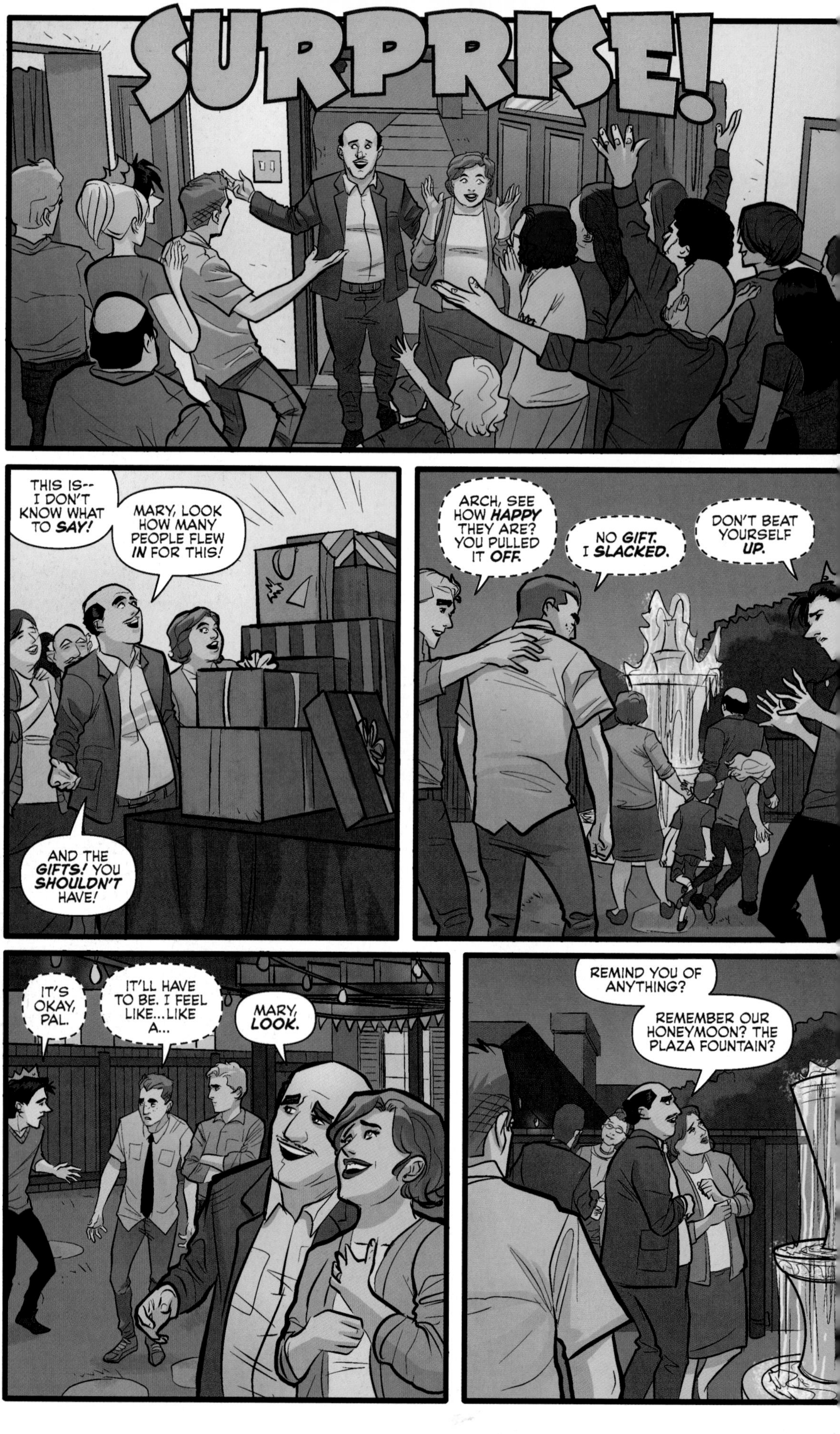
SURPRISE!
THIS IS-- I DON'T KNOW WHAT TO *SAY!*
MARY, LOOK HOW MANY PEOPLE FLEW *IN* FOR THIS!
AND THE *GIFTS!* YOU *SHOULDN'T* HAVE!
ARCH, SEE HOW *HAPPY* THEY ARE? YOU PULLED IT *OFF.*
NO *GIFT.* I *SLACKED.*
DON'T BEAT YOURSELF *UP.*
IT'S OKAY, PAL.
IT'LL HAVE TO BE. I FEEL LIKE...LIKE A...
MARY, *LOOK.*
REMIND YOU OF ANYTHING?
REMEMBER OUR HONEYMOON? THE PLAZA FOUNTAIN?

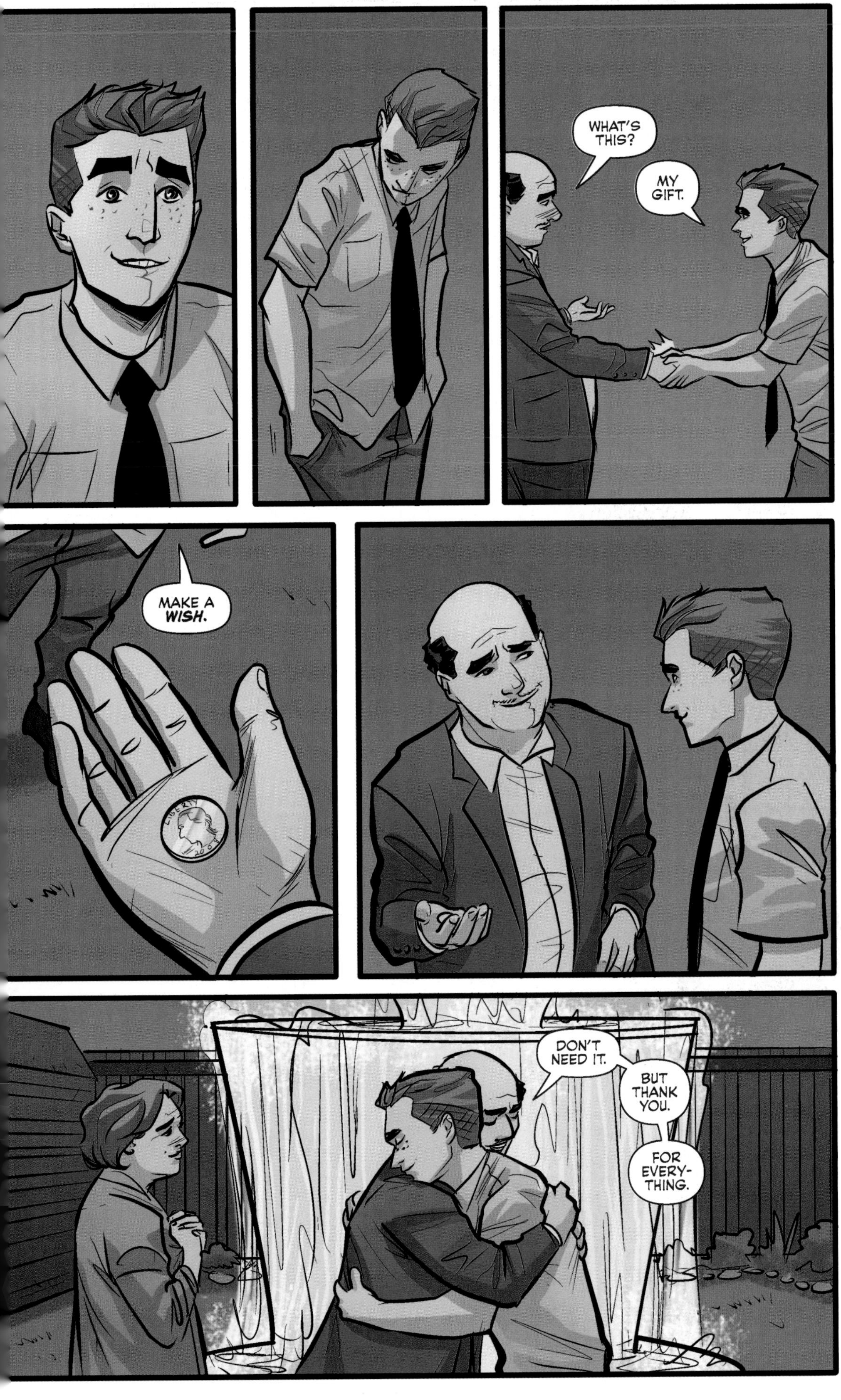
WHAT'S THIS?
MY GIFT.
MAKE A *WISH*.
DON'T NEED IT.
BUT THANK YOU.
FOR EVERY-THING.

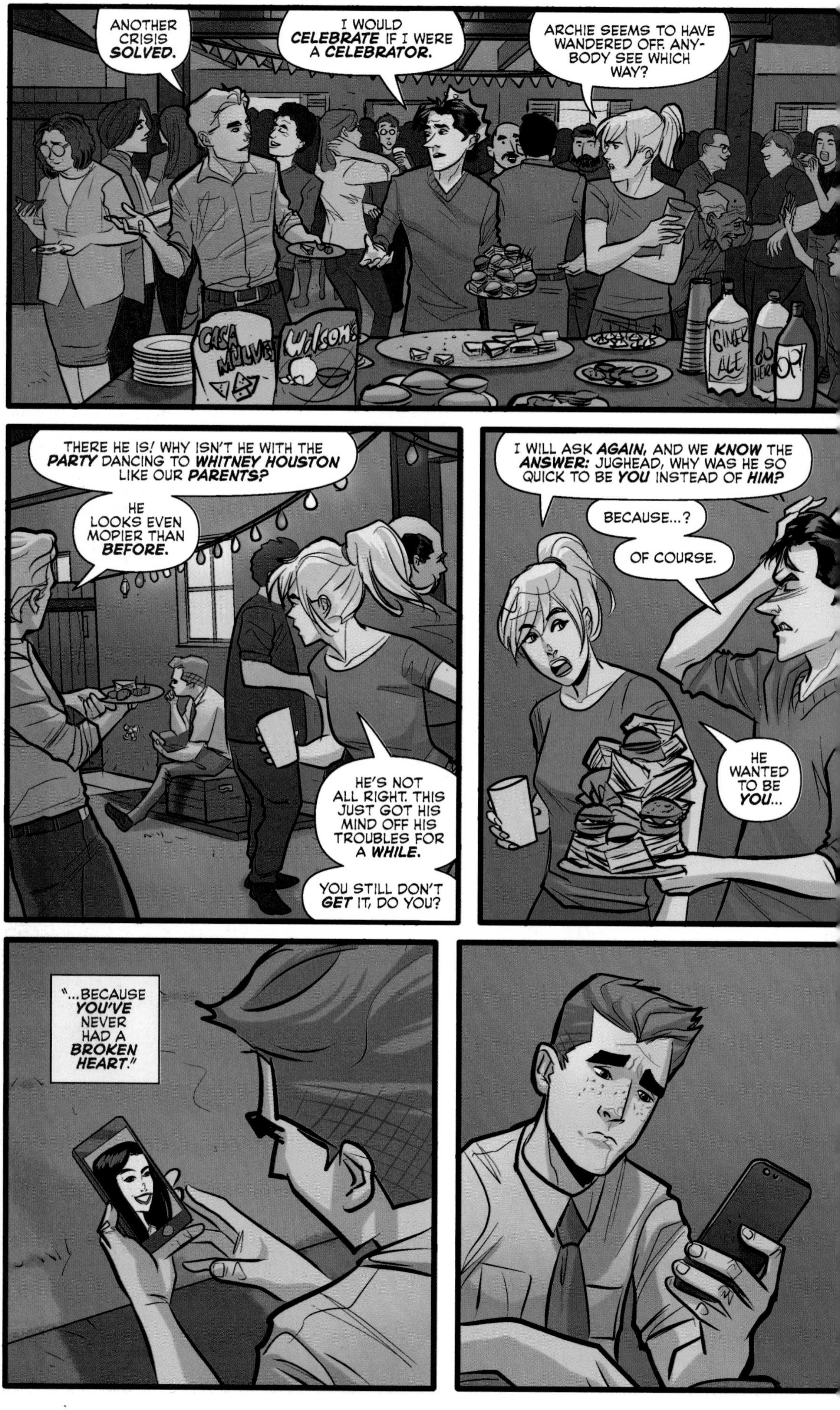
ANOTHER CRISIS SOLVED.
I WOULD CELEBRATE IF I WERE A CELEBRATOR.
ARCHIE SEEMS TO HAVE WANDERED OFF. ANYBODY SEE WHICH WAY?
THERE HE IS! WHY ISN'T HE WITH THE PARTY DANCING TO WHITNEY HOUSTON LIKE OUR PARENTS?
HE LOOKS EVEN MOPIER THAN BEFORE.
HE'S NOT ALL RIGHT. THIS JUST GOT HIS MIND OFF HIS TROUBLES FOR A WHILE.
YOU STILL DON'T GET IT, DO YOU?
I WILL ASK AGAIN, AND WE KNOW THE ANSWER: JUGHEAD, WHY WAS HE SO QUICK TO BE YOU INSTEAD OF HIM?
BECAUSE...?
OF COURSE.
HE WANTED TO BE YOU...
"...BECAUSE YOU'VE NEVER HAD A BROKEN HEART."

# CHAPTER THREE: Swiss Miss

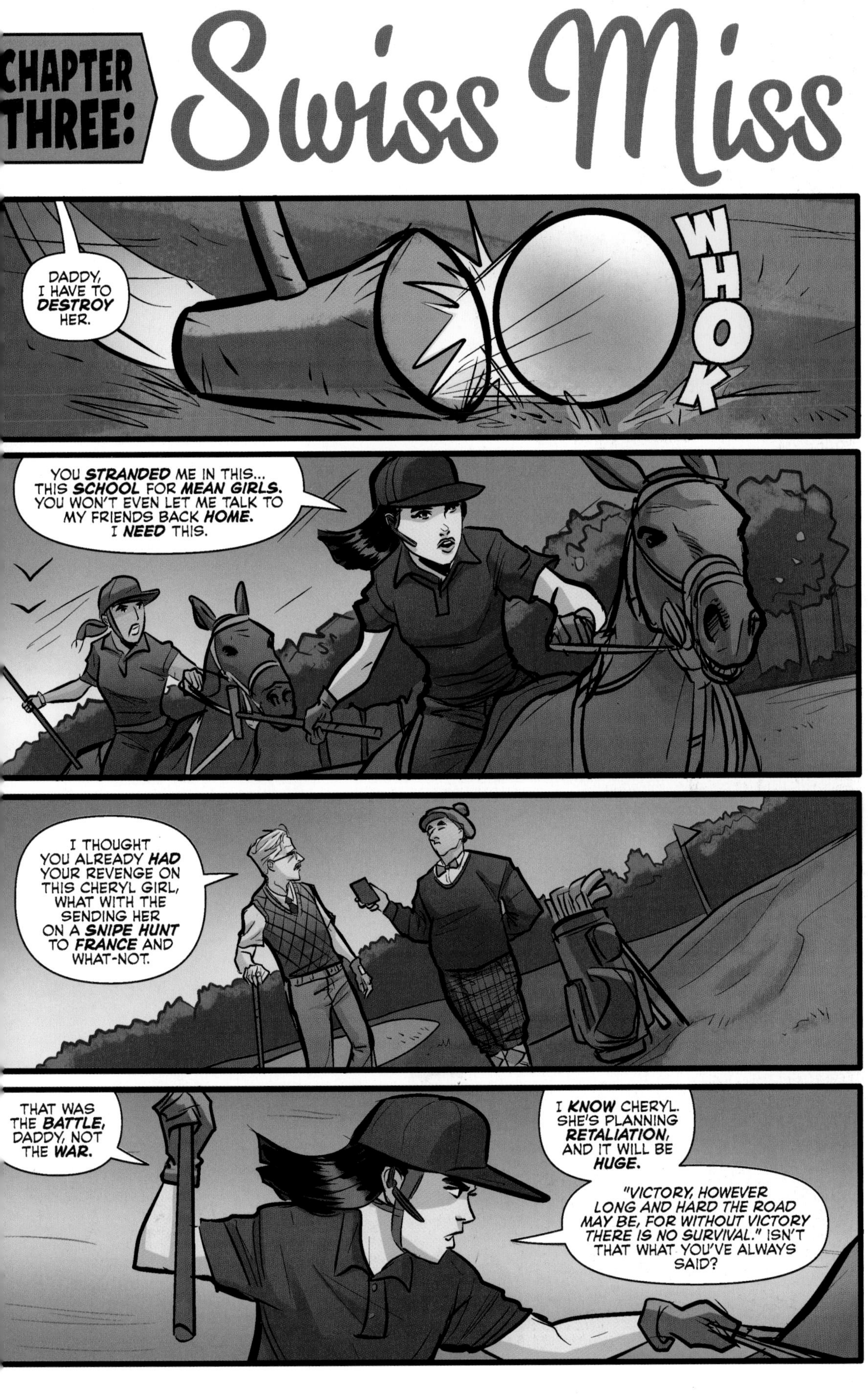
DADDY, I HAVE TO DESTROY HER.
WHOK
YOU STRANDED ME IN THIS... THIS SCHOOL FOR MEAN GIRLS. YOU WON'T EVEN LET ME TALK TO MY FRIENDS BACK HOME. I NEED THIS.
I THOUGHT YOU ALREADY HAD YOUR REVENGE ON THIS CHERYL GIRL, WHAT WITH THE SENDING HER ON A SNIPE HUNT TO FRANCE AND WHAT-NOT.
THAT WAS THE BATTLE, DADDY, NOT THE WAR.
I KNOW CHERYL. SHE'S PLANNING RETALIATION, AND IT WILL BE HUGE.
"VICTORY, HOWEVER LONG AND HARD THE ROAD MAY BE, FOR WITHOUT VICTORY THERE IS NO SURVIVAL." ISN'T THAT WHAT YOU'VE ALWAYS SAID?

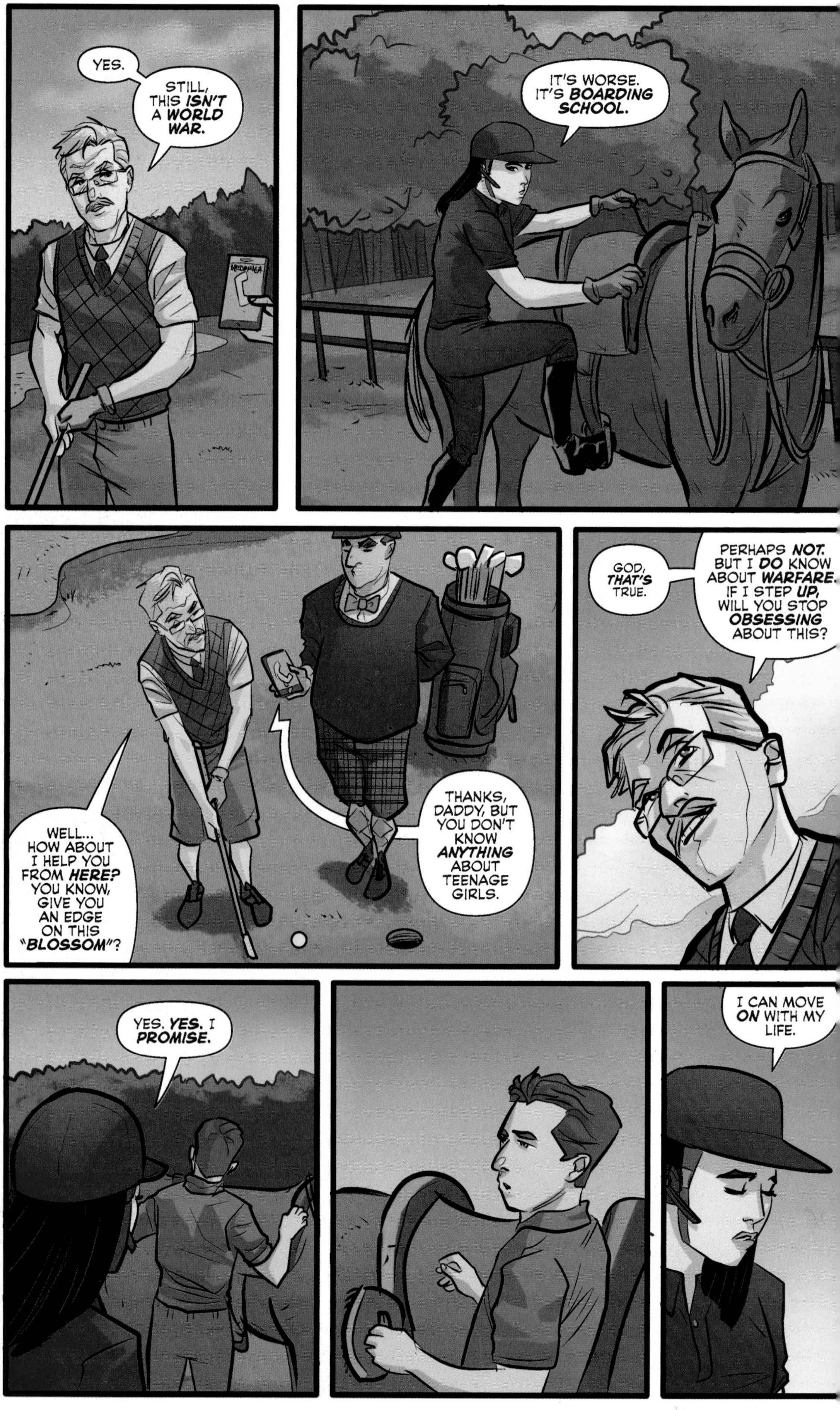
YES.
STILL, THIS ISN'T A WORLD WAR.
IT'S WORSE. IT'S BOARDING SCHOOL.
WELL... HOW ABOUT I HELP YOU FROM HERE? YOU KNOW, GIVE YOU AN EDGE ON THIS "BLOSSOM"?
THANKS, DADDY, BUT YOU DON'T KNOW ANYTHING ABOUT TEENAGE GIRLS.
GOD, THAT'S TRUE.
PERHAPS NOT. BUT I DO KNOW ABOUT WARFARE. IF I STEP UP, WILL YOU STOP OBSESSING ABOUT THIS?
YES. YES. I PROMISE.
I CAN MOVE ON WITH MY LIFE.

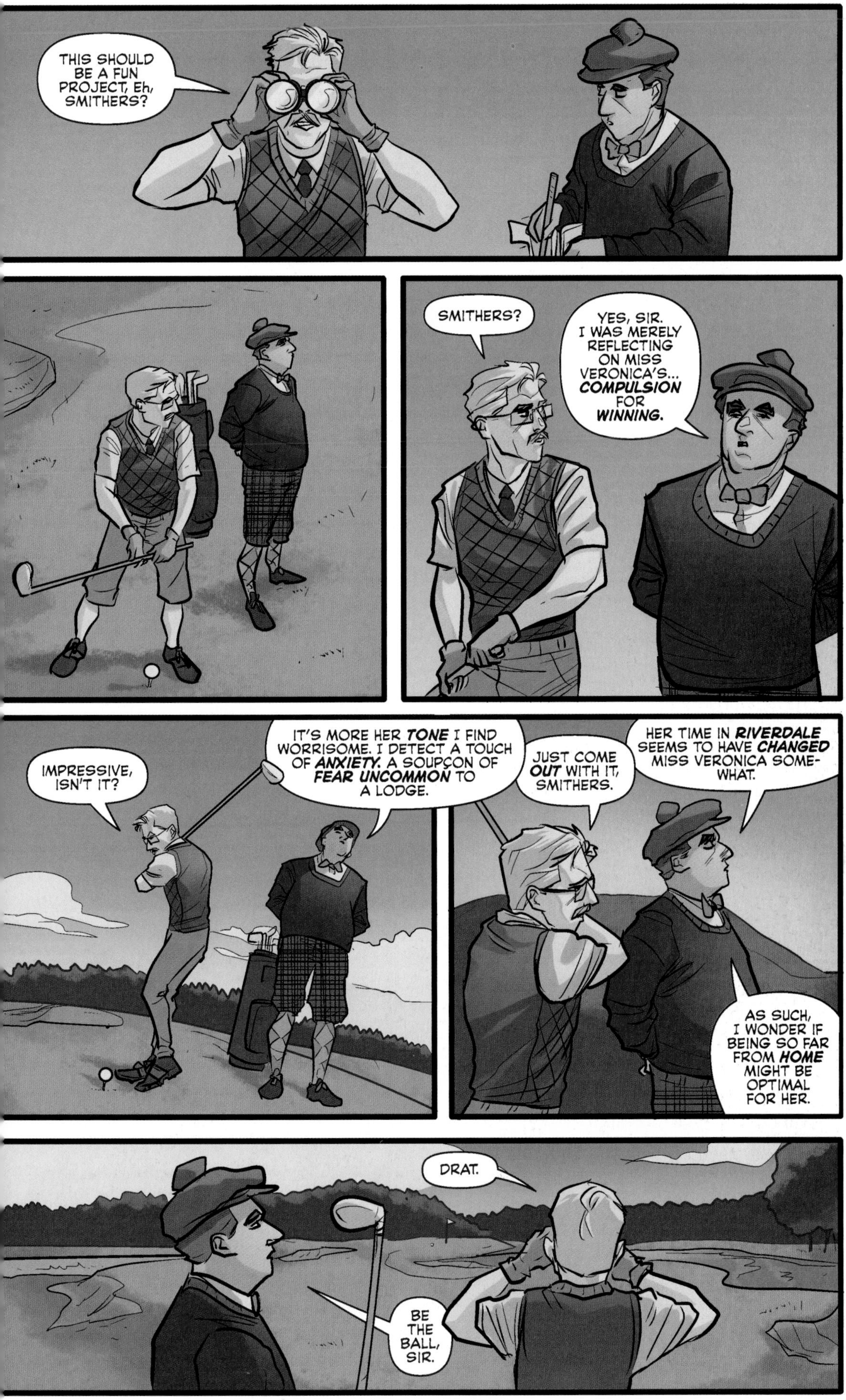

THIS SHOULD BE A FUN PROJECT, Eh, SMITHERS?
SMITHERS?
YES, SIR. I WAS MERELY REFLECTING ON MISS VERONICA'S... **COMPULSION** FOR **WINNING.**
IMPRESSIVE, ISN'T IT?
IT'S MORE HER **TONE** I FIND WORRISOME. I DETECT A TOUCH OF **ANXIETY.** A SOUPÇON OF **FEAR UNCOMMON** TO A LODGE.
JUST COME **OUT** WITH IT, SMITHERS.
HER TIME IN **RIVERDALE** SEEMS TO HAVE **CHANGED** MISS VERONICA SOME-WHAT.
AS SUCH, I WONDER IF BEING SO FAR FROM **HOME** MIGHT BE OPTIMAL FOR HER.
DRAT.
BE THE BALL, SIR.

# CHAPTER FOUR: Here To Gloat?

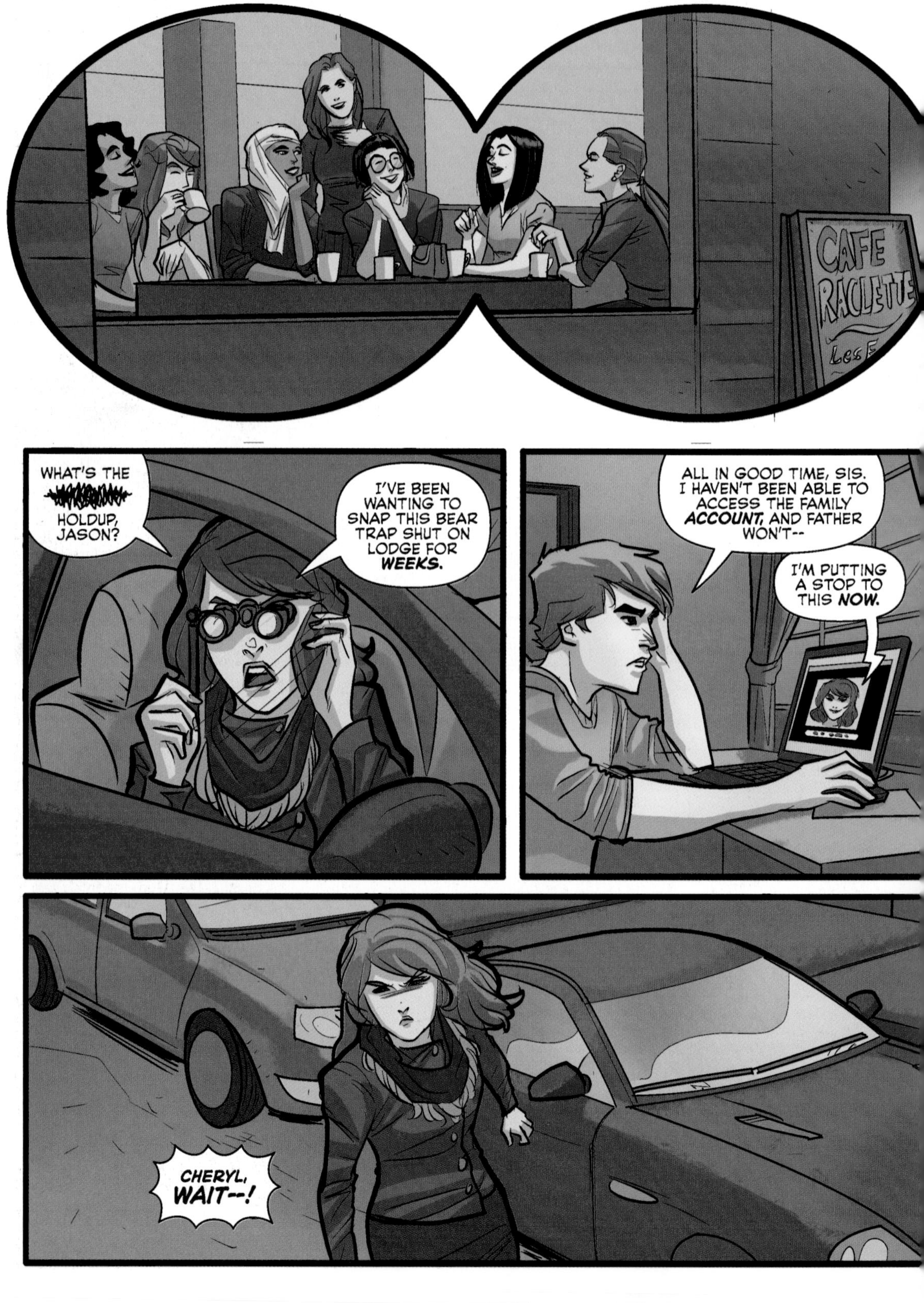
CAFE RACLETTE
WHAT'S THE HOLDUP, JASON?
I'VE BEEN WANTING TO SNAP THIS BEAR TRAP SHUT ON LODGE FOR **WEEKS.**
ALL IN GOOD TIME, SIS. I HAVEN'T BEEN ABLE TO ACCESS THE FAMILY **ACCOUNT,** AND FATHER WON'T--
I'M PUTTING A STOP TO THIS **NOW.**
CHERYL, **WAIT--!**

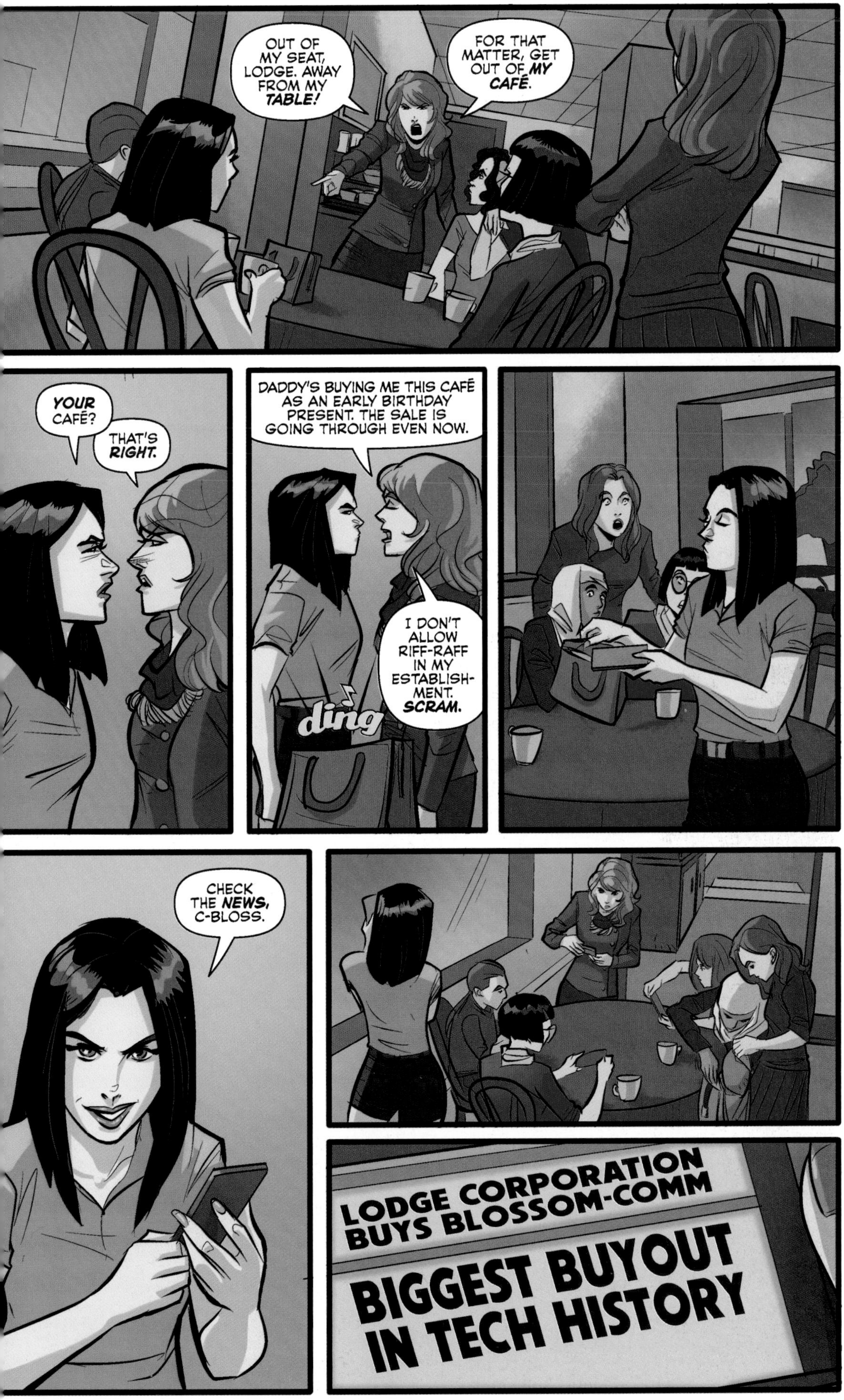
OUT OF MY SEAT, LODGE. AWAY FROM MY TABLE!
FOR THAT MATTER, GET OUT OF MY CAFÉ.
YOUR CAFÉ?
THAT'S RIGHT.
DADDY'S BUYING ME THIS CAFÉ AS AN EARLY BIRTHDAY PRESENT. THE SALE IS GOING THROUGH EVEN NOW.
I DON'T ALLOW RIFF-RAFF IN MY ESTABLISH-MENT. SCRAM.
ding
CHECK THE NEWS, C-BLOSS.
LODGE CORPORATION BUYS BLOSSOM-COMM
BIGGEST BUYOUT IN TECH HISTORY

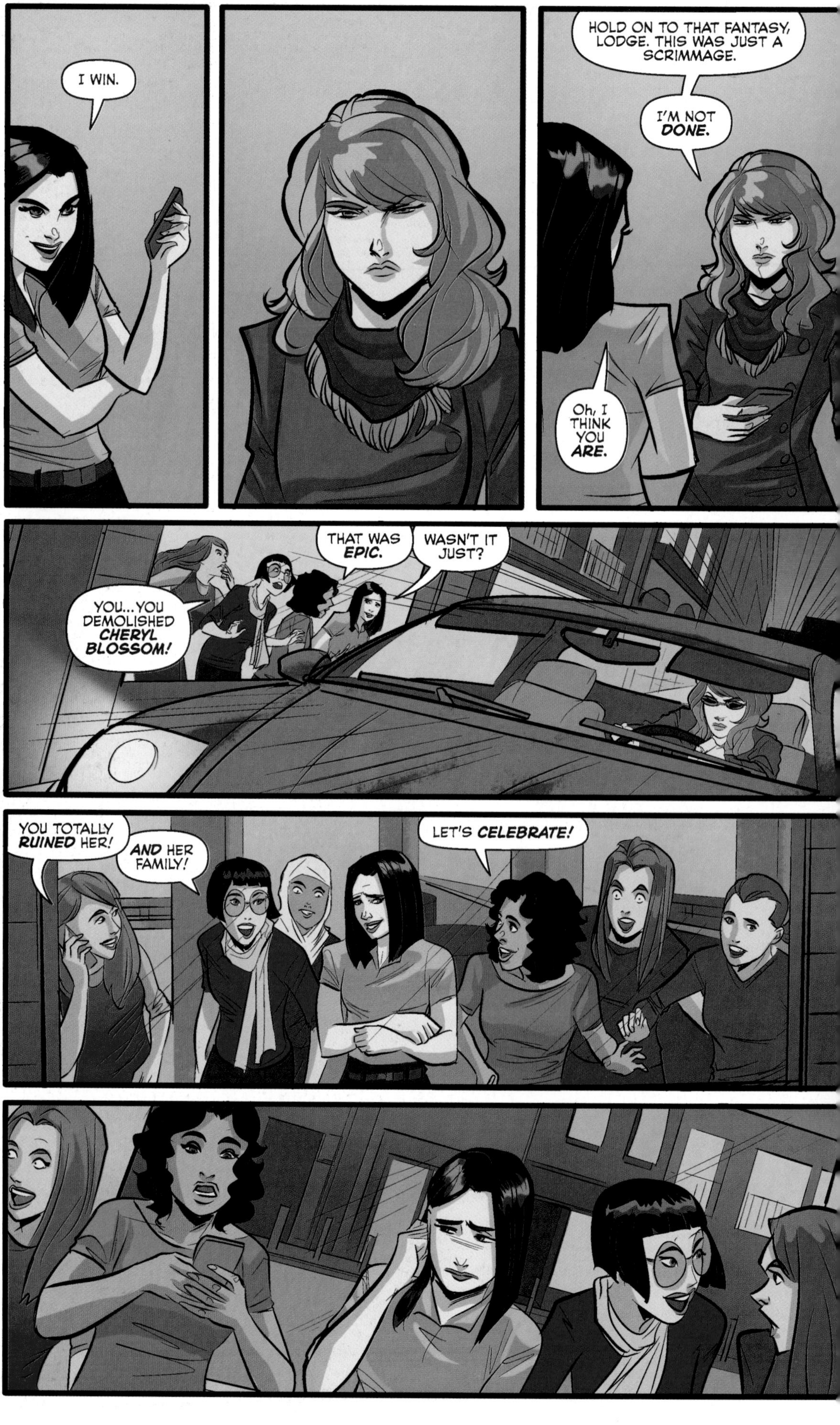

I WIN.
HOLD ON TO THAT FANTASY, LODGE. THIS WAS JUST A SCRIMMAGE.
I'M NOT DONE.
Oh, I THINK YOU ARE.
YOU...YOU DEMOLISHED CHERYL BLOSSOM!
THAT WAS EPIC.
WASN'T IT JUST?
YOU TOTALLY RUINED HER!
AND HER FAMILY!
LET'S CELEBRATE!

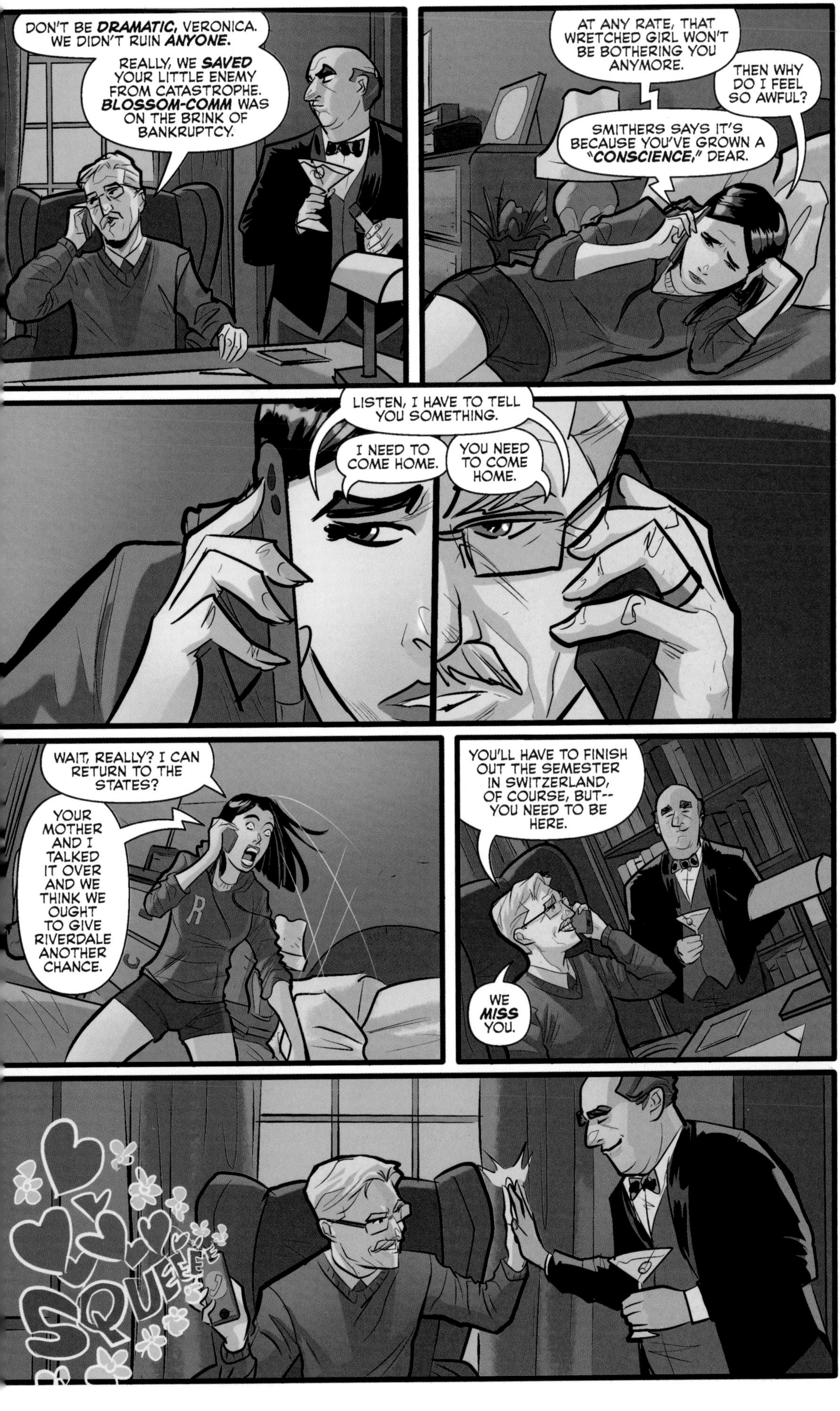
DON'T BE DRAMATIC, VERONICA. WE DIDN'T RUIN ANYONE.
REALLY, WE SAVED YOUR LITTLE ENEMY FROM CATASTROPHE. BLOSSOM-COMM WAS ON THE BRINK OF BANKRUPTCY.
AT ANY RATE, THAT WRETCHED GIRL WON'T BE BOTHERING YOU ANYMORE.
THEN WHY DO I FEEL SO AWFUL?
SMITHERS SAYS IT'S BECAUSE YOU'VE GROWN A "CONSCIENCE," DEAR.
LISTEN, I HAVE TO TELL YOU SOMETHING.
I NEED TO COME HOME.
YOU NEED TO COME HOME.
WAIT, REALLY? I CAN RETURN TO THE STATES?
YOUR MOTHER AND I TALKED IT OVER AND WE THINK WE OUGHT TO GIVE RIVERDALE ANOTHER CHANCE.
YOU'LL HAVE TO FINISH OUT THE SEMESTER IN SWITZERLAND, OF COURSE, BUT-- YOU NEED TO BE HERE.
WE MISS YOU.
SQUEEE

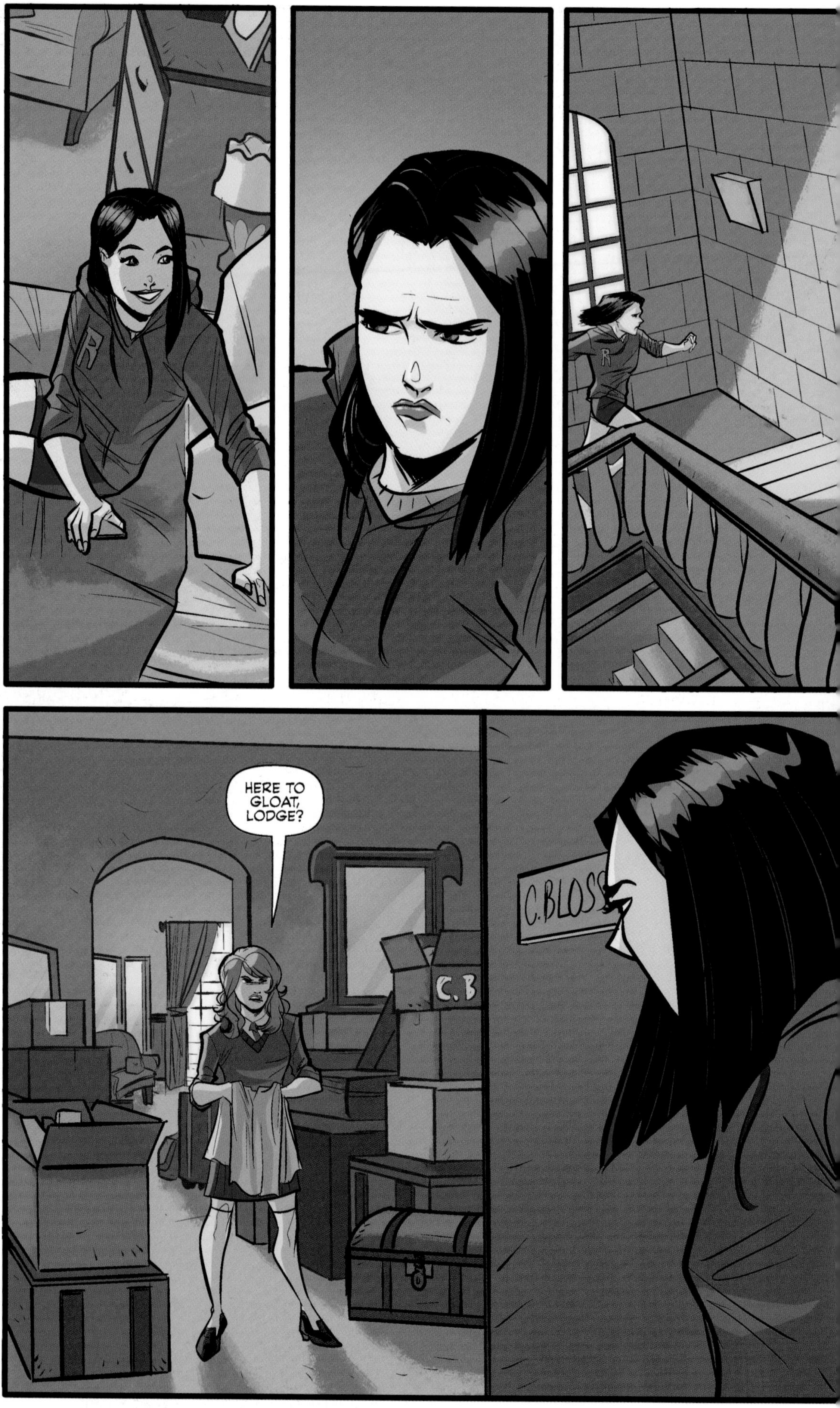
HERE TO GLOAT, LODGE?
C.B
C.BLOSS

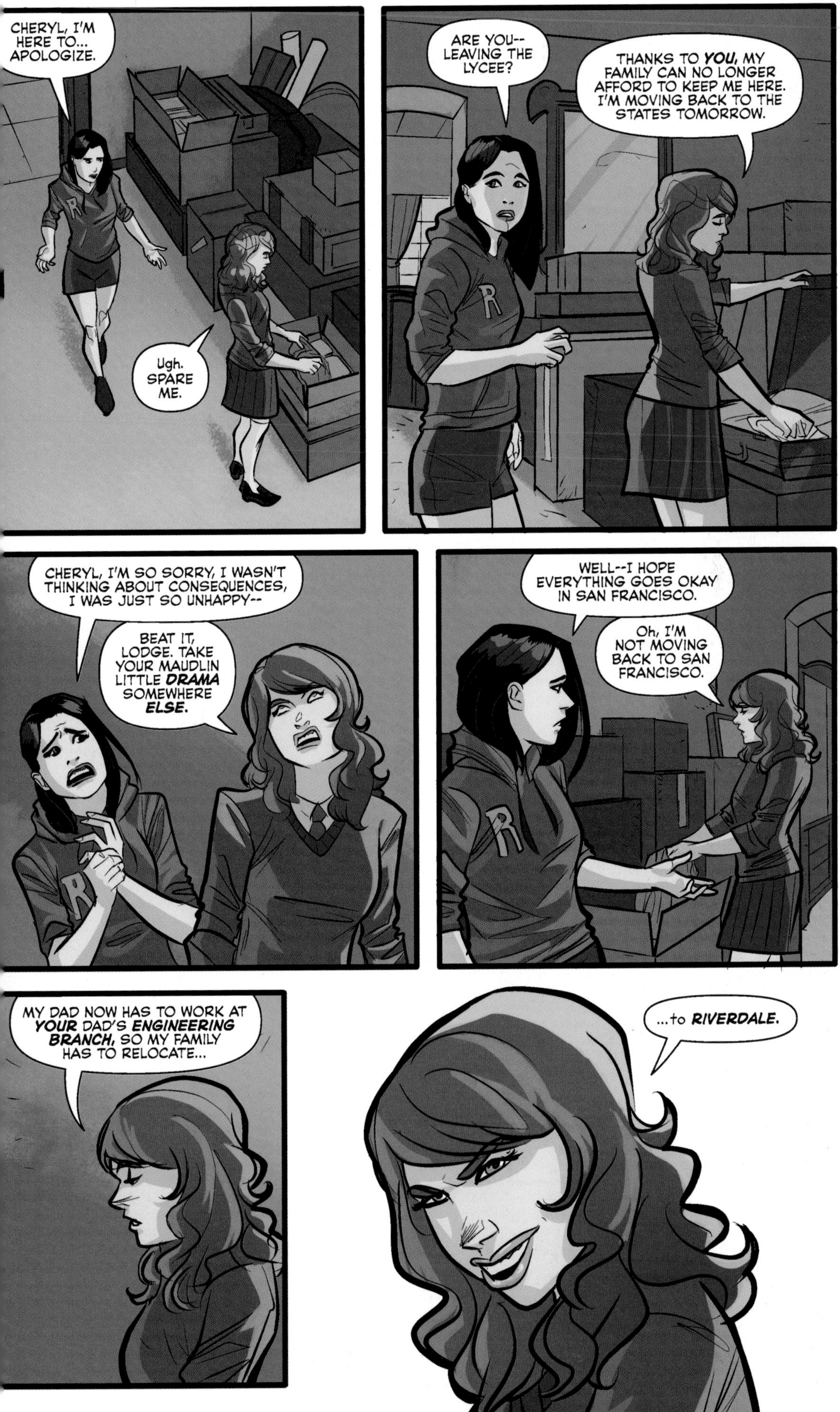

CHERYL, I'M HERE TO... APOLOGIZE.
Ugh. SPARE ME.
ARE YOU-- LEAVING THE LYCEE?
THANKS TO YOU, MY FAMILY CAN NO LONGER AFFORD TO KEEP ME HERE. I'M MOVING BACK TO THE STATES TOMORROW.
CHERYL, I'M SO SORRY, I WASN'T THINKING ABOUT CONSEQUENCES, I WAS JUST SO UNHAPPY--
BEAT IT, LODGE. TAKE YOUR MAUDLIN LITTLE DRAMA SOMEWHERE ELSE.
WELL--I HOPE EVERYTHING GOES OKAY IN SAN FRANCISCO.
Oh, I'M NOT MOVING BACK TO SAN FRANCISCO.
MY DAD NOW HAS TO WORK AT YOUR DAD'S ENGINEERING BRANCH, SO MY FAMILY HAS TO RELOCATE...
...to RIVERDALE.

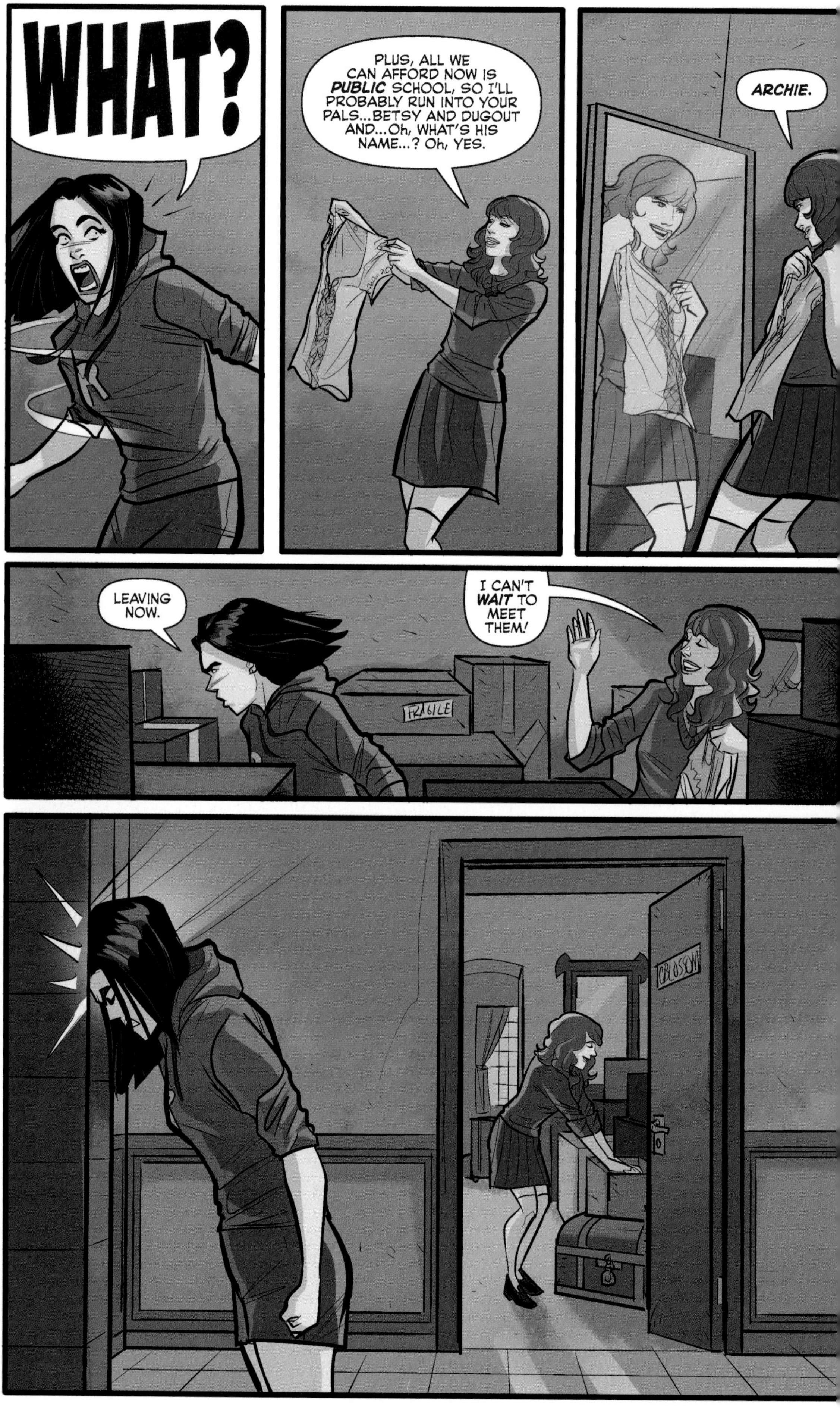
WHAT?
PLUS, ALL WE CAN AFFORD NOW IS PUBLIC SCHOOL, SO I'LL PROBABLY RUN INTO YOUR PALS...BETSY AND DUGOUT AND...Oh, WHAT'S HIS NAME...? Oh, YES.
ARCHIE.
LEAVING NOW.
I CAN'T WAIT TO MEET THEM!
FRAGILE
BLOSSOM

TO BE CONTINUED...

# ISSUE SIXTEEN

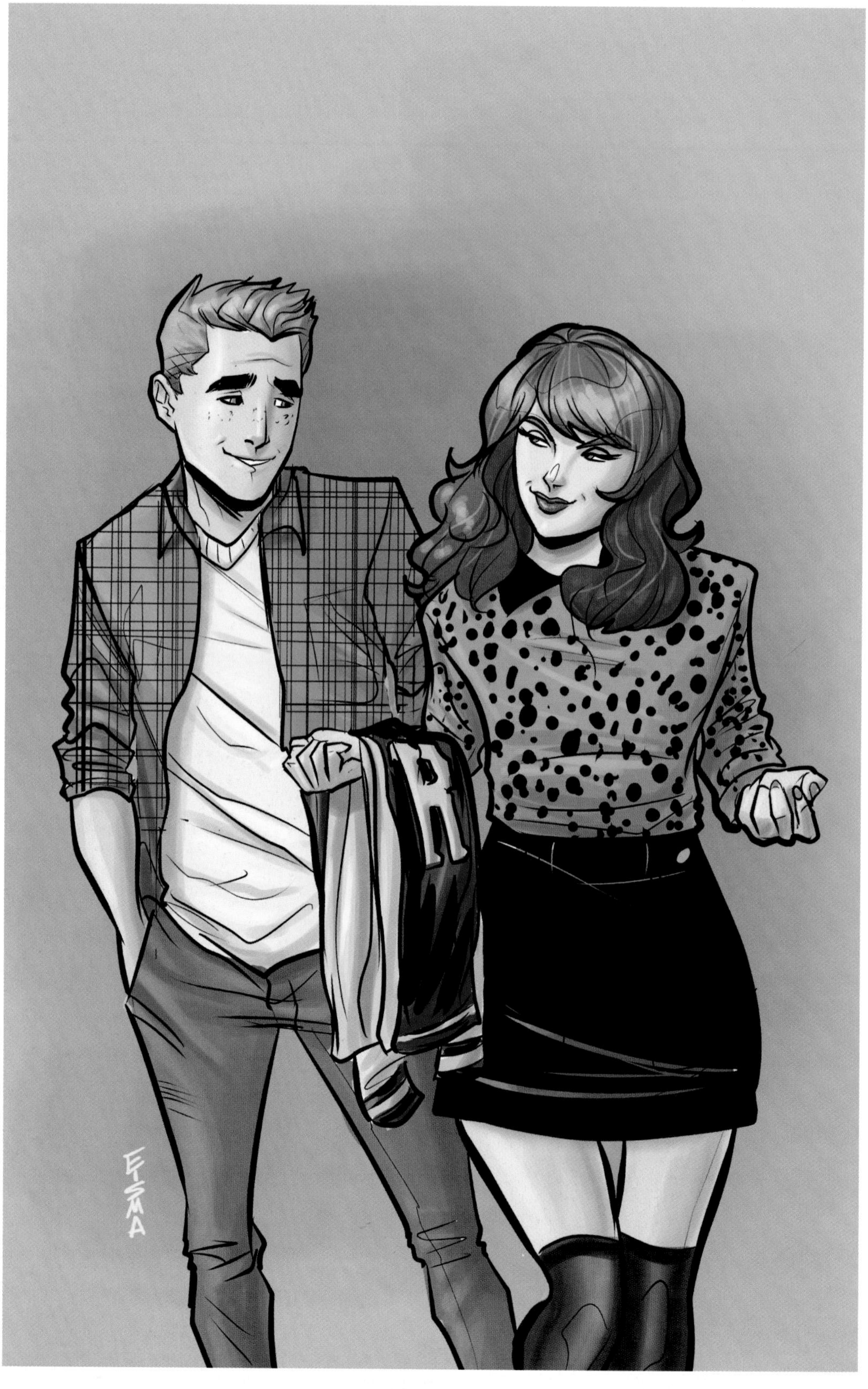
EISMA

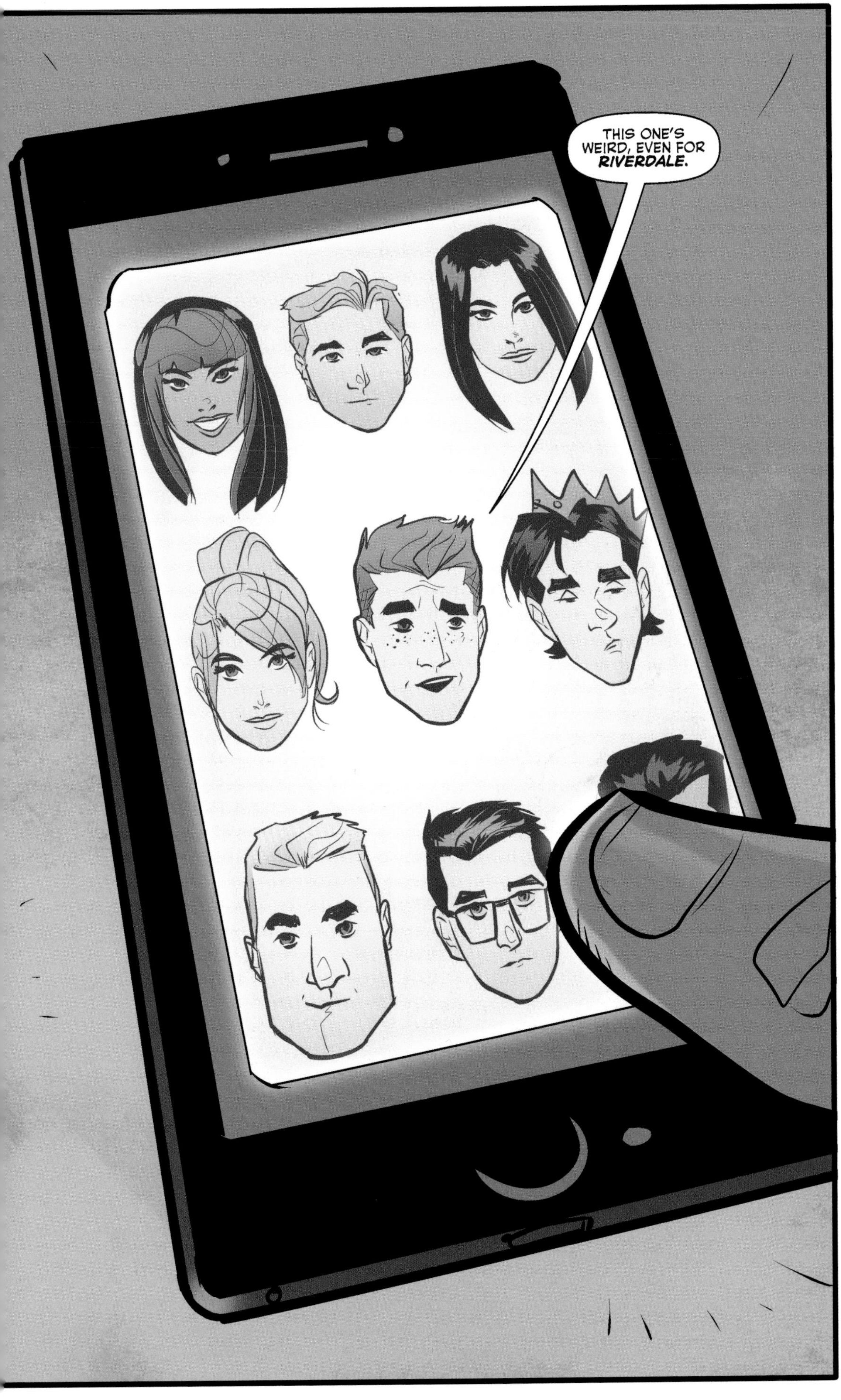
THIS ONE'S WEIRD, EVEN FOR *RIVERDALE*.

# CHAPTER ONE: YOU'VE INVENTED YELP.

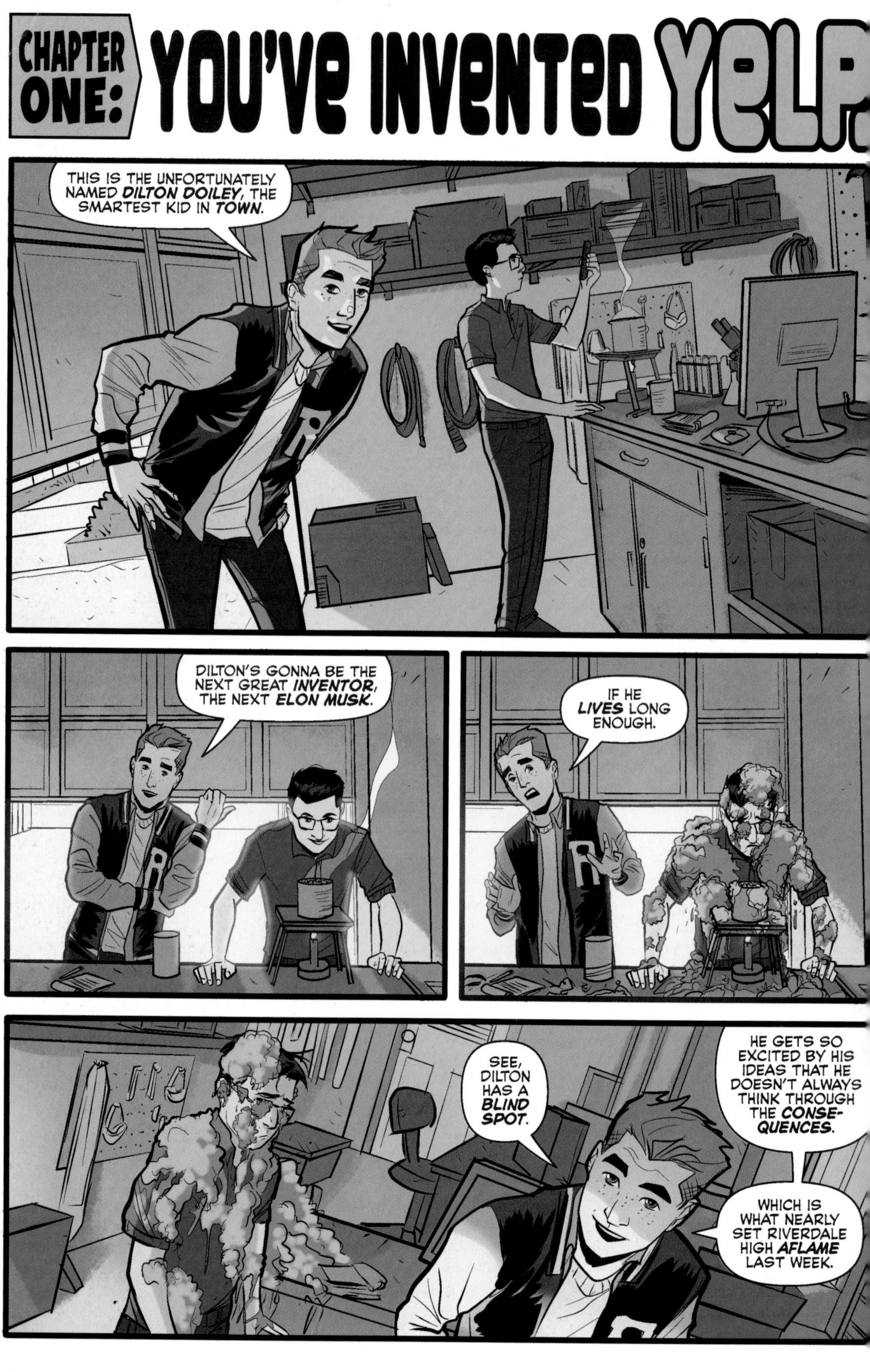
THIS IS THE UNFORTUNATELY NAMED DILTON DOILEY, THE SMARTEST KID IN TOWN.
DILTON'S GONNA BE THE NEXT GREAT INVENTOR, THE NEXT ELON MUSK.
IF HE LIVES LONG ENOUGH.
SEE, DILTON HAS A BLIND SPOT.
HE GETS SO EXCITED BY HIS IDEAS THAT HE DOESN'T ALWAYS THINK THROUGH THE CONSE-QUENCES.
WHICH IS WHAT NEARLY SET RIVERDALE HIGH AFLAME LAST WEEK.

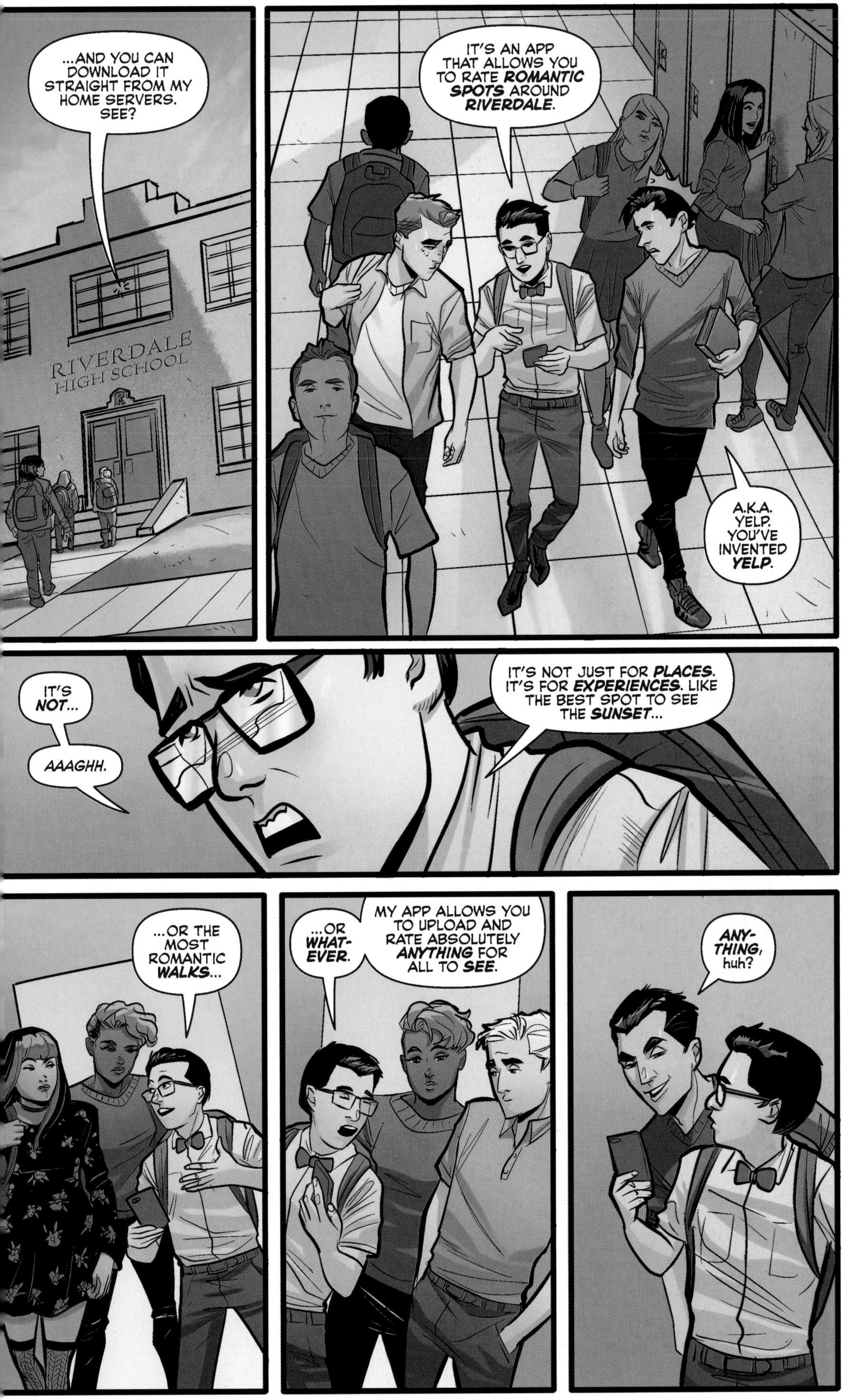
...AND YOU CAN DOWNLOAD IT STRAIGHT FROM MY HOME SERVERS. SEE?
RIVERDALE HIGH SCHOOL
IT'S AN APP THAT ALLOWS YOU TO RATE ROMANTIC SPOTS AROUND RIVERDALE.
A.K.A. YELP. YOU'VE INVENTED YELP.
IT'S NOT...
AAAGHH.
IT'S NOT JUST FOR PLACES. IT'S FOR EXPERIENCES. LIKE THE BEST SPOT TO SEE THE SUNSET...
...OR THE MOST ROMANTIC WALKS...
...OR WHAT-EVER.
MY APP ALLOWS YOU TO UPLOAD AND RATE ABSOLUTELY ANYTHING FOR ALL TO SEE.
ANY-THING, huh?

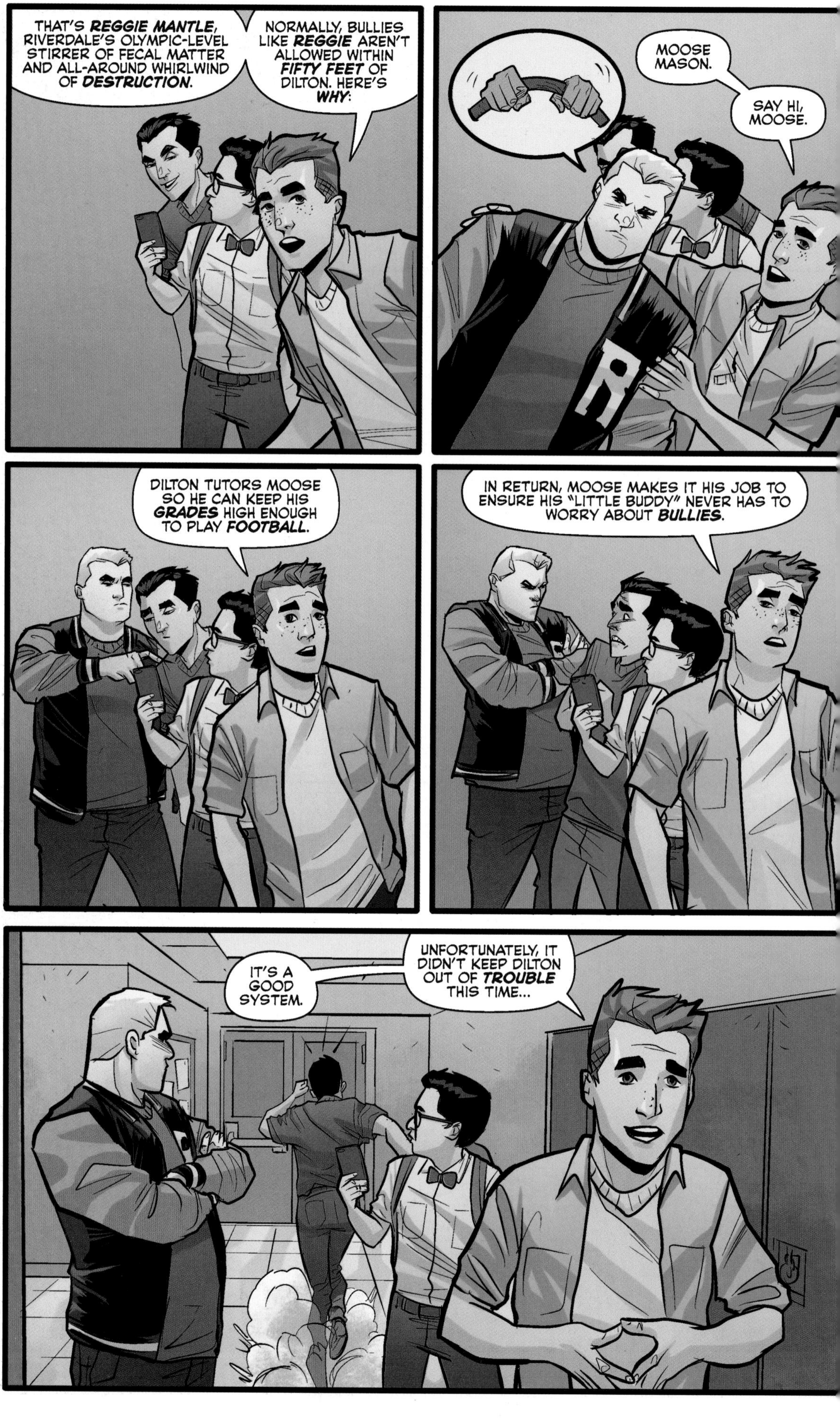
THAT'S REGGIE MANTLE, RIVERDALE'S OLYMPIC-LEVEL STIRRER OF FECAL MATTER AND ALL-AROUND WHIRLWIND OF DESTRUCTION.
NORMALLY, BULLIES LIKE REGGIE AREN'T ALLOWED WITHIN FIFTY FEET OF DILTON. HERE'S WHY:
MOOSE MASON.
SAY HI, MOOSE.
DILTON TUTORS MOOSE SO HE CAN KEEP HIS GRADES HIGH ENOUGH TO PLAY FOOTBALL.
IN RETURN, MOOSE MAKES IT HIS JOB TO ENSURE HIS "LITTLE BUDDY" NEVER HAS TO WORRY ABOUT BULLIES.
IT'S A GOOD SYSTEM.
UNFORTUNATELY, IT DIDN'T KEEP DILTON OUT OF TROUBLE THIS TIME...

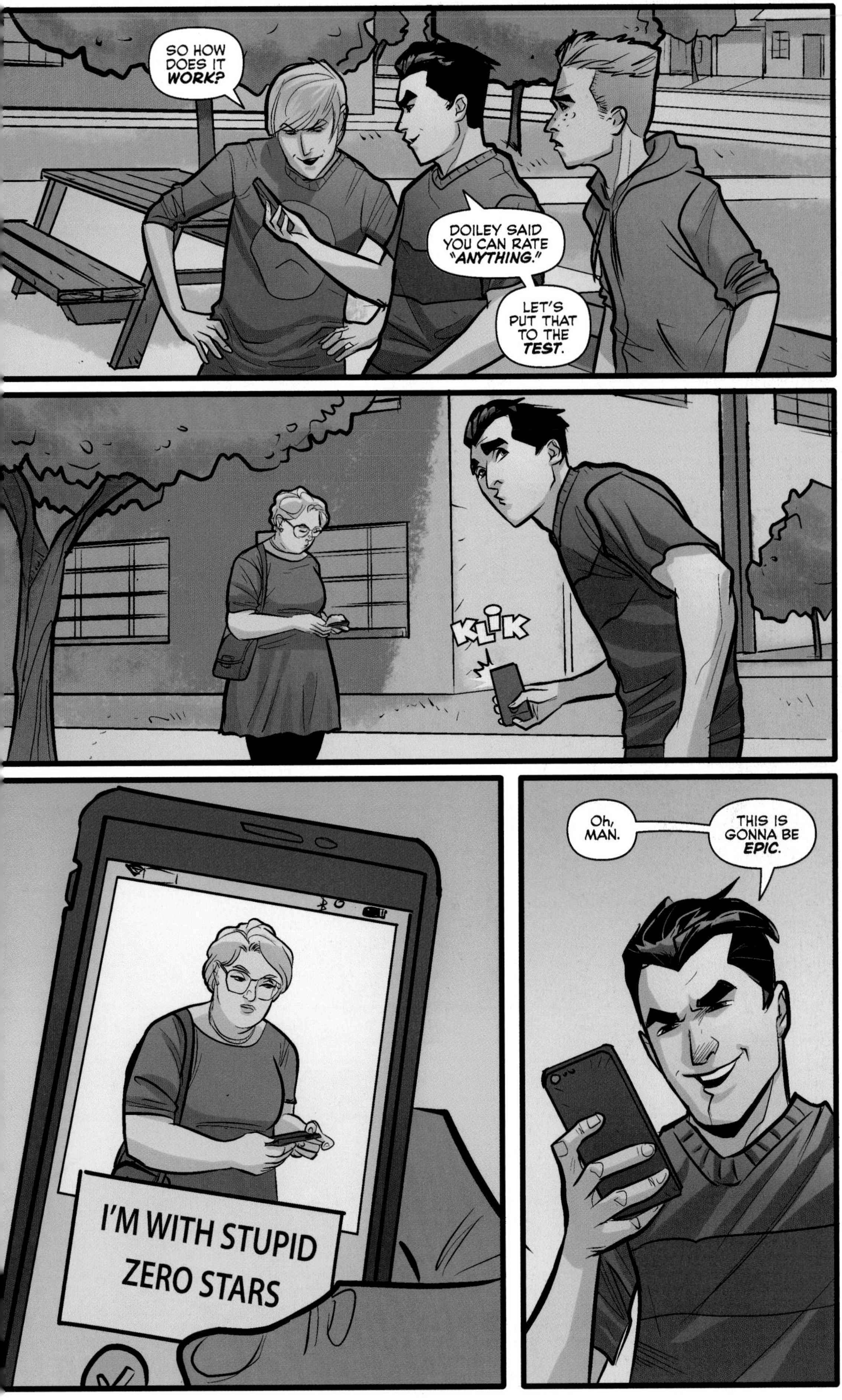
SO HOW DOES IT WORK?
DOILEY SAID YOU CAN RATE "ANYTHING."
LET'S PUT THAT TO THE TEST.
KLIK
I'M WITH STUPID
ZERO STARS
Oh, MAN.
THIS IS GONNA BE EPIC.

# CHAPTER TWO: ELSEWHERE, VERONICA...

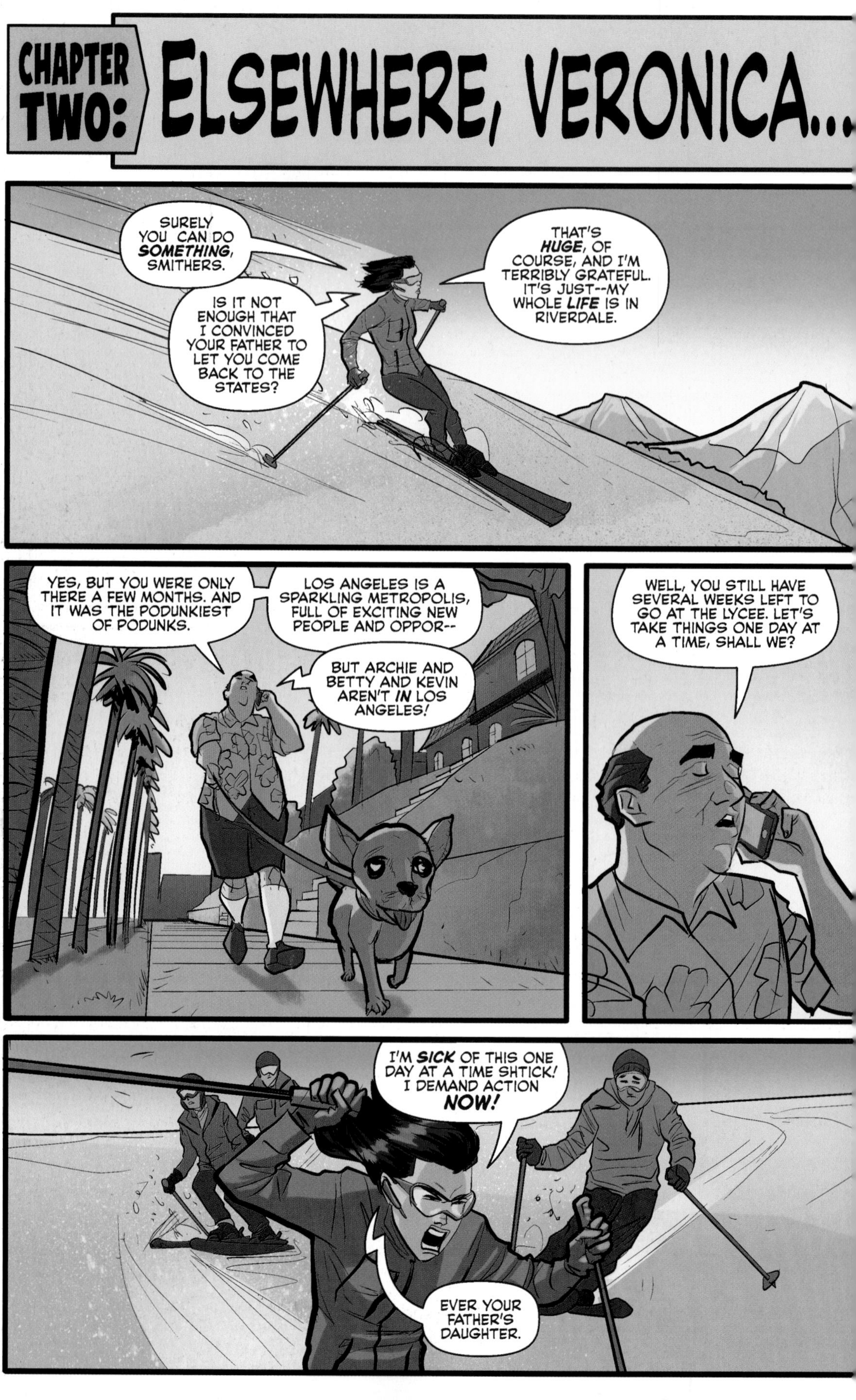
SURELY YOU CAN DO SOMETHING, SMITHERS.
IS IT NOT ENOUGH THAT I CONVINCED YOUR FATHER TO LET YOU COME BACK TO THE STATES?
THAT'S HUGE, OF COURSE, AND I'M TERRIBLY GRATEFUL. IT'S JUST--MY WHOLE LIFE IS IN RIVERDALE.
YES, BUT YOU WERE ONLY THERE A FEW MONTHS. AND IT WAS THE PODUNKIEST OF PODUNKS.
LOS ANGELES IS A SPARKLING METROPOLIS, FULL OF EXCITING NEW PEOPLE AND OPPOR--
BUT ARCHIE AND BETTY AND KEVIN AREN'T IN LOS ANGELES!
WELL, YOU STILL HAVE SEVERAL WEEKS LEFT TO GO AT THE LYCEE. LET'S TAKE THINGS ONE DAY AT A TIME, SHALL WE?
I'M SICK OF THIS ONE DAY AT A TIME SHTICK! I DEMAND ACTION NOW!
EVER YOUR FATHER'S DAUGHTER.

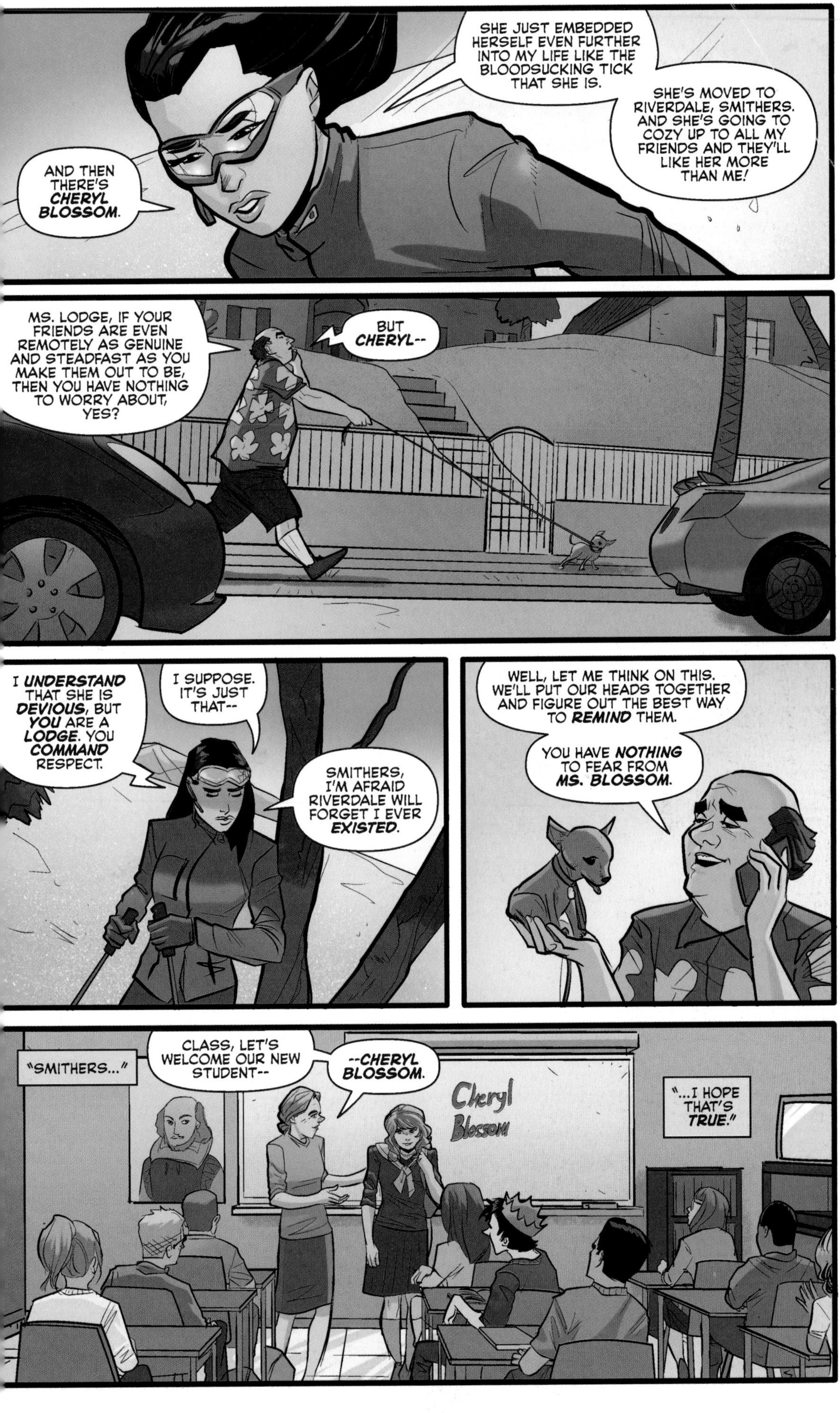

SHE JUST EMBEDDED HERSELF EVEN FURTHER INTO MY LIFE LIKE THE BLOODSUCKING TICK THAT SHE IS.
AND THEN THERE'S CHERYL BLOSSOM.
SHE'S MOVED TO RIVERDALE, SMITHERS. AND SHE'S GOING TO COZY UP TO ALL MY FRIENDS AND THEY'LL LIKE HER MORE THAN ME!
MS. LODGE, IF YOUR FRIENDS ARE EVEN REMOTELY AS GENUINE AND STEADFAST AS YOU MAKE THEM OUT TO BE, THEN YOU HAVE NOTHING TO WORRY ABOUT, YES?
BUT CHERYL--
I UNDERSTAND THAT SHE IS DEVIOUS, BUT YOU ARE A LODGE. YOU COMMAND RESPECT.
I SUPPOSE. IT'S JUST THAT--
SMITHERS, I'M AFRAID RIVERDALE WILL FORGET I EVER EXISTED.
WELL, LET ME THINK ON THIS. WE'LL PUT OUR HEADS TOGETHER AND FIGURE OUT THE BEST WAY TO REMIND THEM.
YOU HAVE NOTHING TO FEAR FROM MS. BLOSSOM.
"SMITHERS..."
CLASS, LET'S WELCOME OUR NEW STUDENT--
--CHERYL BLOSSOM.
Cheryl Blossom
"...I HOPE THAT'S TRUE."

# CHAPTER THREE: The STARS of RIVERDALE

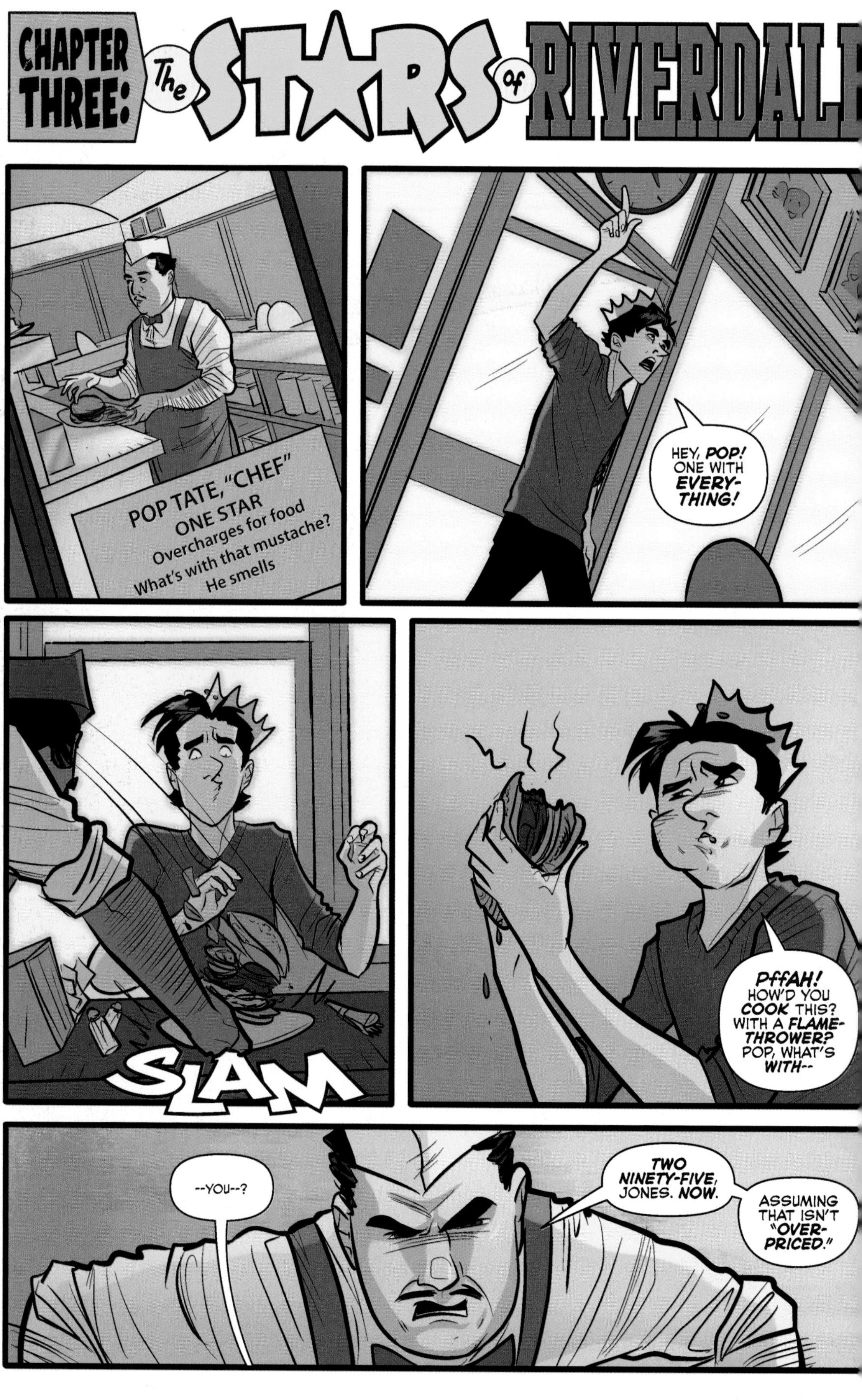

POP TATE, "CHEF"
ONE STAR
Overcharges for food
What's with that mustache?
He smells
HEY, POP! ONE WITH EVERY-THING!
SLAM
PffAH! HOW'D YOU COOK THIS? WITH A FLAME-THROWER? POP, WHAT'S WITH--
--YOU--?
TWO NINETY-FIVE, JONES. NOW.
ASSUMING THAT ISN'T "OVER-PRICED."

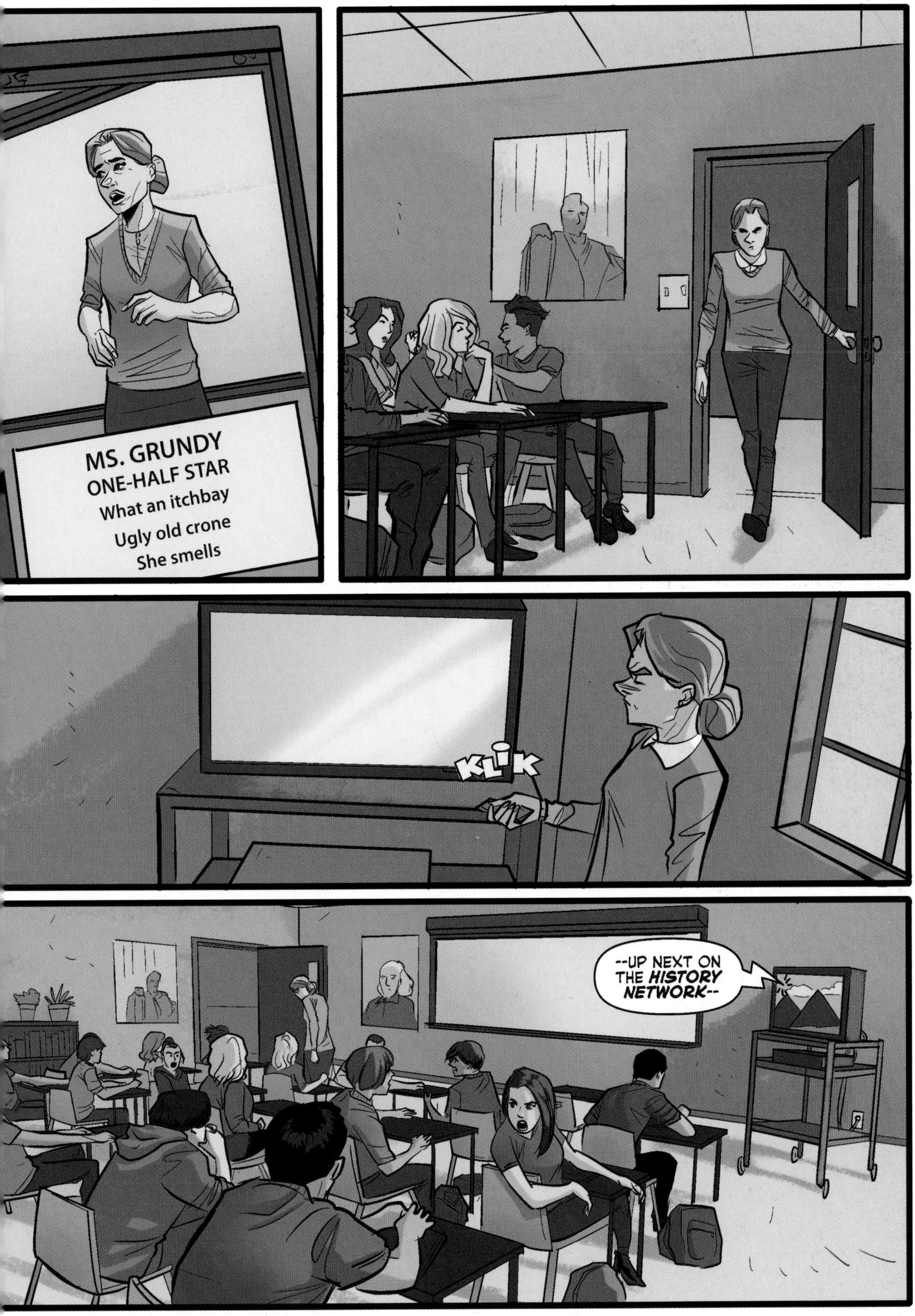
MS. GRUNDY
ONE-HALF STAR
What an itchbay
Ugly old crone
She smells
KLIK
--UP NEXT ON THE HISTORY NETWORK--

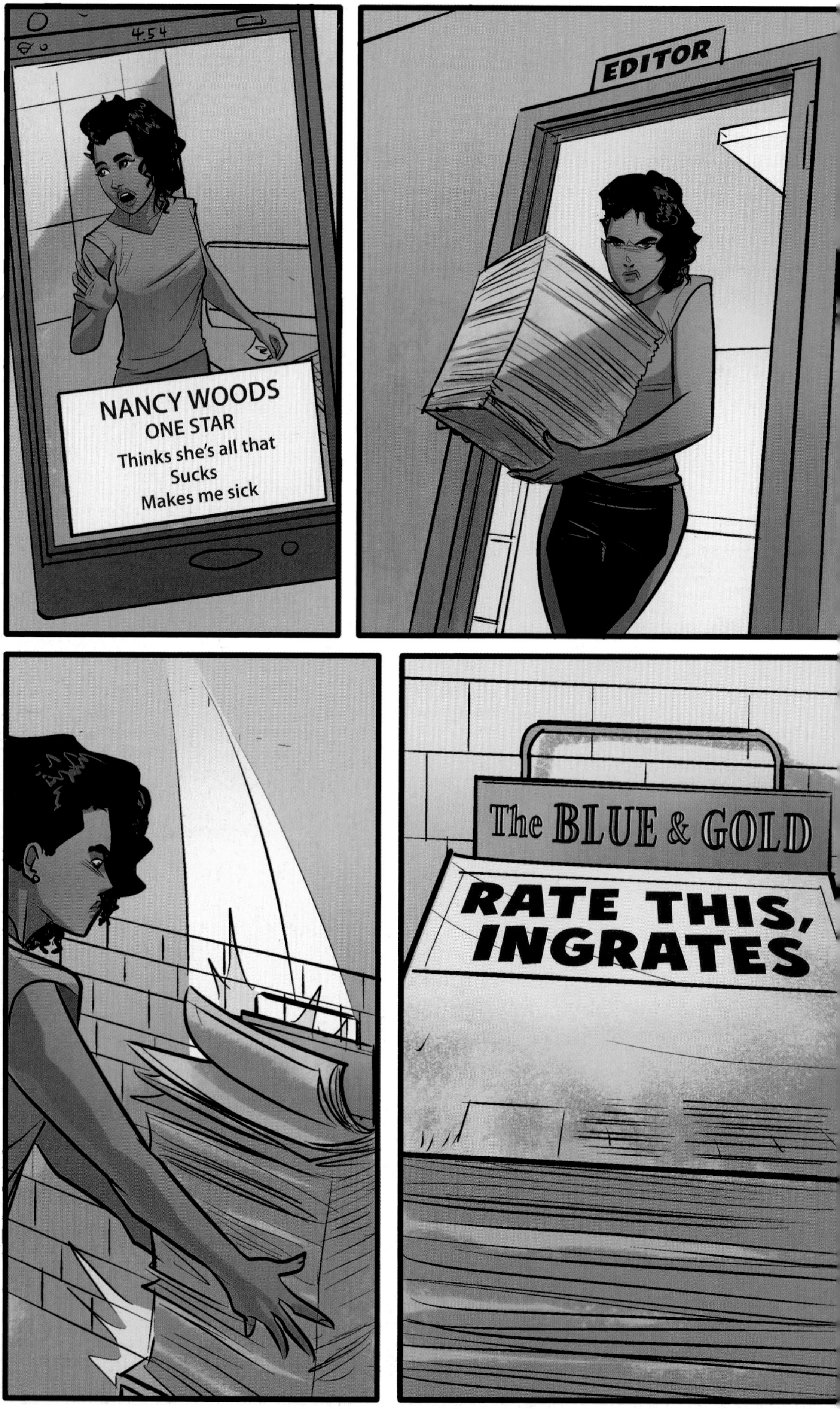
4:54
NANCY WOODS
ONE STAR
Thinks she's all that
Sucks
Makes me sick
EDITOR
The BLUE & GOLD
RATE THIS, INGRATES

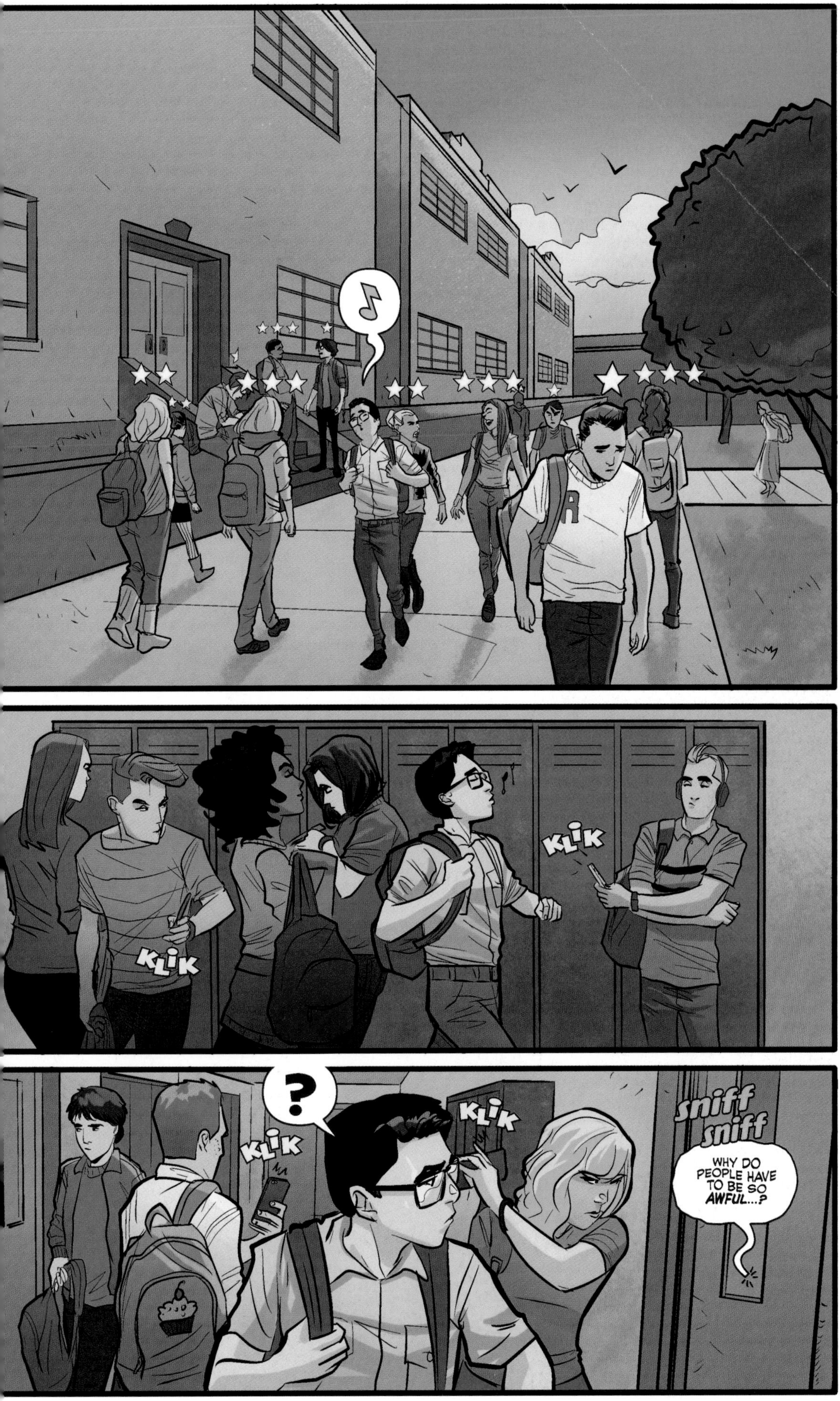
♪
KLIK
KLIK
?
KLIK
KLIK
sniff sniff
WHY DO PEOPLE HAVE TO BE SO *AWFUL*...?

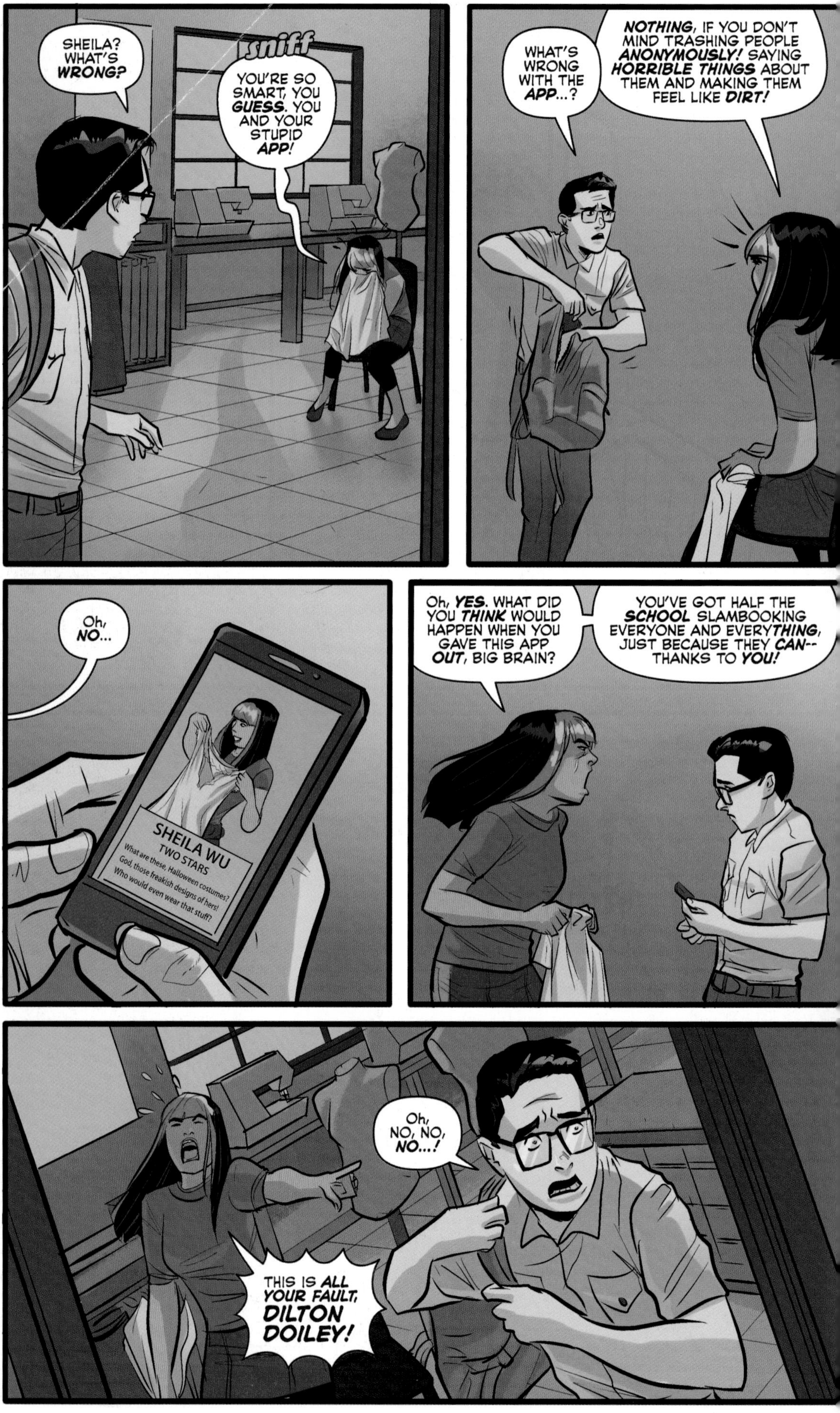

SHEILA? WHAT'S **WRONG?**
sniff
YOU'RE SO SMART, YOU **GUESS**. YOU AND YOUR STUPID **APP!**
WHAT'S WRONG WITH THE **APP**...?
**NOTHING**, IF YOU DON'T MIND TRASHING PEOPLE **ANONYMOUSLY!** SAYING **HORRIBLE THINGS** ABOUT THEM AND MAKING THEM FEEL LIKE **DIRT!**
Oh, **NO**...
SHEILA WU
TWO STARS
What are these, Halloween costumes? God, those freakish designs of hers! Who would even wear that stuff?
Oh, **YES**. WHAT DID YOU **THINK** WOULD HAPPEN WHEN YOU GAVE THIS APP **OUT**, BIG BRAIN?
YOU'VE GOT HALF THE **SCHOOL** SLAMBOOKING EVERYONE AND EVERY**THING**, JUST BECAUSE THEY **CAN**-- THANKS TO **YOU!**
Oh, NO, NO, **NO...!**
THIS IS **ALL YOUR FAULT, DILTON DOILEY!**

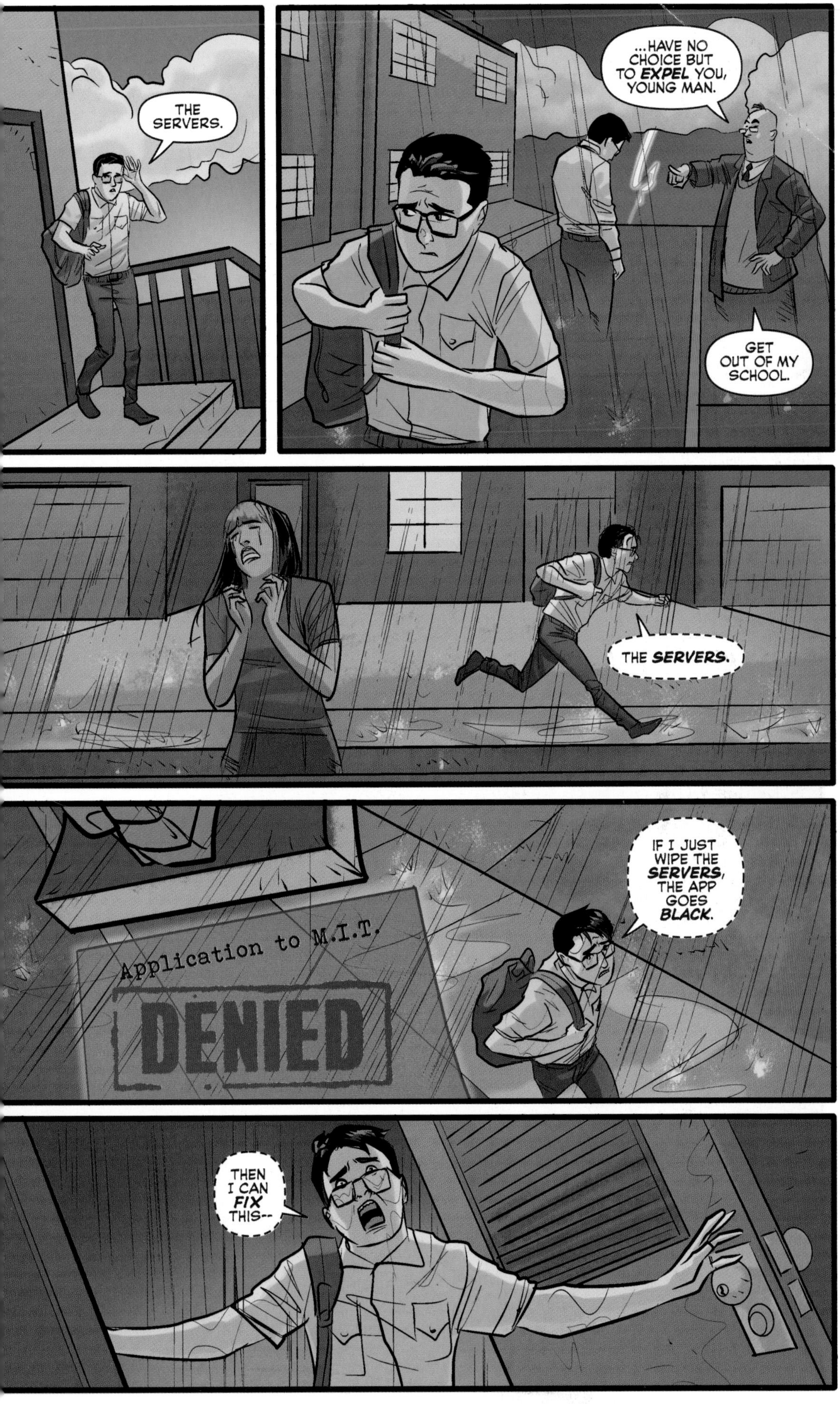
THE SERVERS.
...HAVE NO CHOICE BUT TO EXPEL YOU, YOUNG MAN.
GET OUT OF MY SCHOOL.
THE SERVERS.
IF I JUST WIPE THE SERVERS, THE APP GOES BLACK.
Application to M.I.T.
DENIED
THEN I CAN FIX THIS--

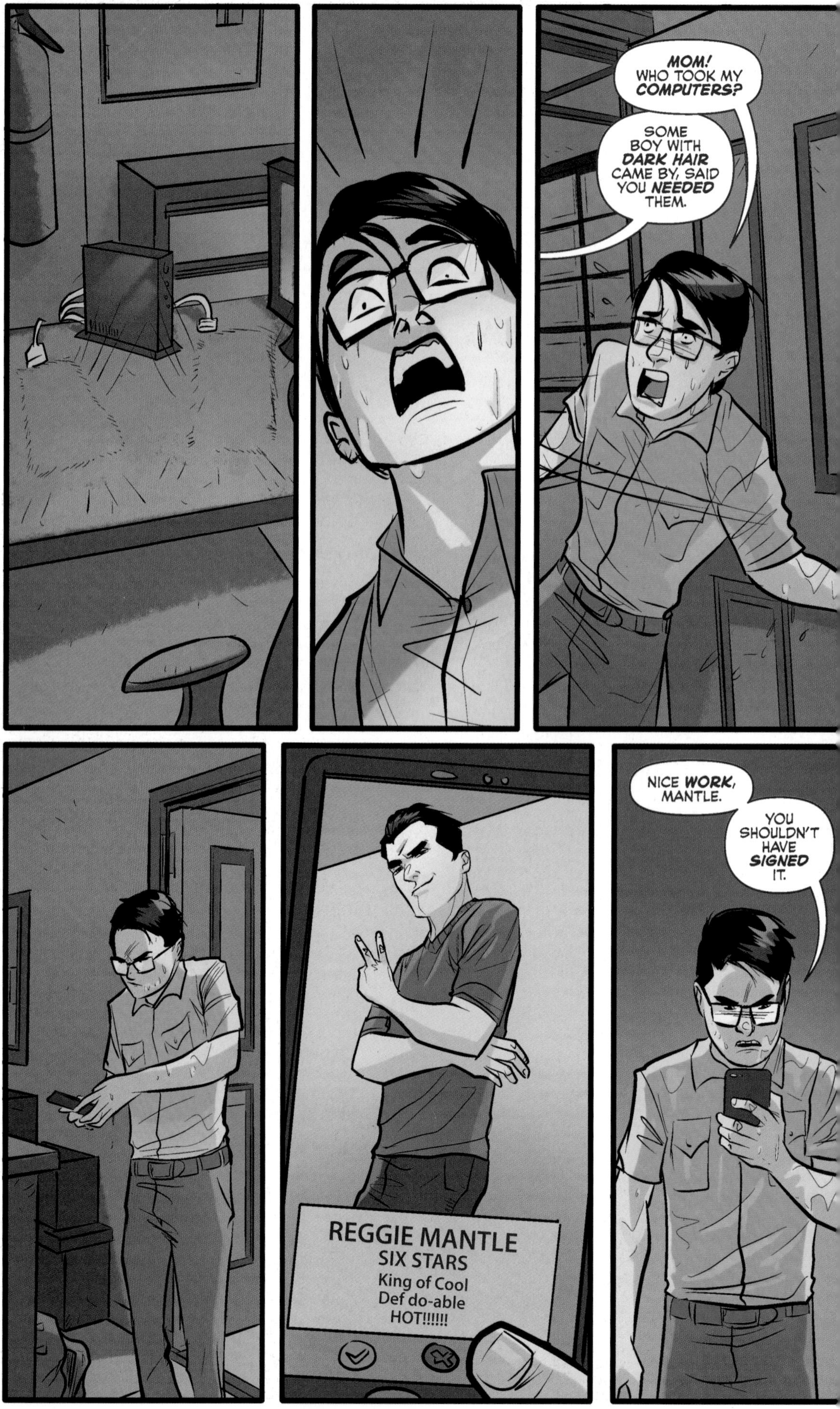

MOM! WHO TOOK MY COMPUTERS?
SOME BOY WITH DARK HAIR CAME BY, SAID YOU NEEDED THEM.
REGGIE MANTLE
SIX STARS
King of Cool
Def do-able
HOT!!!!!!
NICE WORK, MANTLE.
YOU SHOULDN'T HAVE SIGNED IT.

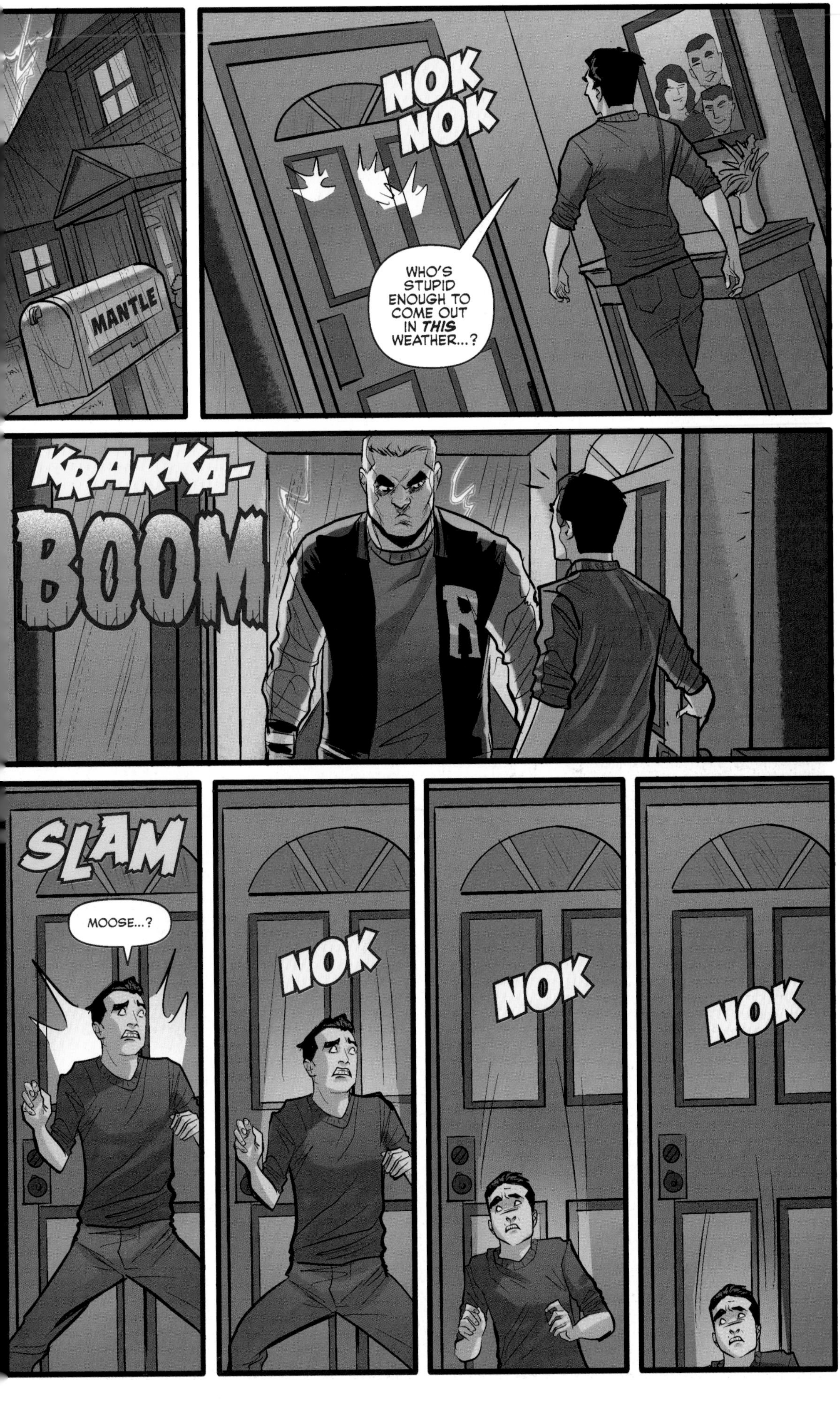
MANTLE
NOK NOK
WHO'S STUPID ENOUGH TO COME OUT IN THIS WEATHER...?
KRAKKA-BOOM
SLAM
MOOSE...?
NOK
NOK
NOK

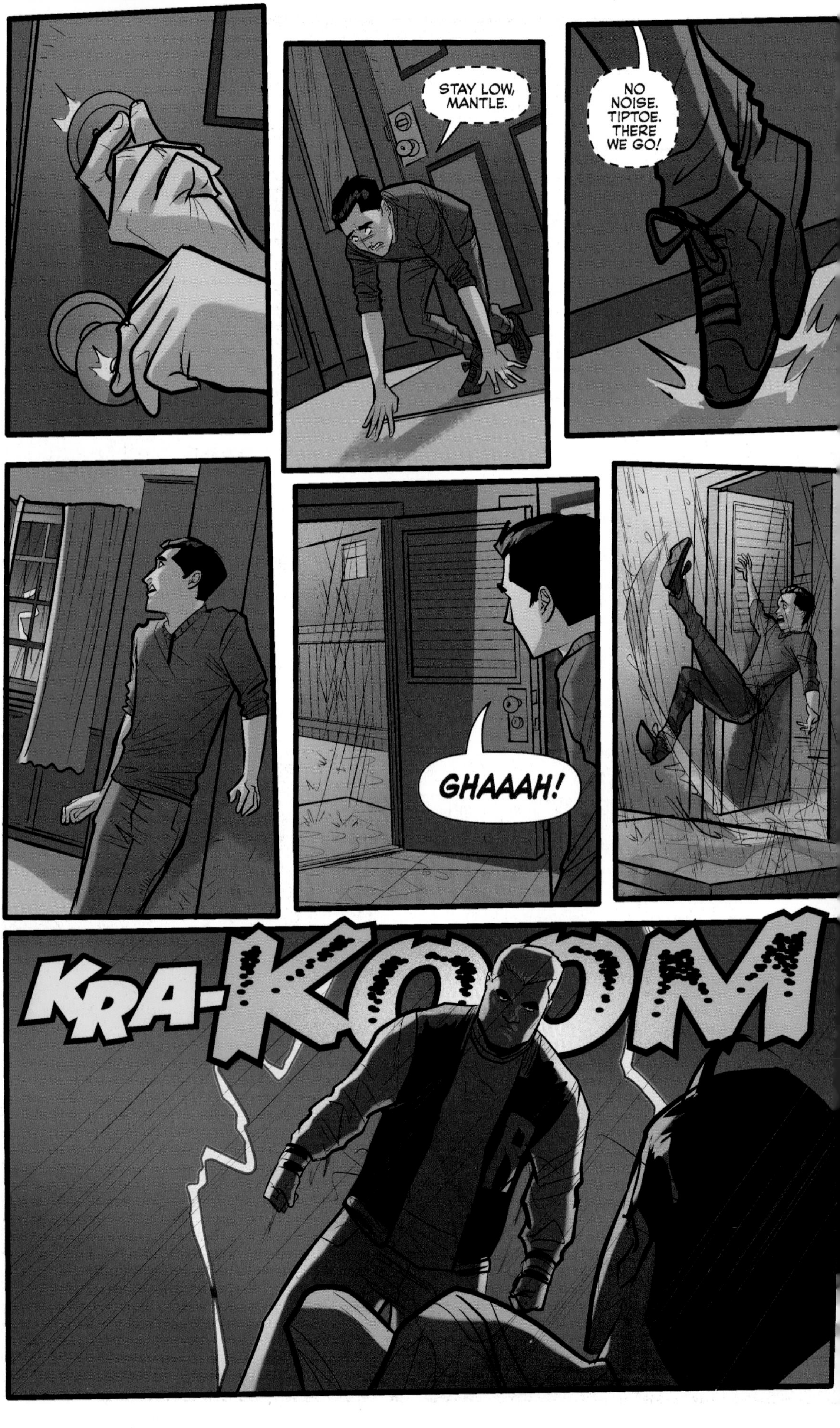
STAY LOW, MANTLE.
NO NOISE. TIPTOE. THERE WE GO!
GHAAAH!
KRA-KOOM

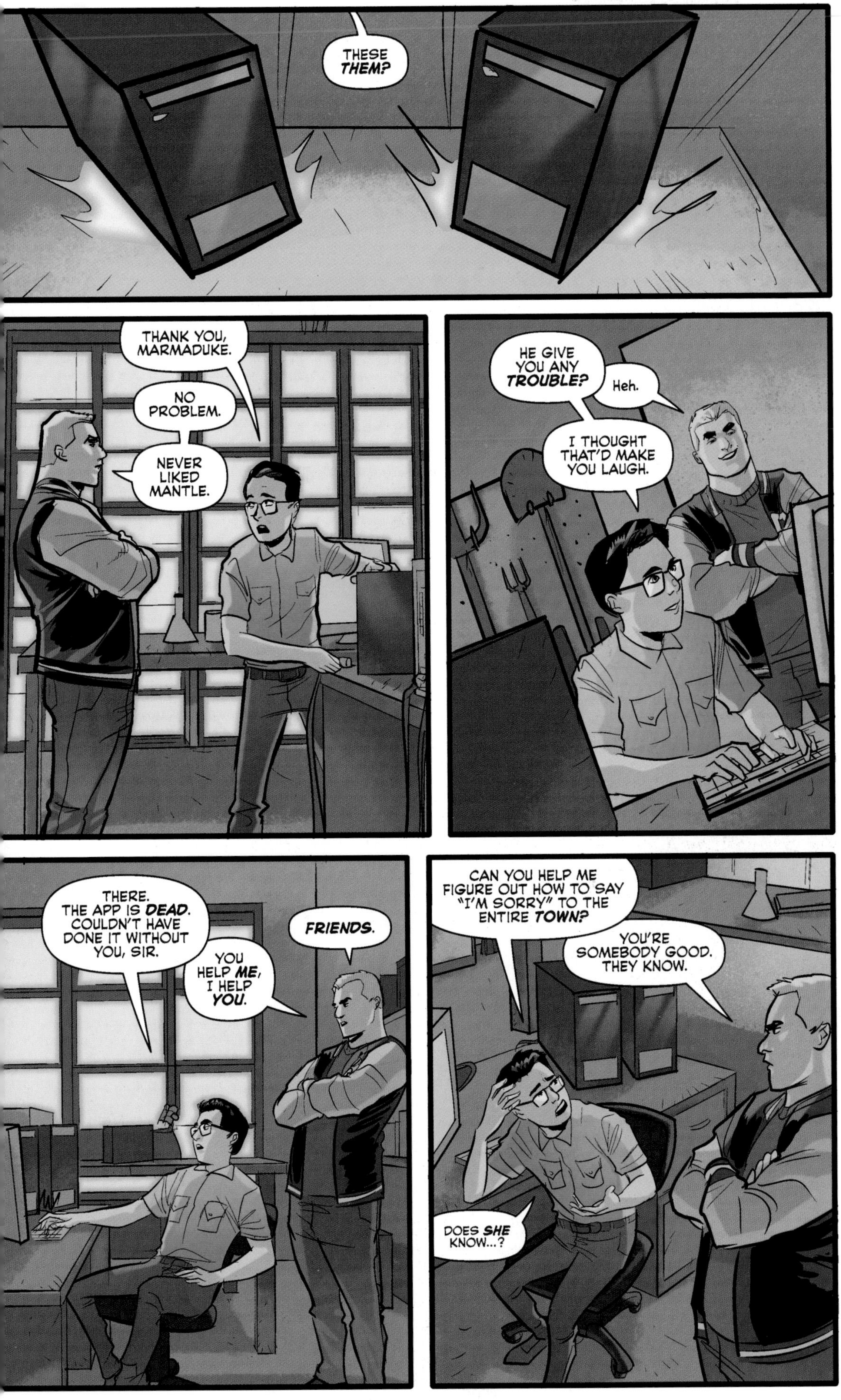
THESE *THEM?*
THANK YOU, MARMADUKE.
NO PROBLEM.
NEVER LIKED MANTLE.
HE GIVE YOU ANY *TROUBLE?*
Heh.
I THOUGHT THAT'D MAKE YOU LAUGH.
THERE. THE APP IS *DEAD*. COULDN'T HAVE DONE IT WITHOUT YOU, SIR.
YOU HELP *ME*, I HELP *YOU*.
*FRIENDS*.
CAN YOU HELP ME FIGURE OUT HOW TO SAY "I'M SORRY" TO THE ENTIRE *TOWN?*
YOU'RE SOMEBODY GOOD. THEY KNOW.
DOES *SHE* KNOW...?

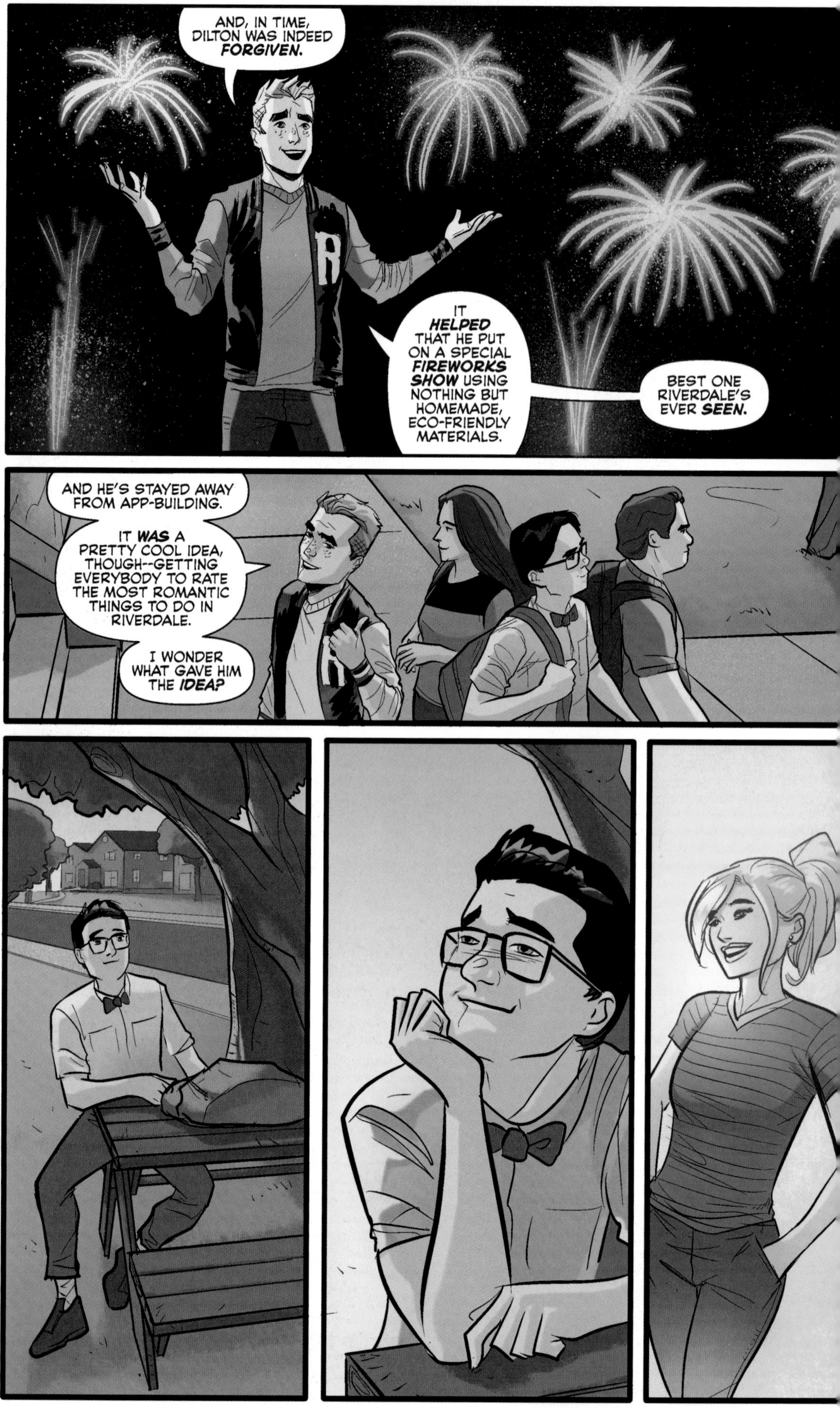
AND, IN TIME, DILTON WAS INDEED **FORGIVEN.**
IT **HELPED** THAT HE PUT ON A SPECIAL **FIREWORKS SHOW** USING NOTHING BUT HOMEMADE, ECO-FRIENDLY MATERIALS.
BEST ONE RIVERDALE'S EVER **SEEN.**
AND HE'S STAYED AWAY FROM APP-BUILDING.
IT ***WAS*** A PRETTY COOL IDEA, THOUGH--GETTING EVERYBODY TO RATE THE MOST ROMANTIC THINGS TO DO IN RIVERDALE.
I WONDER WHAT GAVE HIM THE ***IDEA?***

# EPILOGUE: PROLOGUE

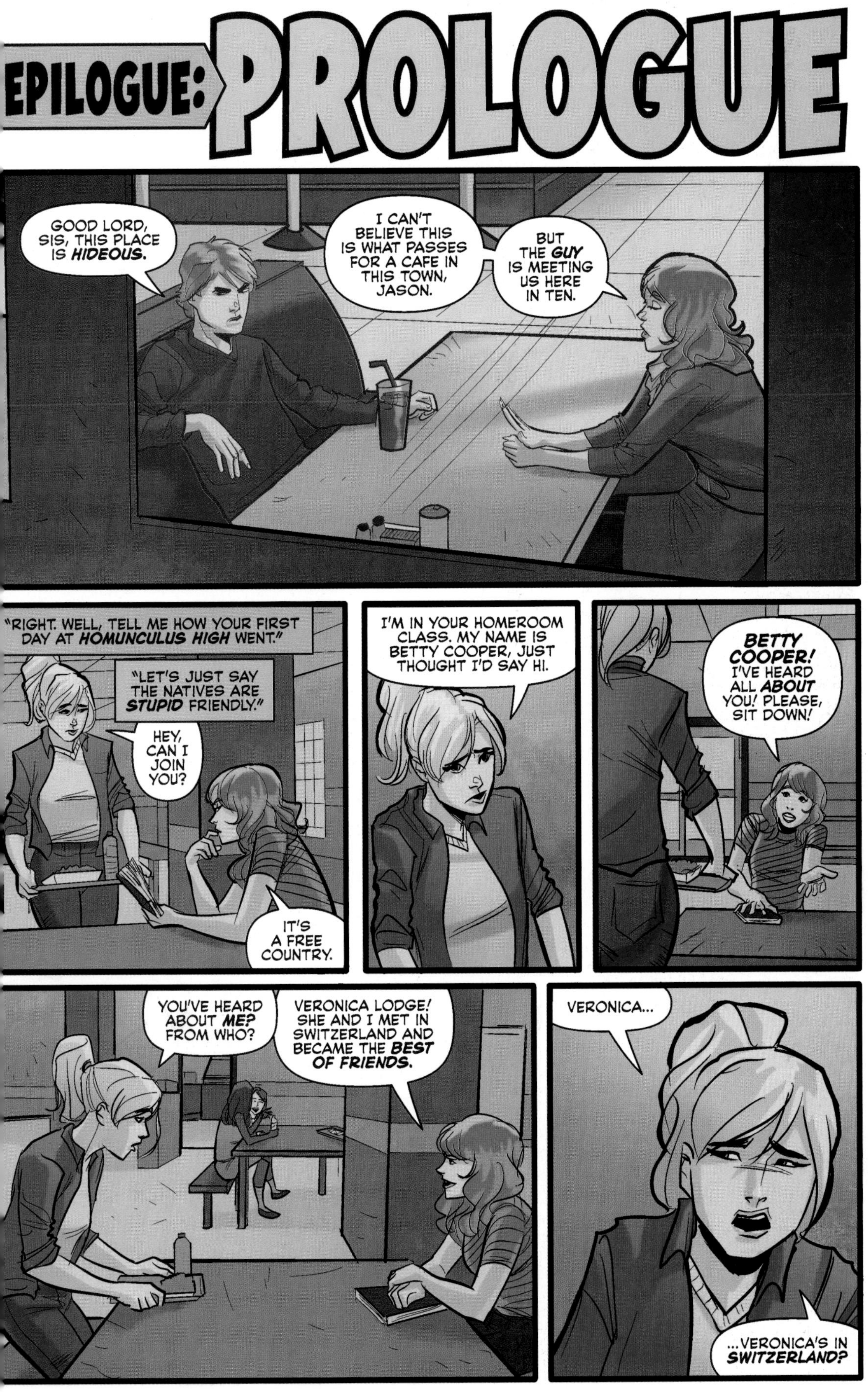
GOOD LORD, SIS, THIS PLACE IS *HIDEOUS.*
I CAN'T BELIEVE THIS IS WHAT PASSES FOR A CAFE IN THIS TOWN, JASON.
BUT THE *GUY* IS MEETING US HERE IN TEN.
"RIGHT. WELL, TELL ME HOW YOUR FIRST DAY AT *HOMUNCULUS HIGH* WENT."
"LET'S JUST SAY THE NATIVES ARE *STUPID* FRIENDLY."
HEY, CAN I JOIN YOU?
IT'S A FREE COUNTRY.
I'M IN YOUR HOMEROOM CLASS. MY NAME IS BETTY COOPER, JUST THOUGHT I'D SAY HI.
*BETTY COOPER!* I'VE HEARD ALL *ABOUT* YOU! PLEASE, SIT DOWN!
YOU'VE HEARD ABOUT *ME?* FROM WHO?
VERONICA LODGE! SHE AND I MET IN SWITZERLAND AND BECAME THE *BEST OF FRIENDS.*
VERONICA...
...VERONICA'S IN *SWITZERLAND?*

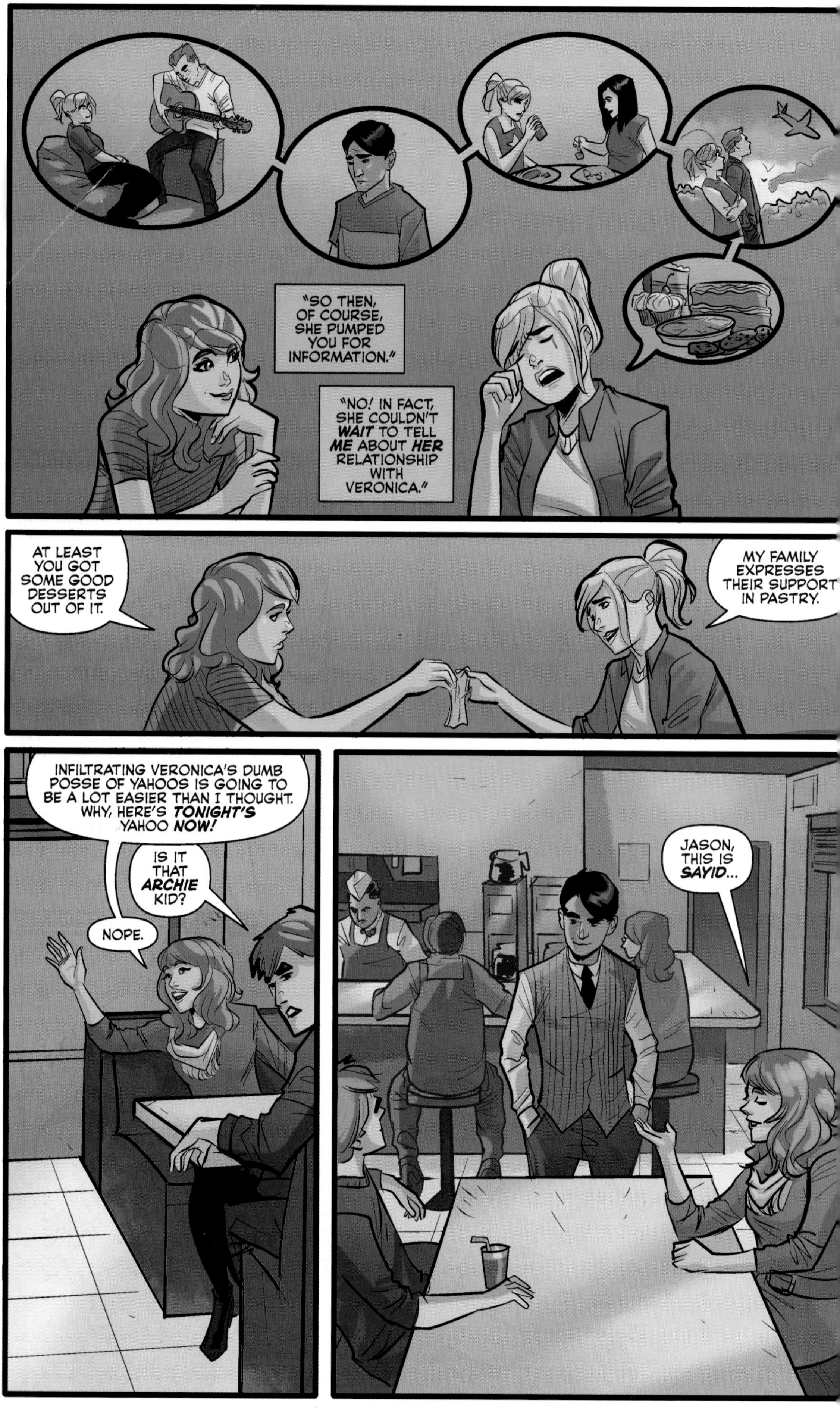

"SO THEN, OF COURSE, SHE PUMPED YOU FOR INFORMATION."
"NO! IN FACT, SHE COULDN'T WAIT TO TELL ME ABOUT HER RELATIONSHIP WITH VERONICA."
AT LEAST YOU GOT SOME GOOD DESSERTS OUT OF IT.
MY FAMILY EXPRESSES THEIR SUPPORT IN PASTRY.
INFILTRATING VERONICA'S DUMB POSSE OF YAHOOS IS GOING TO BE A LOT EASIER THAN I THOUGHT. WHY, HERE'S TONIGHT'S YAHOO NOW!
IS IT THAT ARCHIE KID?
NOPE.
JASON, THIS IS SAYID...

TO BE CONTINUED...

# ISSUE SEVENTEEN

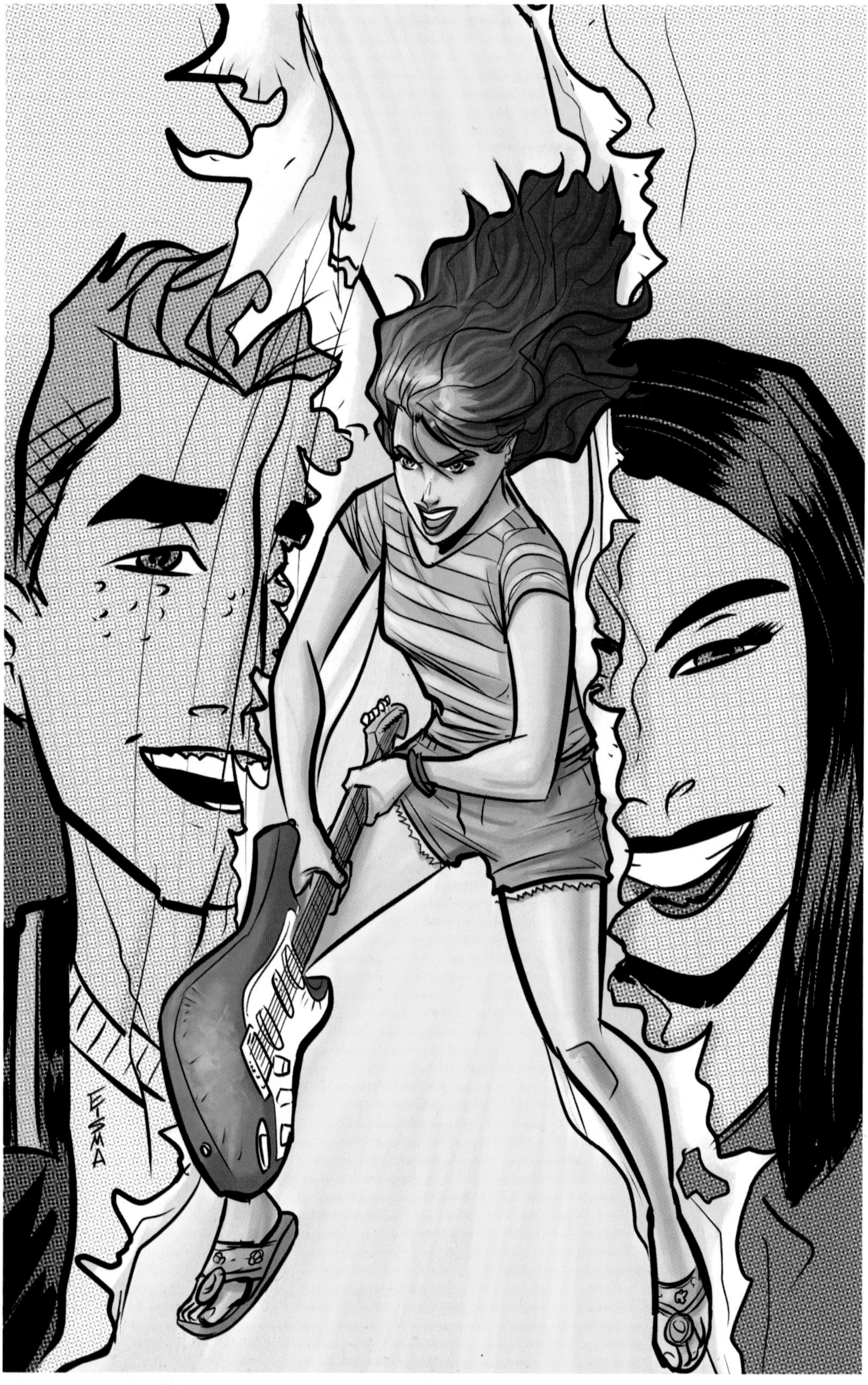
EISMA

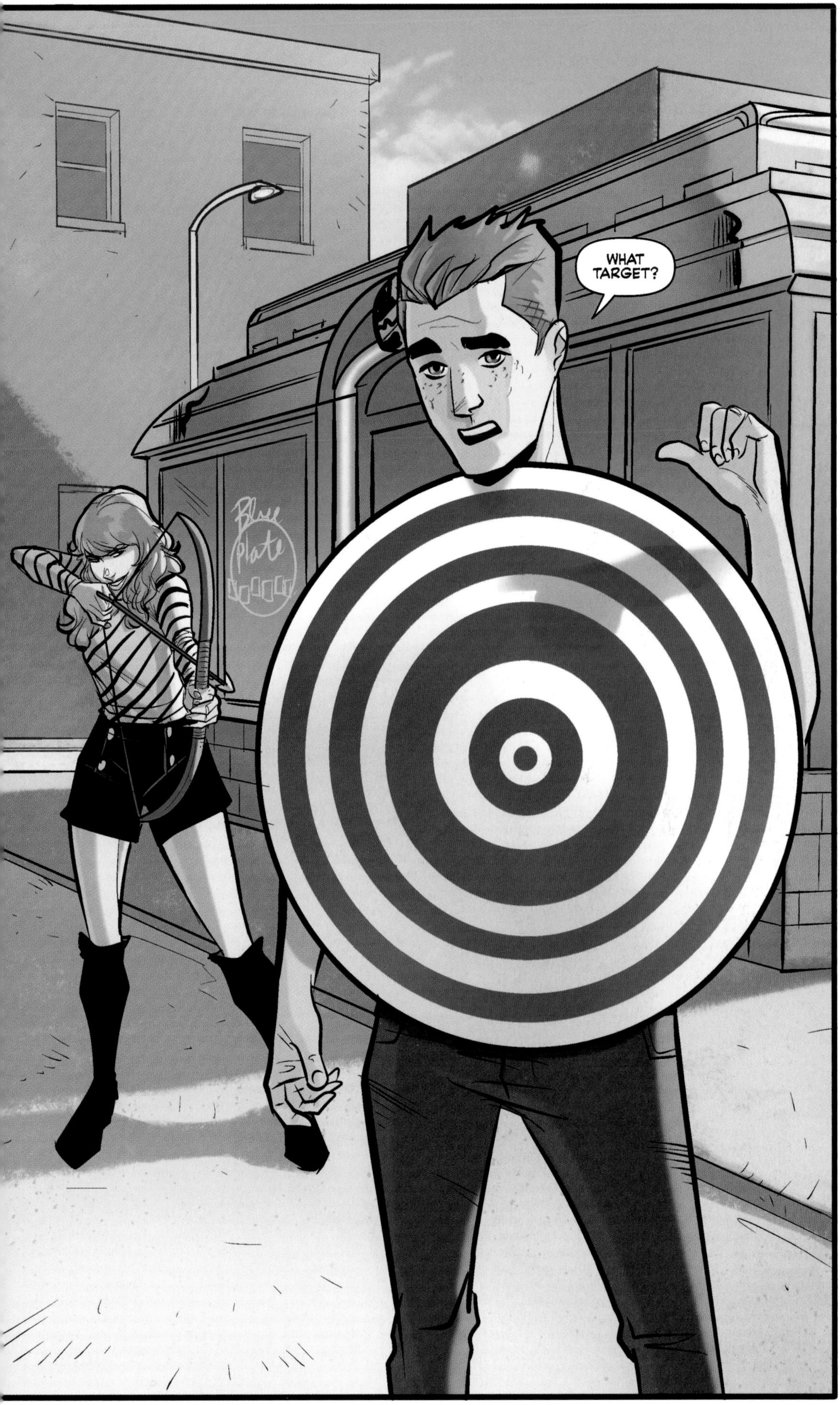
WHAT TARGET?
Blue plate

# CHAPTER ONE: Get your head outta the RAINCLOUDS

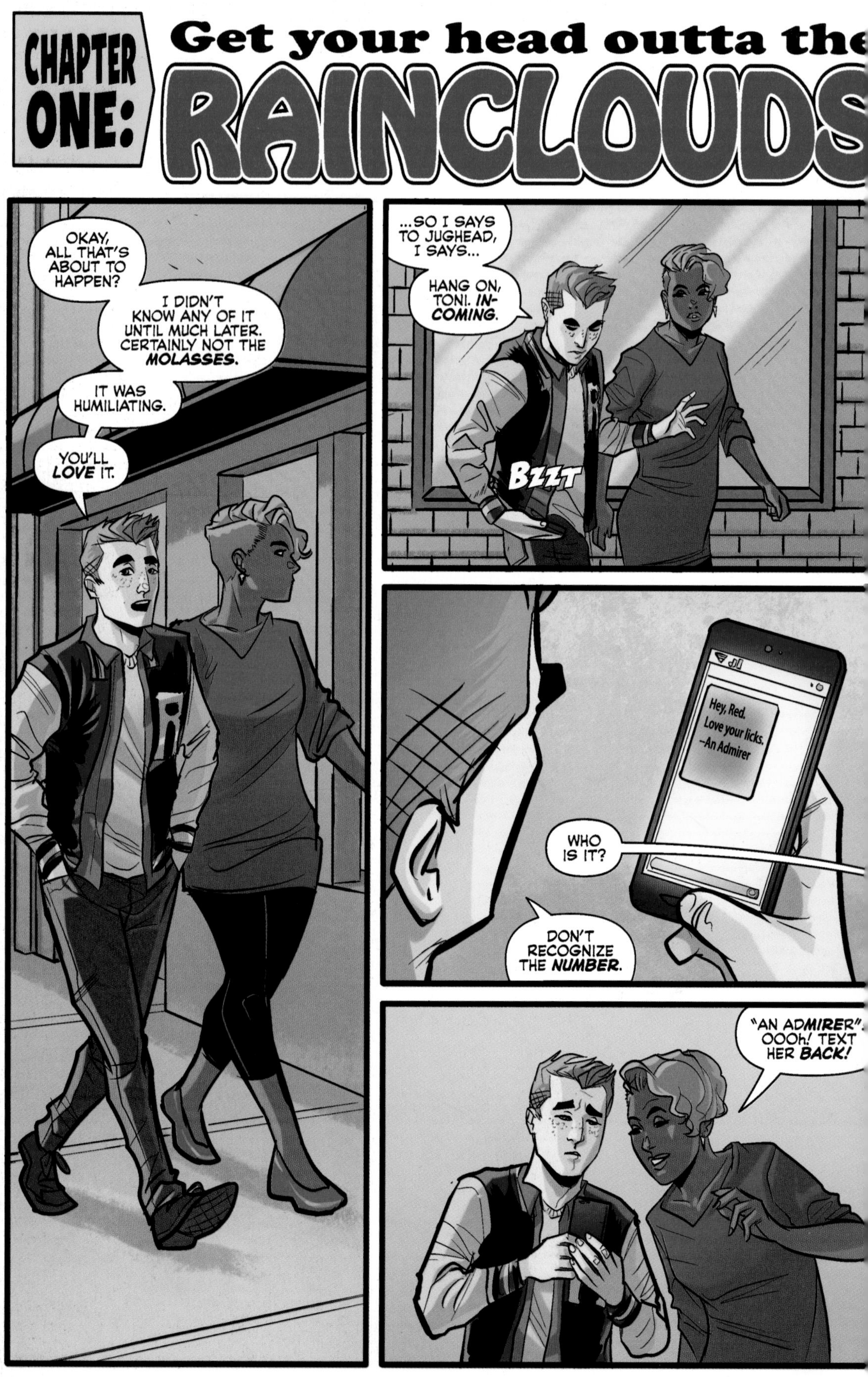
OKAY, ALL THAT'S ABOUT TO HAPPEN?
I DIDN'T KNOW ANY OF IT UNTIL MUCH LATER. CERTAINLY NOT THE MOLASSES.
IT WAS HUMILIATING.
YOU'LL LOVE IT.
...SO I SAYS TO JUGHEAD, I SAYS...
HANG ON, TONI. IN-COMING.
BZZT
Hey, Red. Love your licks. -An Admirer
WHO IS IT?
DON'T RECOGNIZE THE NUMBER.
"AN ADMIRER". OOOh! TEXT HER BACK!

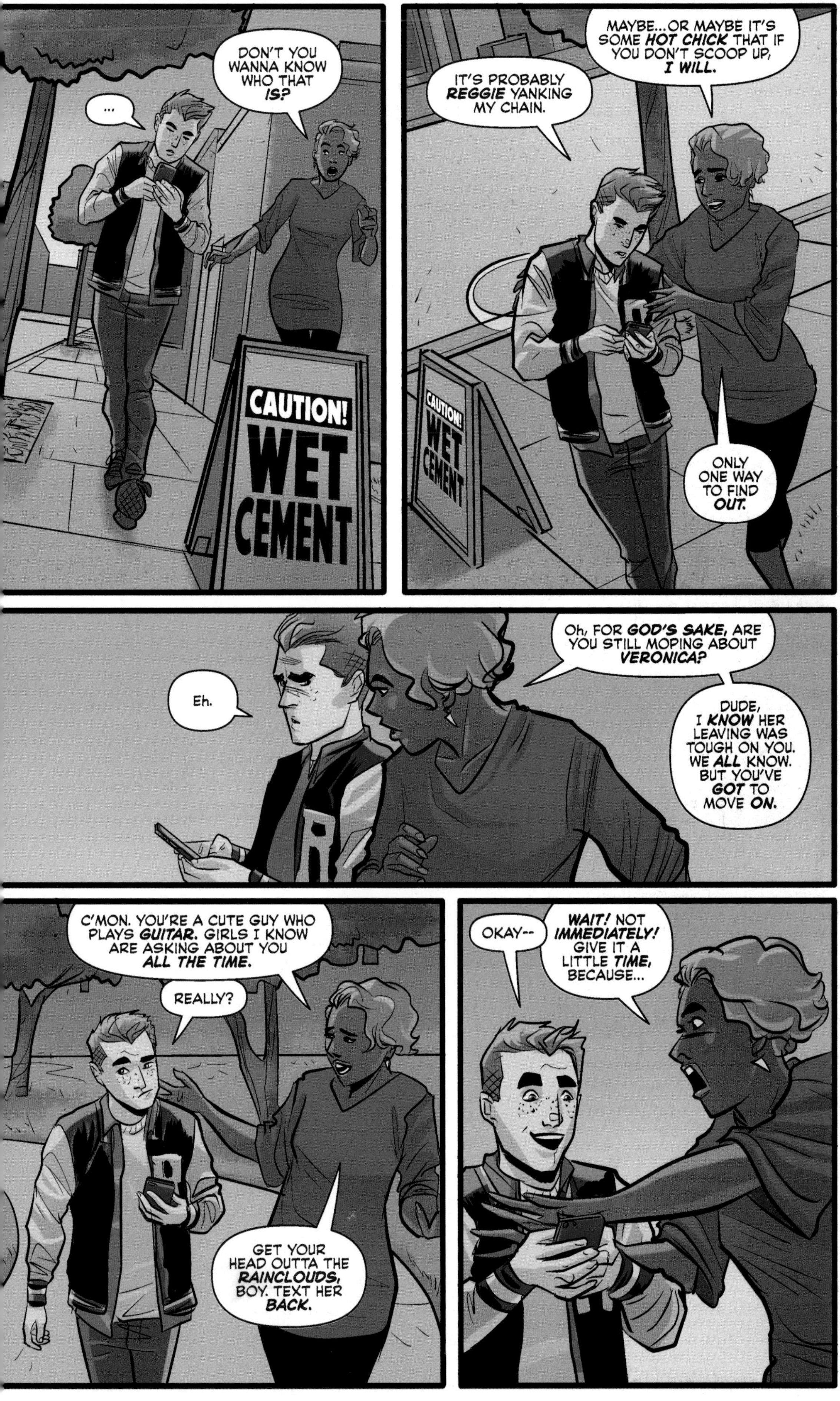
DON'T YOU WANNA KNOW WHO THAT *IS?*
...
CAUTION! WET CEMENT
IT'S PROBABLY *REGGIE* YANKING MY CHAIN.
MAYBE...OR MAYBE IT'S SOME *HOT CHICK* THAT IF YOU DON'T SCOOP UP, *I WILL.*
ONLY ONE WAY TO FIND *OUT.*
CAUTION! WET CEMENT
Eh.
Oh, FOR *GOD'S SAKE,* ARE YOU STILL MOPING ABOUT *VERONICA?*
DUDE, I *KNOW* HER LEAVING WAS TOUGH ON YOU. WE *ALL* KNOW. BUT YOU'VE *GOT* TO MOVE *ON.*
C'MON. YOU'RE A CUTE GUY WHO PLAYS *GUITAR.* GIRLS I KNOW ARE ASKING ABOUT YOU *ALL THE TIME.*
REALLY?
GET YOUR HEAD OUTTA THE *RAINCLOUDS,* BOY. TEXT HER *BACK.*
OKAY--
*WAIT!* NOT *IMMEDIATELY!* GIVE IT A LITTLE *TIME,* BECAUSE...

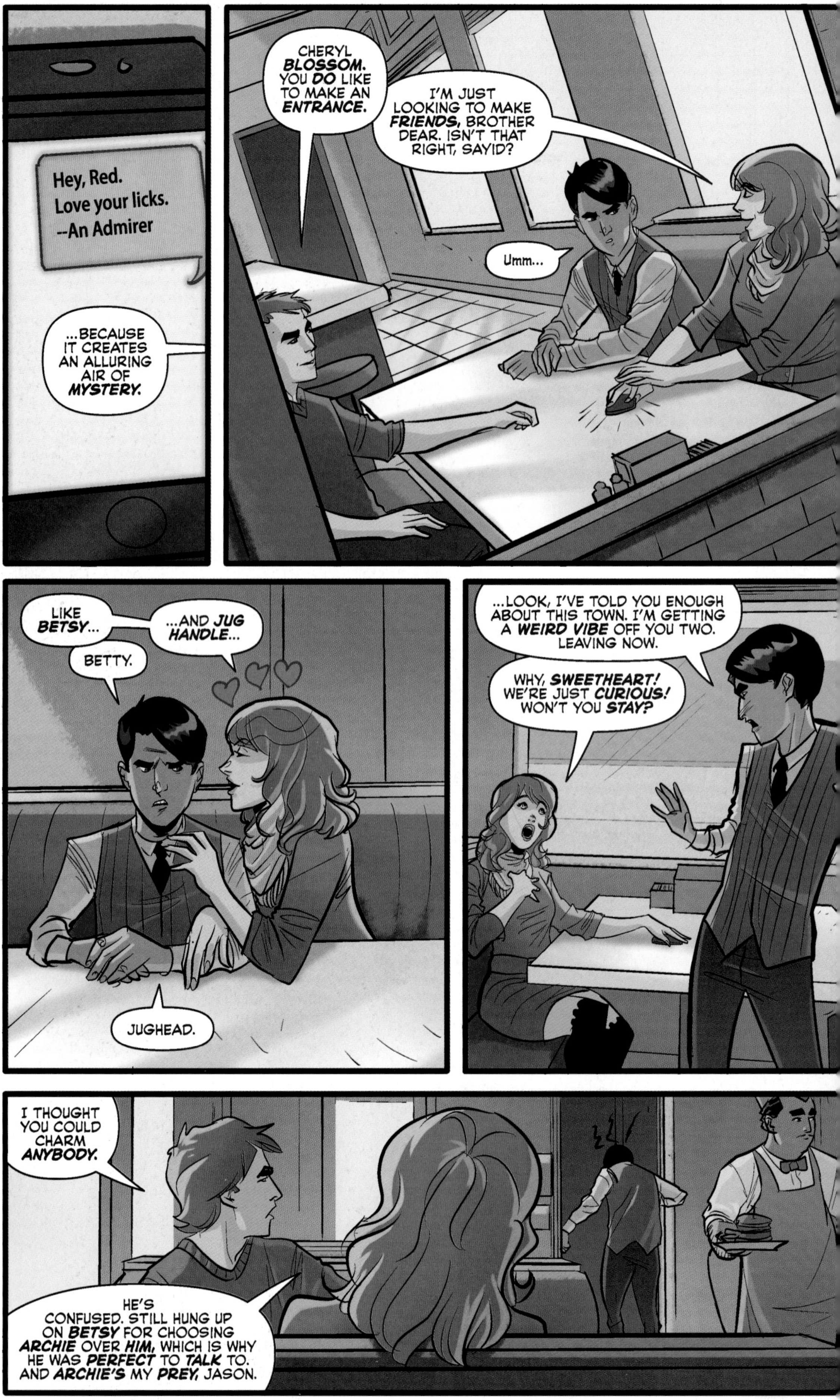
Hey, Red.
Love your licks.
--An Admirer
...BECAUSE IT CREATES AN ALLURING AIR OF MYSTERY.
CHERYL BLOSSOM. YOU DO LIKE TO MAKE AN ENTRANCE.
I'M JUST LOOKING TO MAKE FRIENDS, BROTHER DEAR. ISN'T THAT RIGHT, SAYID?
Umm...
LIKE BETSY...
BETTY.
...AND JUG HANDLE...
JUGHEAD.
...LOOK, I'VE TOLD YOU ENOUGH ABOUT THIS TOWN. I'M GETTING A WEIRD VIBE OFF YOU TWO. LEAVING NOW.
WHY, SWEETHEART! WE'RE JUST CURIOUS! WON'T YOU STAY?
I THOUGHT YOU COULD CHARM ANYBODY.
HE'S CONFUSED. STILL HUNG UP ON BETSY FOR CHOOSING ARCHIE OVER HIM, WHICH IS WHY HE WAS PERFECT TO TALK TO. AND ARCHIE'S MY PREY, JASON.

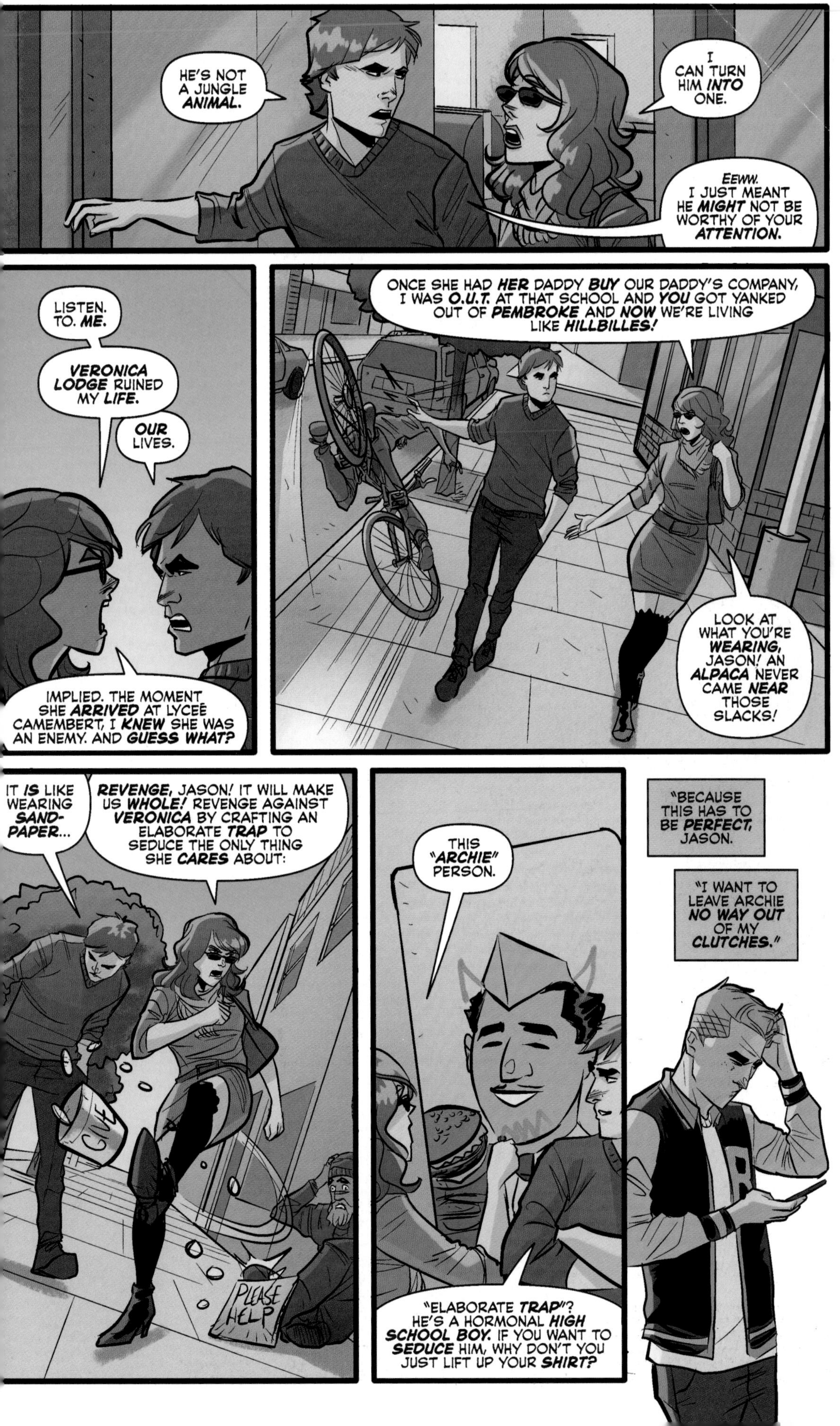

HE'S NOT A JUNGLE ANIMAL.
I CAN TURN HIM INTO ONE.
EEWW. I JUST MEANT HE MIGHT NOT BE WORTHY OF YOUR ATTENTION.
LISTEN. TO. ME.
VERONICA LODGE RUINED MY LIFE.
OUR LIVES.
IMPLIED. THE MOMENT SHE ARRIVED AT LYCEÉ CAMEMBERT, I KNEW SHE WAS AN ENEMY. AND GUESS WHAT?
ONCE SHE HAD HER DADDY BUY OUR DADDY'S COMPANY, I WAS O.U.T. AT THAT SCHOOL AND YOU GOT YANKED OUT OF PEMBROKE AND NOW WE'RE LIVING LIKE HILLBILLES!
LOOK AT WHAT YOU'RE WEARING, JASON! AN ALPACA NEVER CAME NEAR THOSE SLACKS!
IT IS LIKE WEARING SAND-PAPER...
REVENGE, JASON! IT WILL MAKE US WHOLE! REVENGE AGAINST VERONICA BY CRAFTING AN ELABORATE TRAP TO SEDUCE THE ONLY THING SHE CARES ABOUT:
GIVE
PLEASE HELP
THIS "ARCHIE" PERSON.
"ELABORATE TRAP"? HE'S A HORMONAL HIGH SCHOOL BOY. IF YOU WANT TO SEDUCE HIM, WHY DON'T YOU JUST LIFT UP YOUR SHIRT?
"BECAUSE THIS HAS TO BE PERFECT, JASON.
"I WANT TO LEAVE ARCHIE NO WAY OUT OF MY CLUTCHES."

# CHAPTER TWO: Swiss Miss

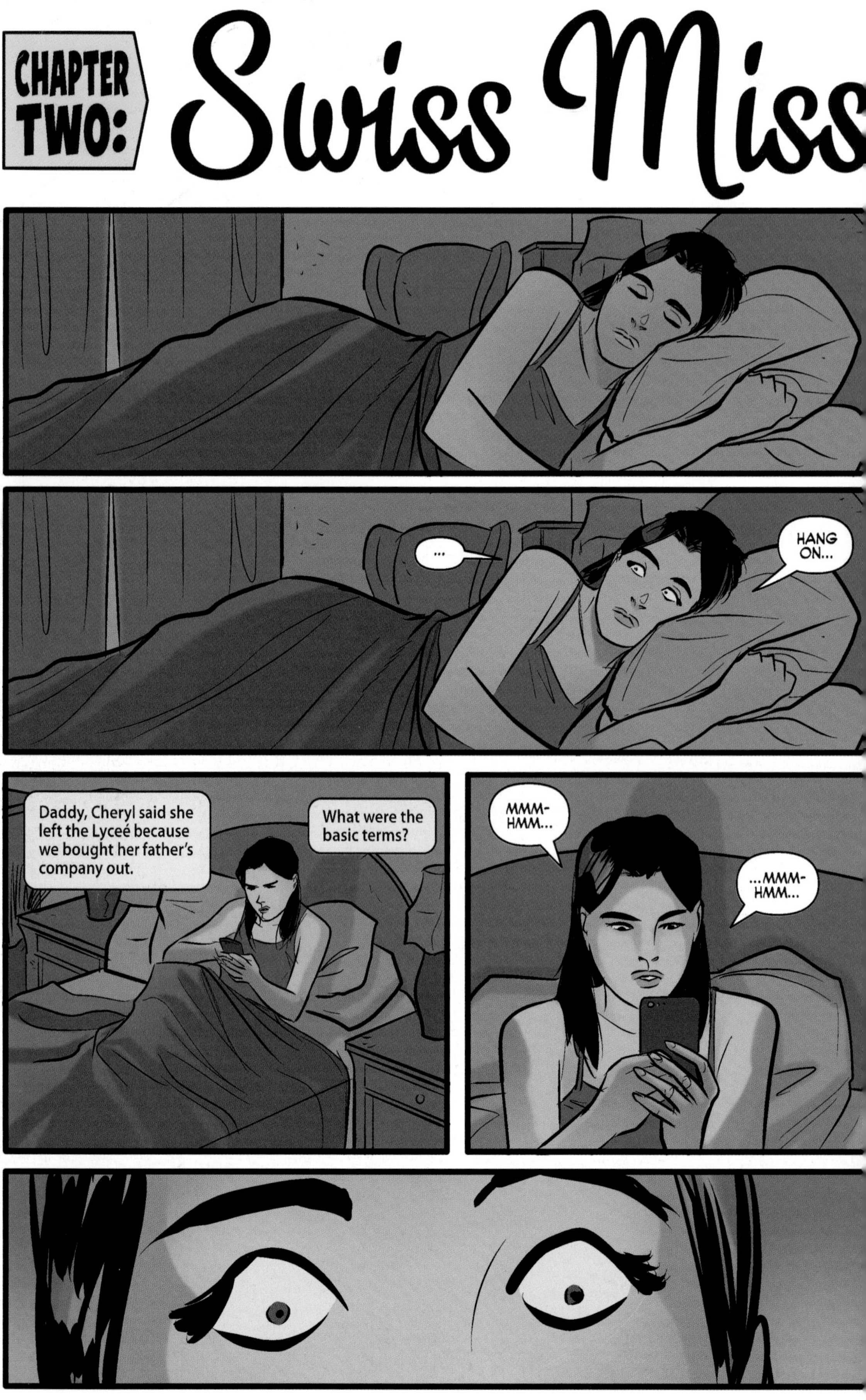
...
HANG ON...
Daddy, Cheryl said she left the Lyceé because we bought her father's company out.
What were the basic terms?
MMM-HMM...
...MMM-HMM...

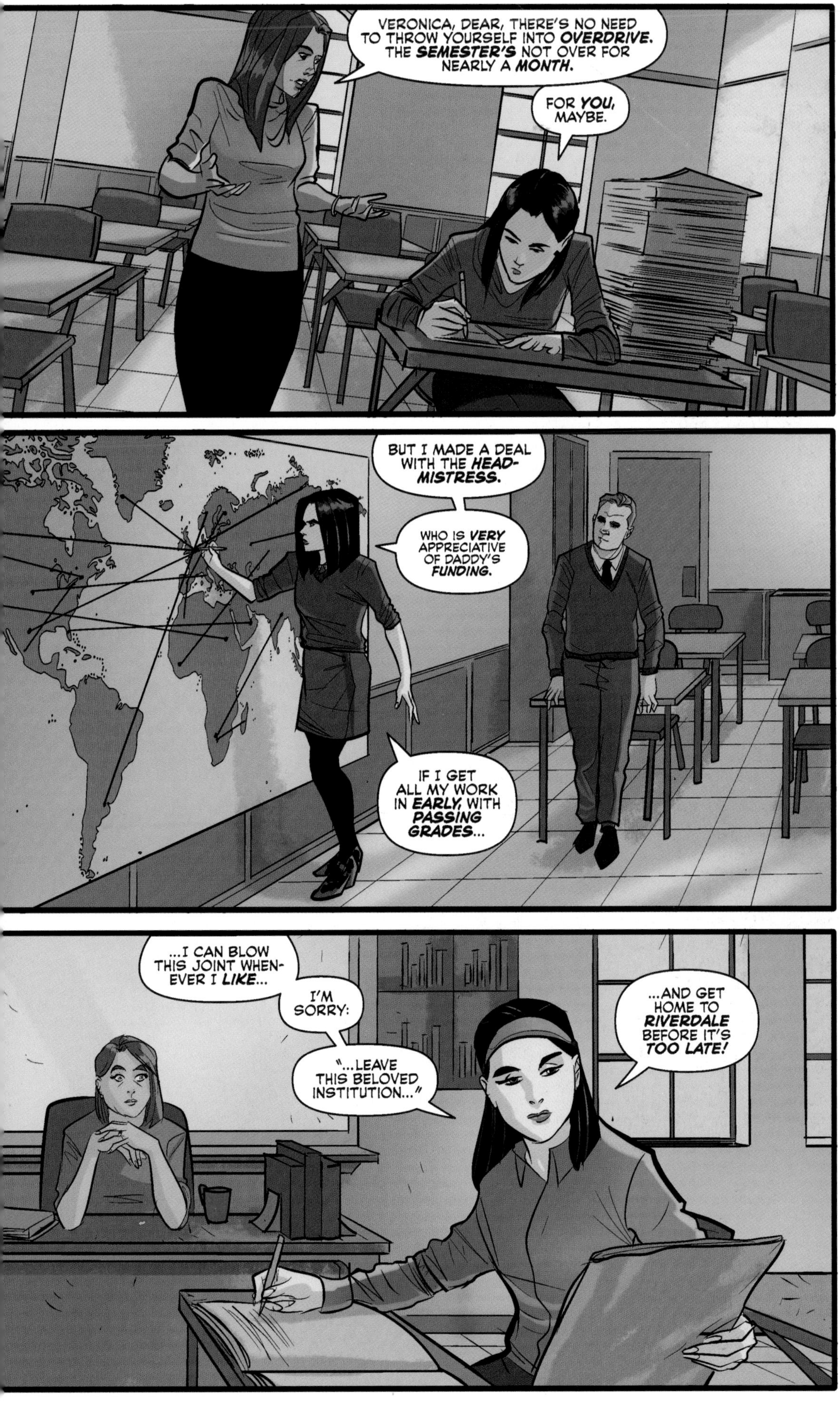

VERONICA, DEAR, THERE'S NO NEED TO THROW YOURSELF INTO OVERDRIVE. THE SEMESTER'S NOT OVER FOR NEARLY A MONTH.
FOR YOU, MAYBE.
BUT I MADE A DEAL WITH THE HEAD-MISTRESS.
WHO IS VERY APPRECIATIVE OF DADDY'S FUNDING.
IF I GET ALL MY WORK IN EARLY, WITH PASSING GRADES...
...I CAN BLOW THIS JOINT WHEN-EVER I LIKE...
I'M SORRY:
"...LEAVE THIS BELOVED INSTITUTION..."
...AND GET HOME TO RIVERDALE BEFORE IT'S TOO LATE!

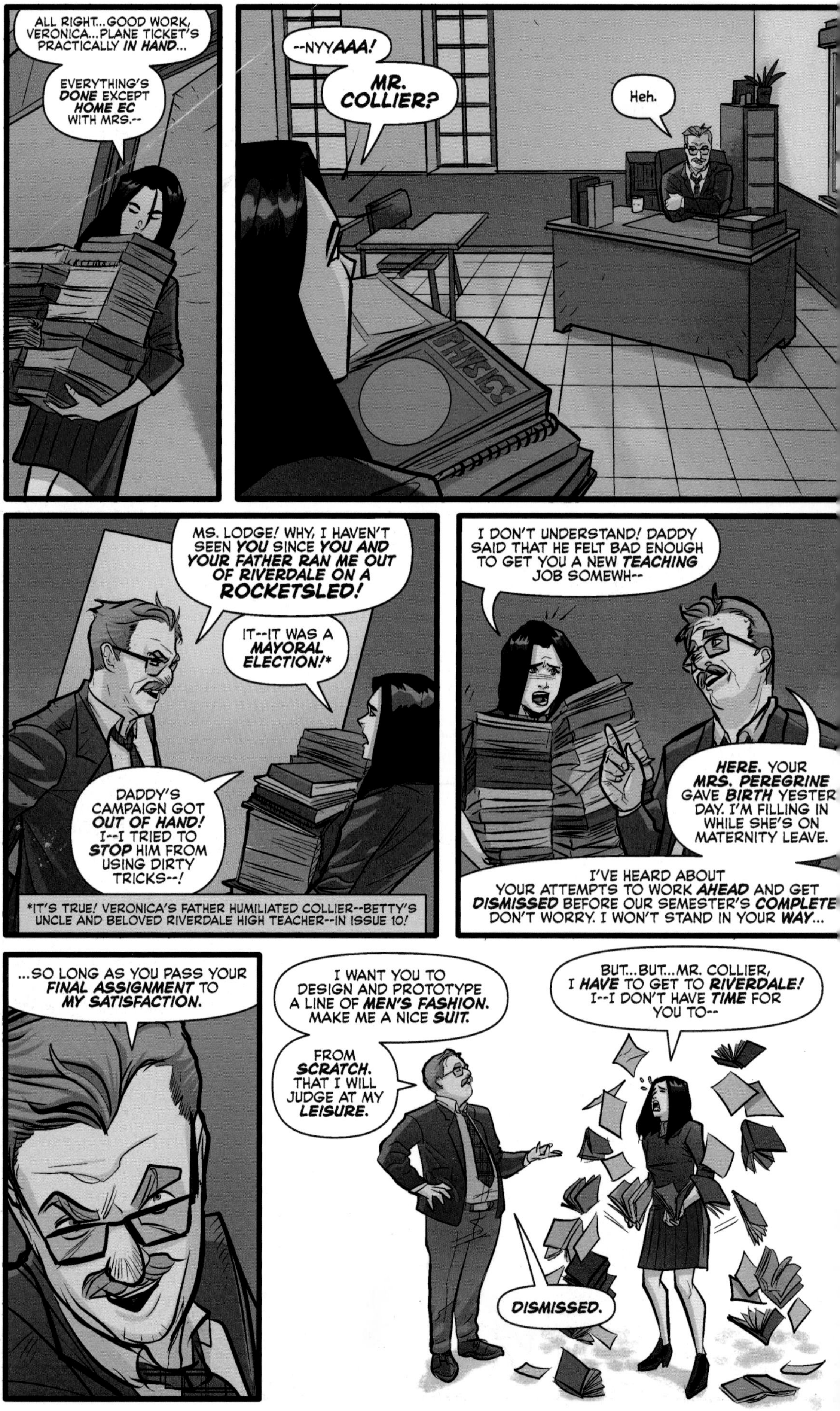
ALL RIGHT...GOOD WORK, VERONICA...PLANE TICKET'S PRACTICALLY IN HAND...
EVERYTHING'S DONE EXCEPT HOME EC WITH MRS.--
--NYYAAA!
MR. COLLIER?
Heh.
PHYSICS
MS. LODGE! WHY, I HAVEN'T SEEN YOU SINCE YOU AND YOUR FATHER RAN ME OUT OF RIVERDALE ON A ROCKETSLED!
IT--IT WAS A MAYORAL ELECTION!*
DADDY'S CAMPAIGN GOT OUT OF HAND! I--I TRIED TO STOP HIM FROM USING DIRTY TRICKS--!
*IT'S TRUE! VERONICA'S FATHER HUMILIATED COLLIER--BETTY'S UNCLE AND BELOVED RIVERDALE HIGH TEACHER--IN ISSUE 10!
I DON'T UNDERSTAND! DADDY SAID THAT HE FELT BAD ENOUGH TO GET YOU A NEW TEACHING JOB SOMEWH--
HERE. YOUR MRS. PEREGRINE GAVE BIRTH YESTER DAY. I'M FILLING IN WHILE SHE'S ON MATERNITY LEAVE.
I'VE HEARD ABOUT YOUR ATTEMPTS TO WORK AHEAD AND GET DISMISSED BEFORE OUR SEMESTER'S COMPLETE. DON'T WORRY. I WON'T STAND IN YOUR WAY...
...SO LONG AS YOU PASS YOUR FINAL ASSIGNMENT TO MY SATISFACTION.
I WANT YOU TO DESIGN AND PROTOTYPE A LINE OF MEN'S FASHION. MAKE ME A NICE SUIT.
FROM SCRATCH. THAT I WILL JUDGE AT MY LEISURE.
BUT...BUT...MR. COLLIER, I HAVE TO GET TO RIVERDALE! I--I DON'T HAVE TIME FOR YOU TO--
DISMISSED.

# HAPTER HREE: The Seduction of Archie Andrews

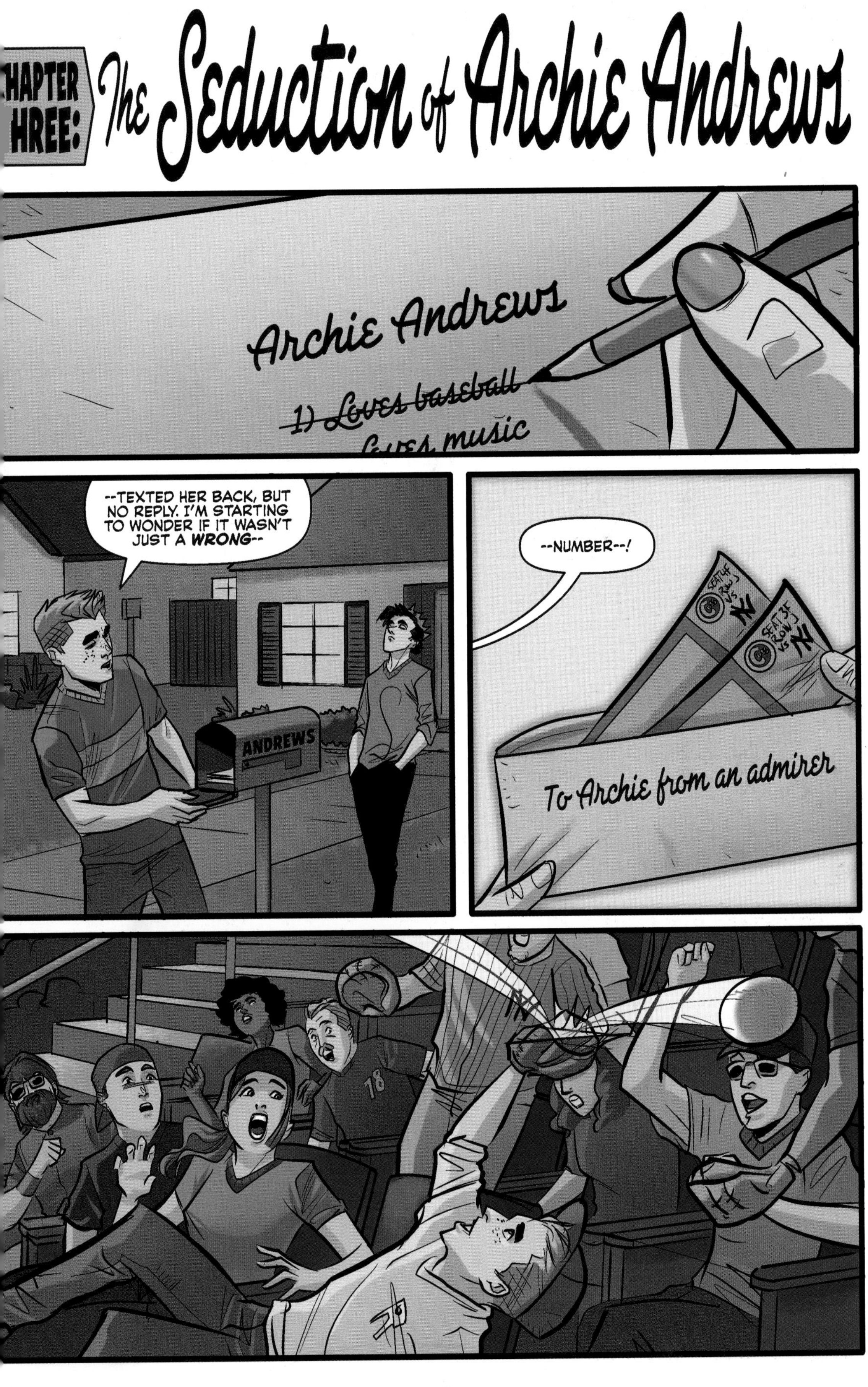

Archie Andrews
1) Loves baseball
Loves music
--TEXTED HER BACK, BUT NO REPLY. I'M STARTING TO WONDER IF IT WASN'T JUST A *WRONG*--
ANDREWS
--NUMBER--!
To Archie from an admirer
18

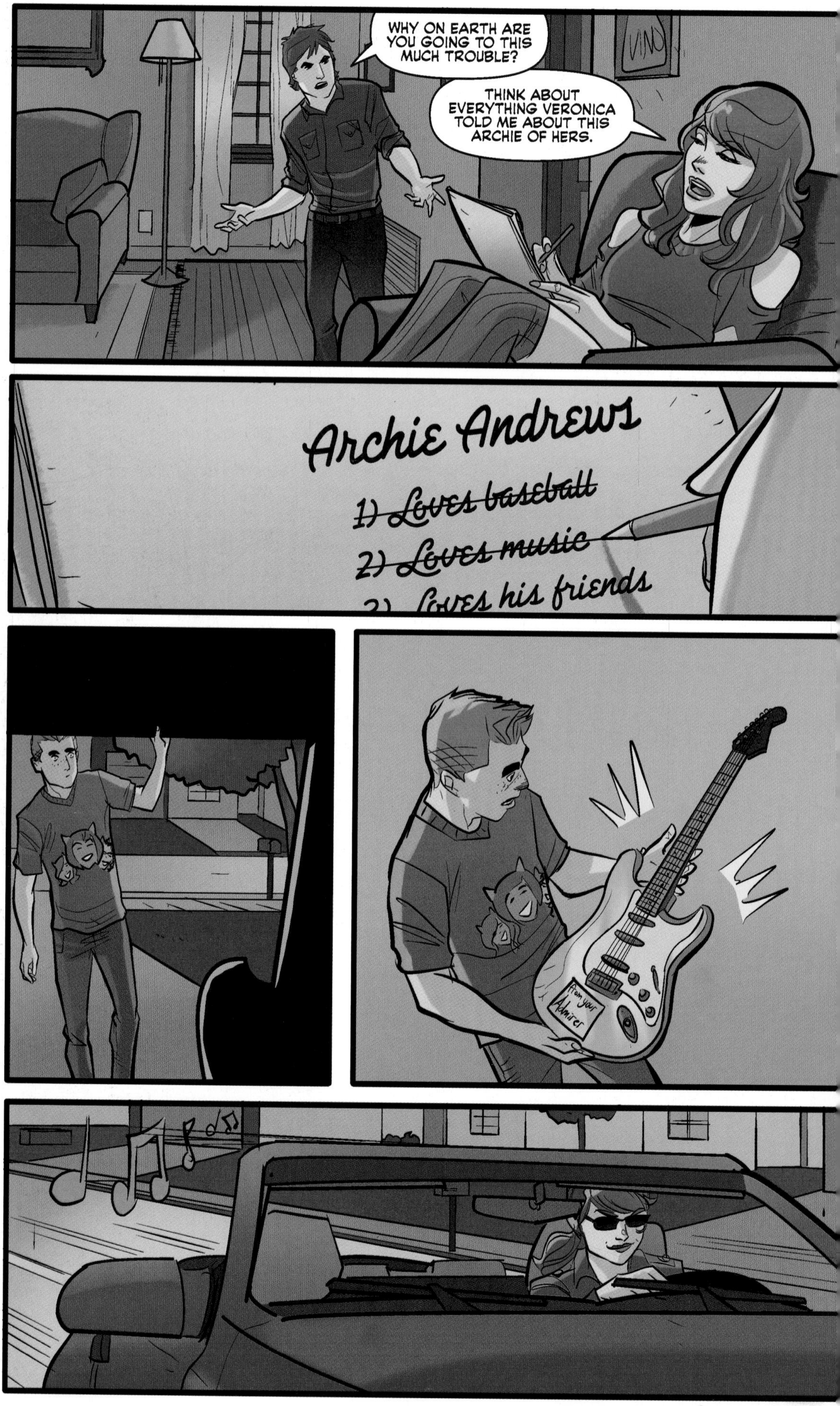
WHY ON EARTH ARE YOU GOING TO THIS MUCH TROUBLE?
THINK ABOUT EVERYTHING VERONICA TOLD ME ABOUT THIS ARCHIE OF HERS.
VINO
Archie Andrews
1) Loves baseball
2) Loves music
3) Loves his friends
From your Admirer

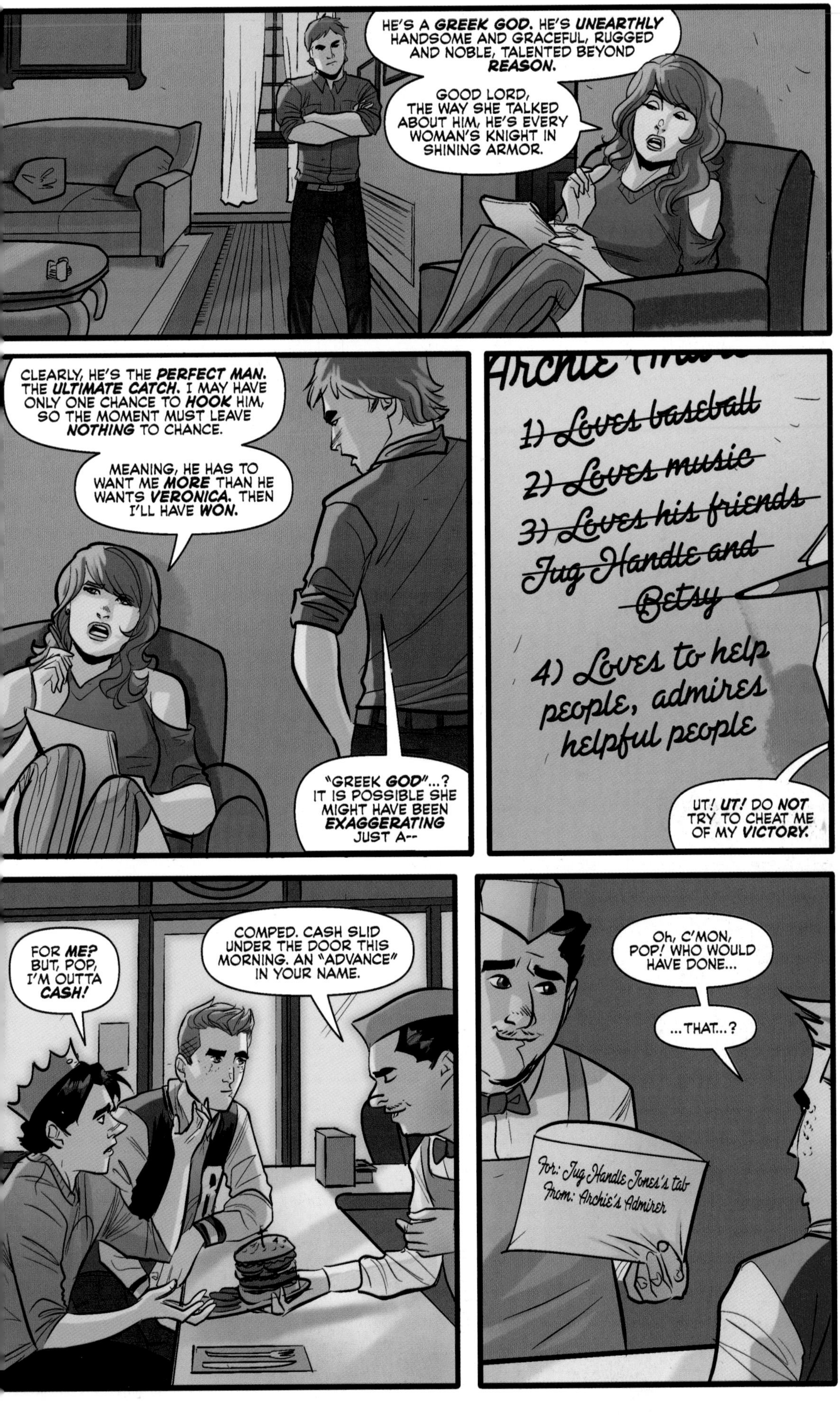
HE'S A GREEK GOD. HE'S UNEARTHLY HANDSOME AND GRACEFUL, RUGGED AND NOBLE, TALENTED BEYOND REASON.
GOOD LORD, THE WAY SHE TALKED ABOUT HIM, HE'S EVERY WOMAN'S KNIGHT IN SHINING ARMOR.
CLEARLY, HE'S THE PERFECT MAN. THE ULTIMATE CATCH. I MAY HAVE ONLY ONE CHANCE TO HOOK HIM, SO THE MOMENT MUST LEAVE NOTHING TO CHANCE.
MEANING, HE HAS TO WANT ME MORE THAN HE WANTS VERONICA. THEN I'LL HAVE WON.
"GREEK GOD"...? IT IS POSSIBLE SHE MIGHT HAVE BEEN EXAGGERATING JUST A--
1) Loves baseball
2) Loves music
3) Loves his friends Jug Handle and Betsy
4) Loves to help people, admires helpful people
UT! UT! DO NOT TRY TO CHEAT ME OF MY VICTORY.
FOR ME? BUT, POP, I'M OUTTA CASH!
COMPED. CASH SLID UNDER THE DOOR THIS MORNING. AN "ADVANCE" IN YOUR NAME.
OH, C'MON, POP! WHO WOULD HAVE DONE...
...THAT...?
For: Jug Handle Jones's tab
From: Archie's Admirer

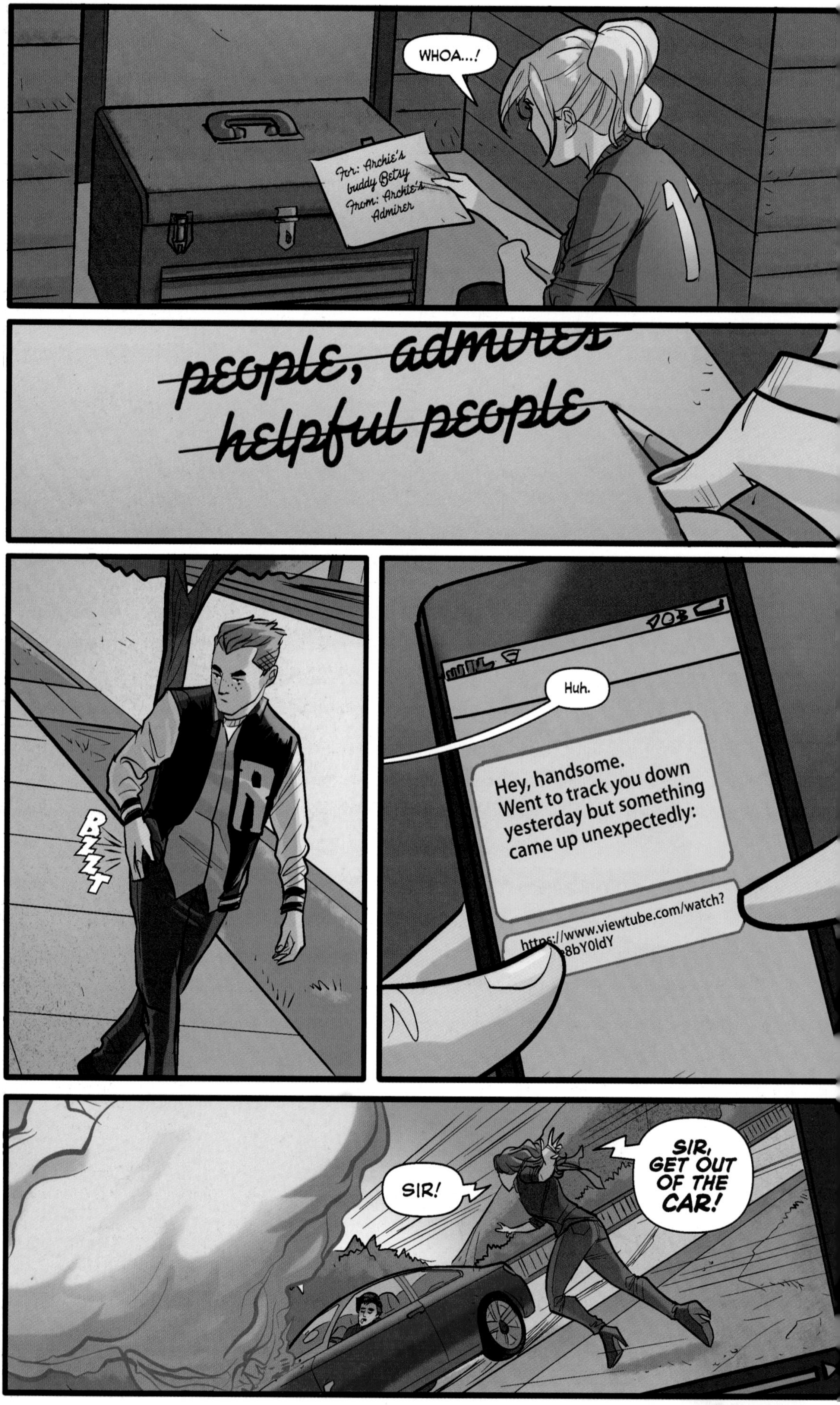
WHOA...!
For: Archie's buddy Betsy
From: Archie's Admirer
people, admirer
helpful people
BZZZT
Huh.
Hey, handsome.
Went to track you down yesterday but something came up unexpectedly:
https://www.viewtube.com/watch?
SIR!
SIR, GET OUT OF THE CAR!

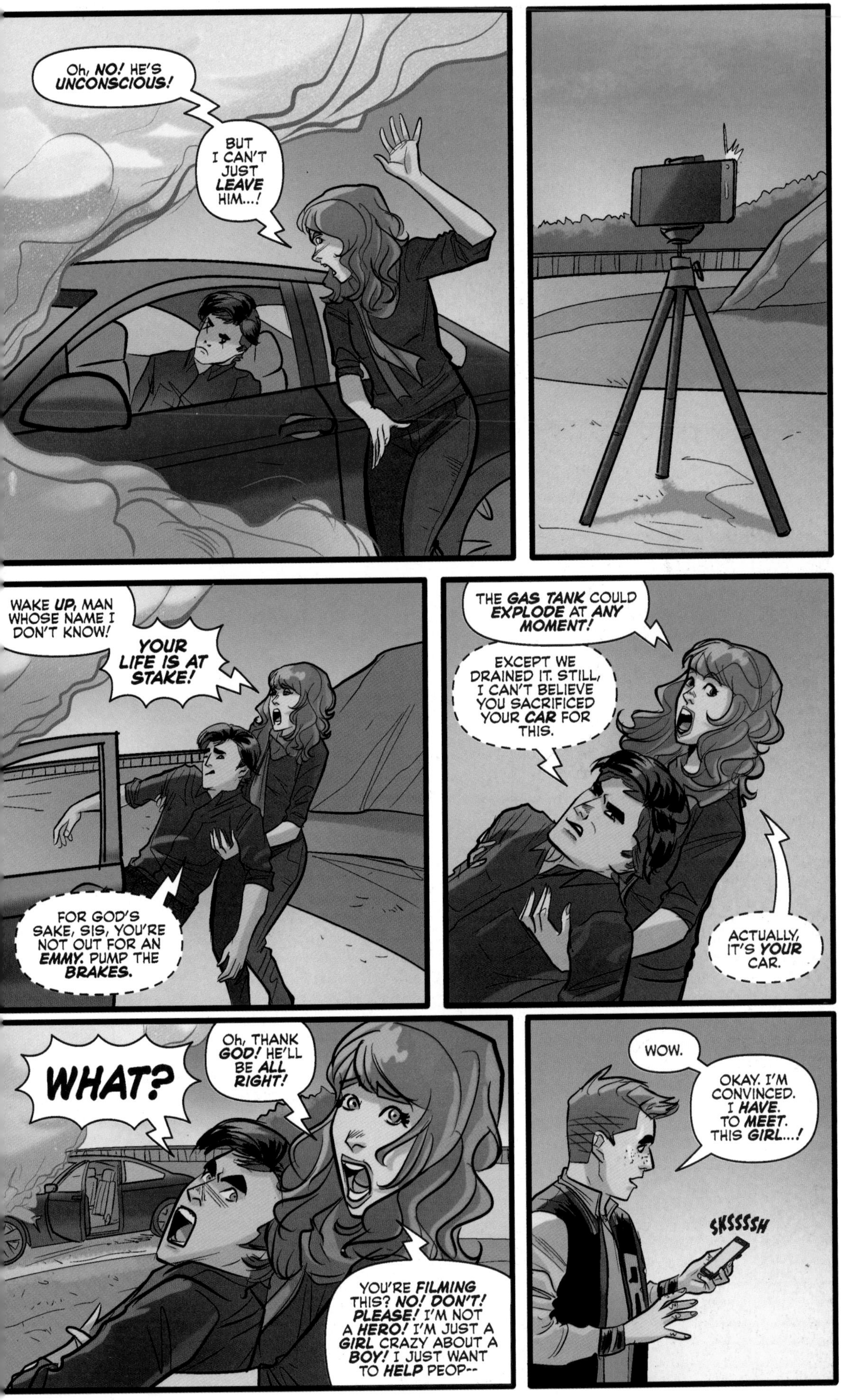
Oh, NO! HE'S UNCONSCIOUS!
BUT I CAN'T JUST LEAVE HIM...!
WAKE UP, MAN WHOSE NAME I DON'T KNOW!
YOUR LIFE IS AT STAKE!
FOR GOD'S SAKE, SIS, YOU'RE NOT OUT FOR AN EMMY. PUMP THE BRAKES.
THE GAS TANK COULD EXPLODE AT ANY MOMENT!
EXCEPT WE DRAINED IT. STILL, I CAN'T BELIEVE YOU SACRIFICED YOUR CAR FOR THIS.
ACTUALLY, IT'S YOUR CAR.
WHAT?
Oh, THANK GOD! HE'LL BE ALL RIGHT!
YOU'RE FILMING THIS? NO! DON'T! PLEASE! I'M NOT A HERO! I'M JUST A GIRL CRAZY ABOUT A BOY! I JUST WANT TO HELP PEOP--
WOW.
OKAY. I'M CONVINCED. I HAVE. TO MEET. THIS GIRL...!
SKSSSSH

# CHAPTER FOUR: Blasted LAMP

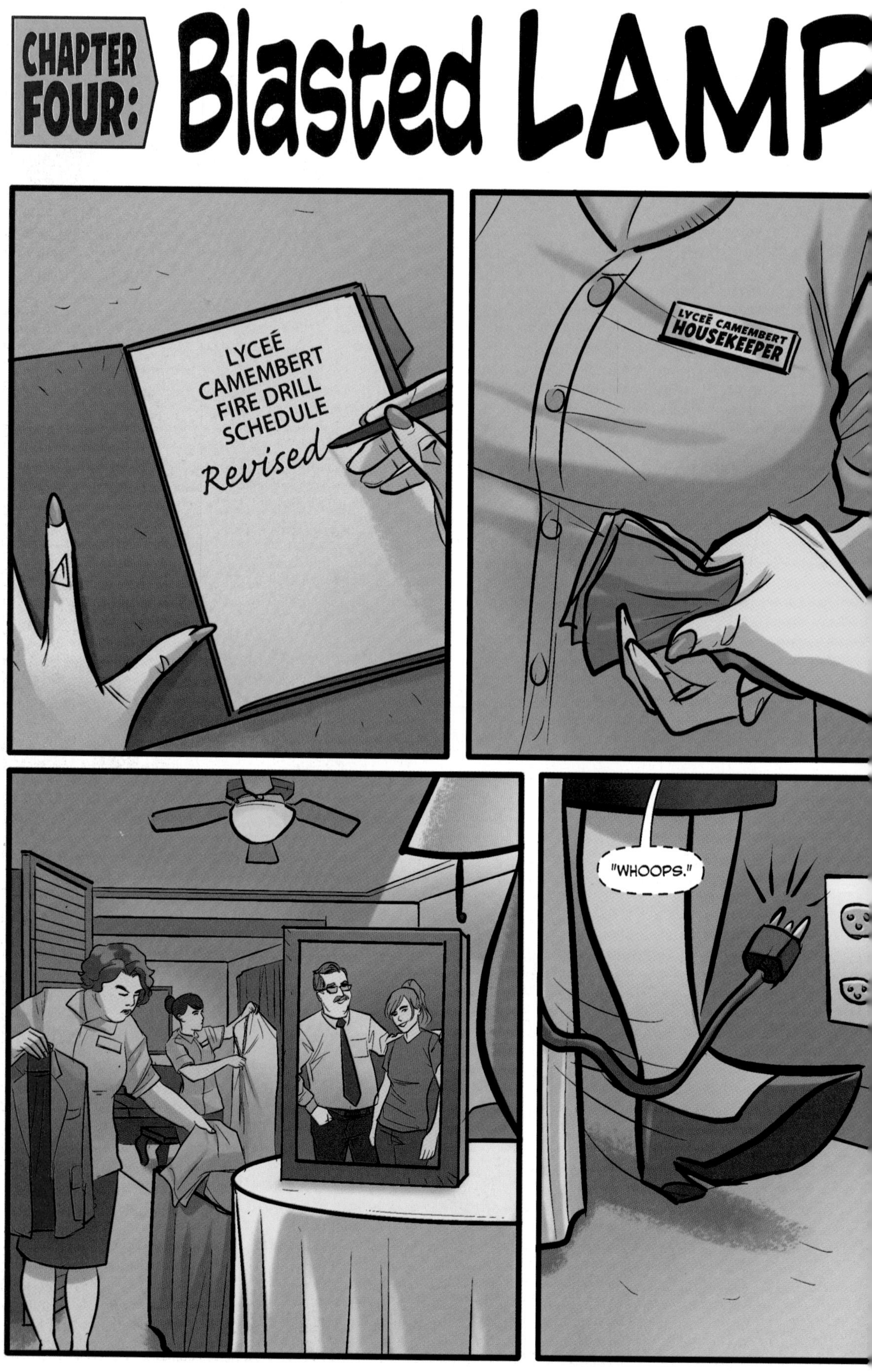
LYCEÉ
CAMEMBERT
FIRE DRILL
SCHEDULE
Revised
LYCEĒ CAMEMBERT
HOUSEKEEPER
"WHOOPS."

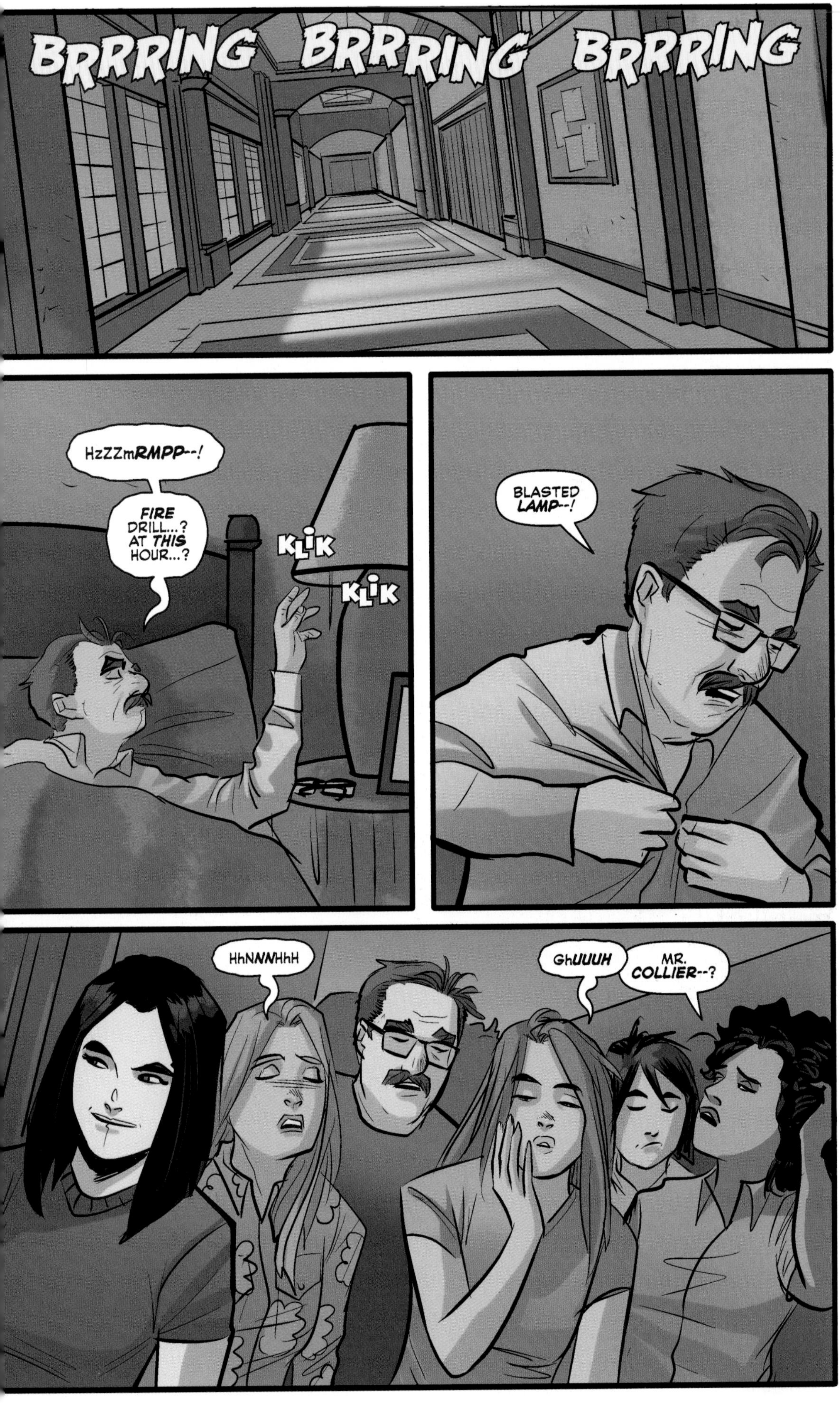
BRRRING BRRRING BRRRING
HzZZmRMPP--!
FIRE DRILL...? AT THIS HOUR...?
KLIK
KLIK
BLASTED LAMP--!
HhNNNhhH
GhUUUH
MR. COLLIER--?

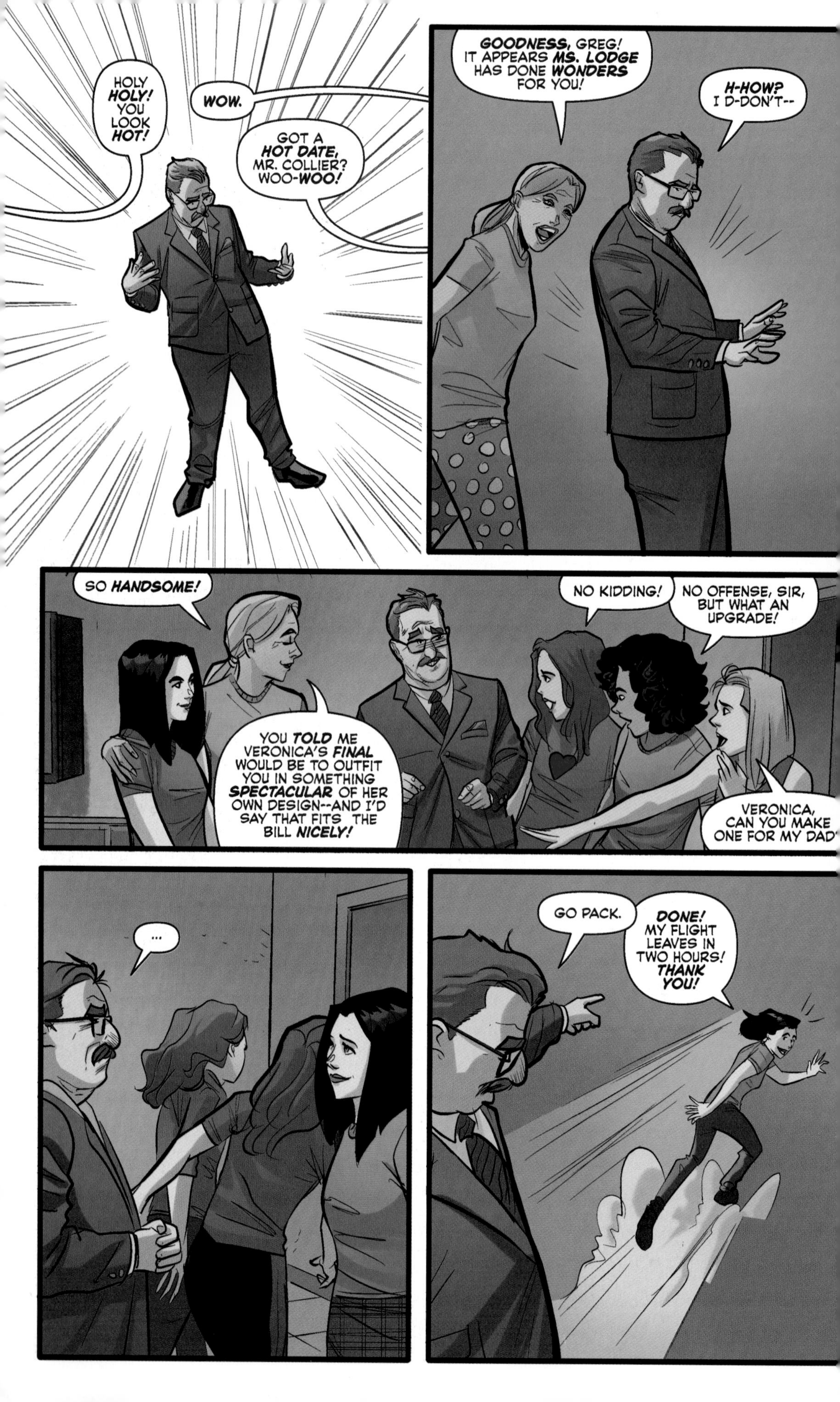
HOLY HOLY! YOU LOOK HOT!
WOW.
GOT A HOT DATE, MR. COLLIER? WOO-WOO!
GOODNESS, GREG! IT APPEARS MS. LODGE HAS DONE WONDERS FOR YOU!
H-HOW? I D-DON'T--
SO HANDSOME!
YOU TOLD ME VERONICA'S FINAL WOULD BE TO OUTFIT YOU IN SOMETHING SPECTACULAR OF HER OWN DESIGN--AND I'D SAY THAT FITS THE BILL NICELY!
NO KIDDING!
NO OFFENSE, SIR, BUT WHAT AN UPGRADE!
VERONICA, CAN YOU MAKE ONE FOR MY DAD
...
GO PACK.
DONE! MY FLIGHT LEAVES IN TWO HOURS! THANK YOU!

# CHAPTER FIVE: BABY PENGUINS

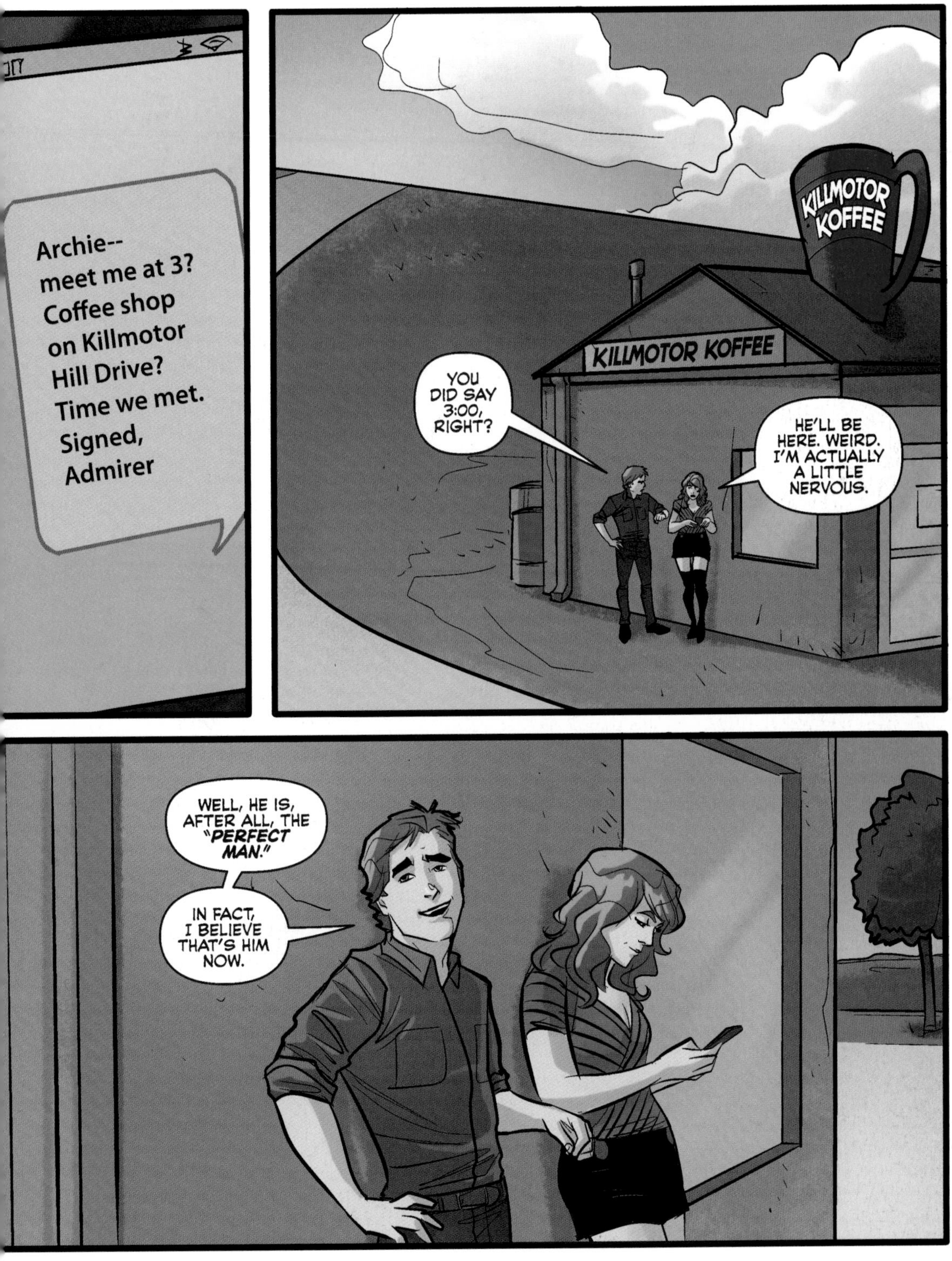
Archie--
meet me at 3?
Coffee shop
on Killmotor
Hill Drive?
Time we met.
Signed,
Admirer
KILLMOTOR KOFFEE
KILLMOTOR KOFFEE
YOU DID SAY 3:00, RIGHT?
HE'LL BE HERE. WEIRD. I'M ACTUALLY A LITTLE NERVOUS.
WELL, HE IS, AFTER ALL, THE "PERFECT MAN."
IN FACT, I BELIEVE THAT'S HIM NOW.

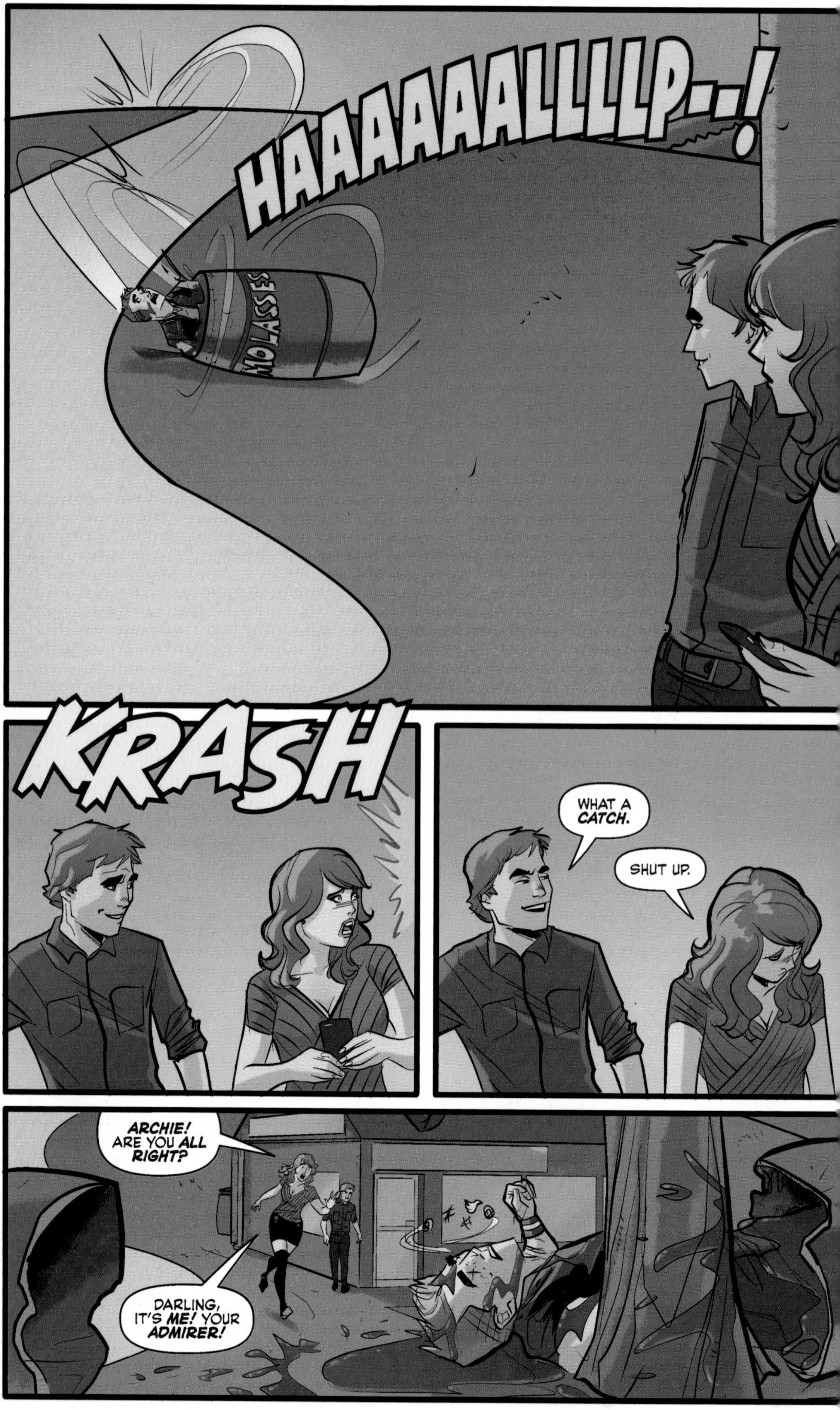

MOLASSES
HAAAAAALLLLP..!
KRASH
WHAT A *CATCH.*
SHUT UP.
***ARCHIE!*** ARE YOU ***ALL RIGHT?***
DARLING, IT'S ***ME!*** YOUR ***ADMIRER!***

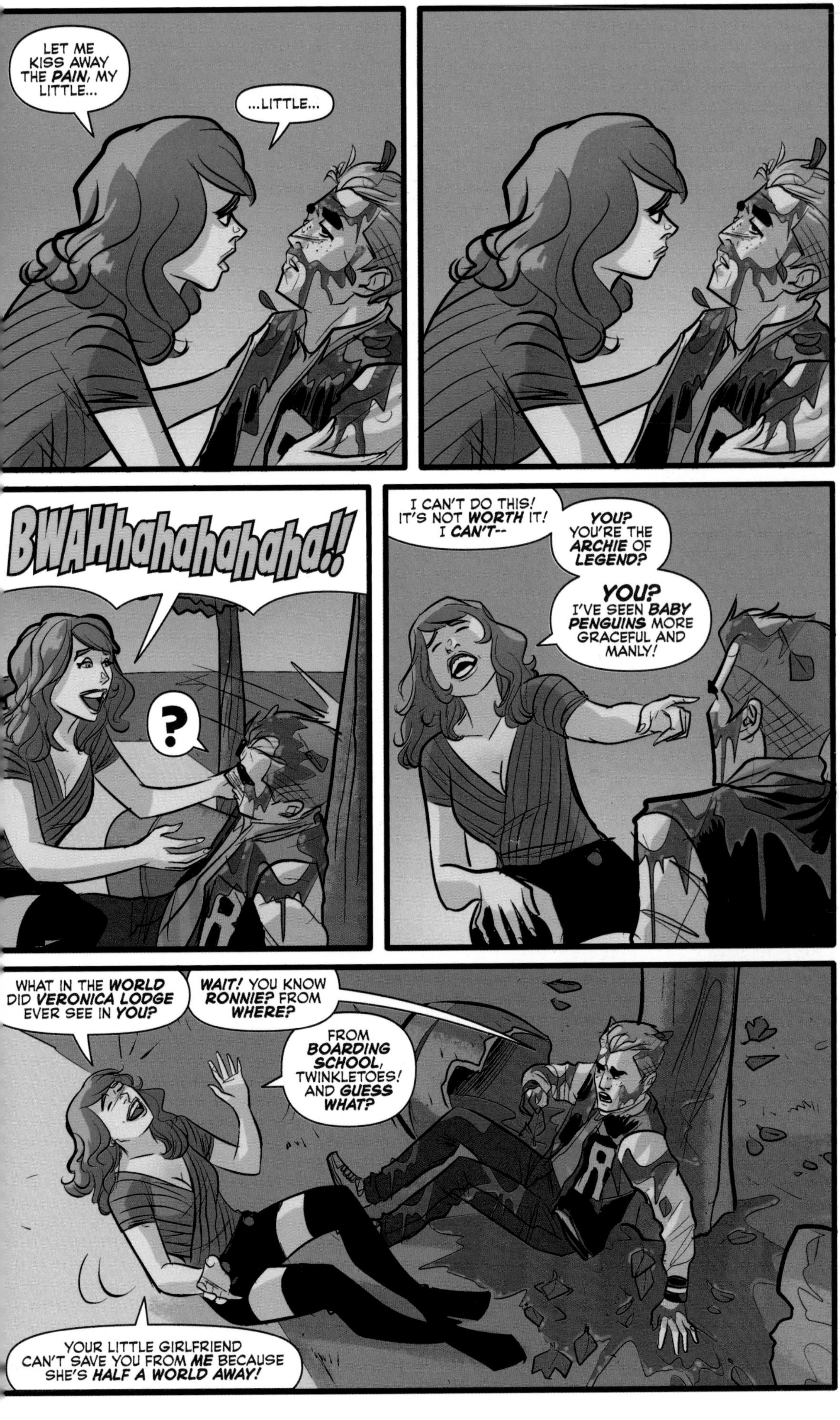

LET ME KISS AWAY THE PAIN, MY LITTLE...
...LITTLE...
BWAHhahahahaha!!
?
I CAN'T DO THIS! IT'S NOT WORTH IT! I CAN'T--
YOU? YOU'RE THE ARCHIE OF LEGEND?
YOU? I'VE SEEN BABY PENGUINS MORE GRACEFUL AND MANLY!
WHAT IN THE WORLD DID VERONICA LODGE EVER SEE IN YOU?
WAIT! YOU KNOW RONNIE? FROM WHERE?
FROM BOARDING SCHOOL, TWINKLETOES! AND GUESS WHAT?
YOUR LITTLE GIRLFRIEND CAN'T SAVE YOU FROM ME BECAUSE SHE'S HALF A WORLD AWAY!

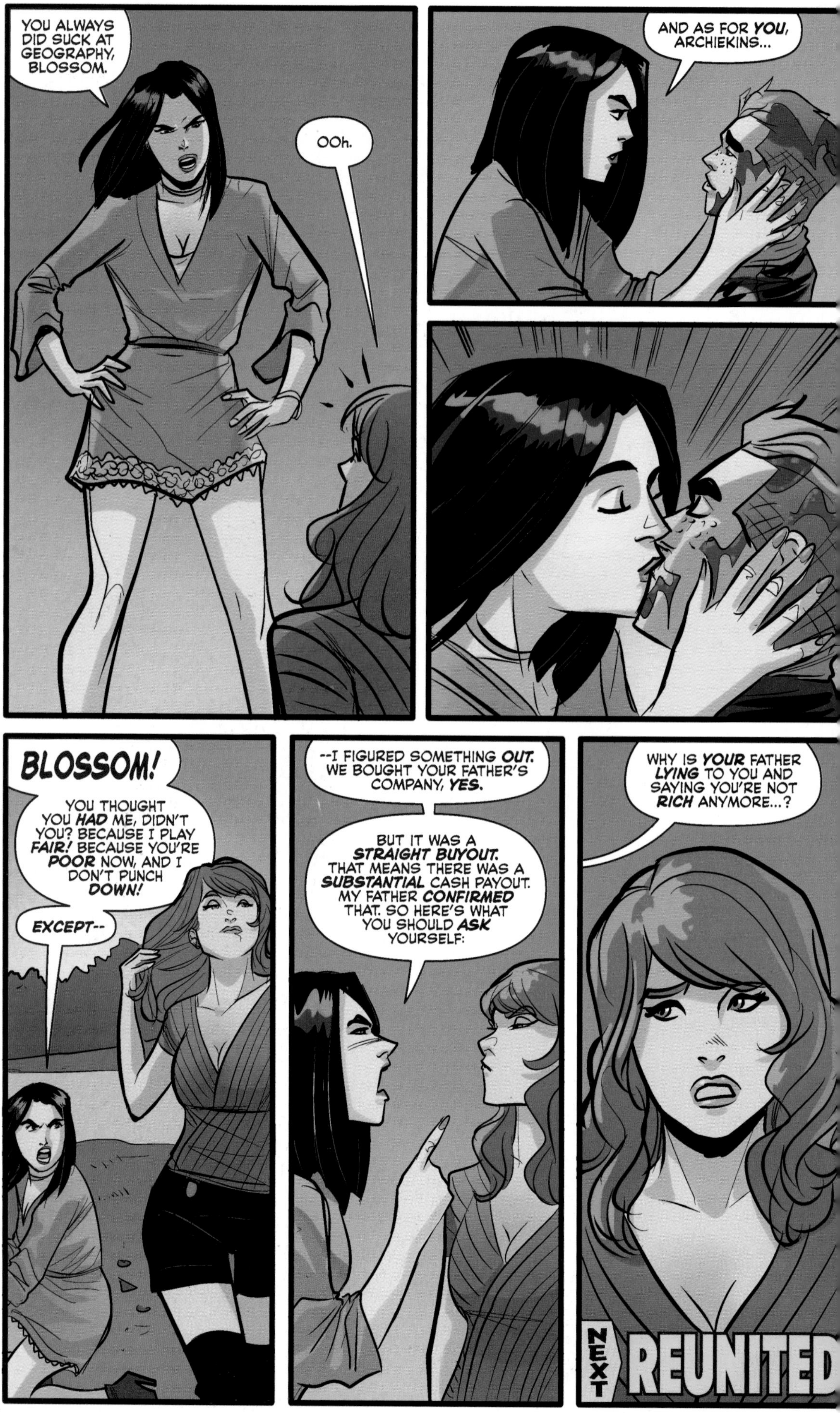
YOU ALWAYS DID SUCK AT GEOGRAPHY, BLOSSOM.
OOh.
AND AS FOR *YOU*, ARCHIEKINS...
BLOSSOM!
YOU THOUGHT YOU *HAD* ME, DIDN'T YOU? BECAUSE I PLAY *FAIR!* BECAUSE YOU'RE *POOR* NOW, AND I DON'T PUNCH *DOWN!*
*EXCEPT--*
--I FIGURED SOMETHING *OUT.* WE BOUGHT YOUR FATHER'S COMPANY, *YES.*
BUT IT WAS A *STRAIGHT BUYOUT.* THAT MEANS THERE WAS A *SUBSTANTIAL* CASH PAYOUT. MY FATHER *CONFIRMED* THAT. SO HERE'S WHAT YOU SHOULD *ASK* YOURSELF:
WHY IS *YOUR* FATHER *LYING* TO YOU AND SAYING YOU'RE NOT *RICH* ANYMORE...?
NEXT REUNITED

# ARCHIE®

## SPECIAL FEATURES

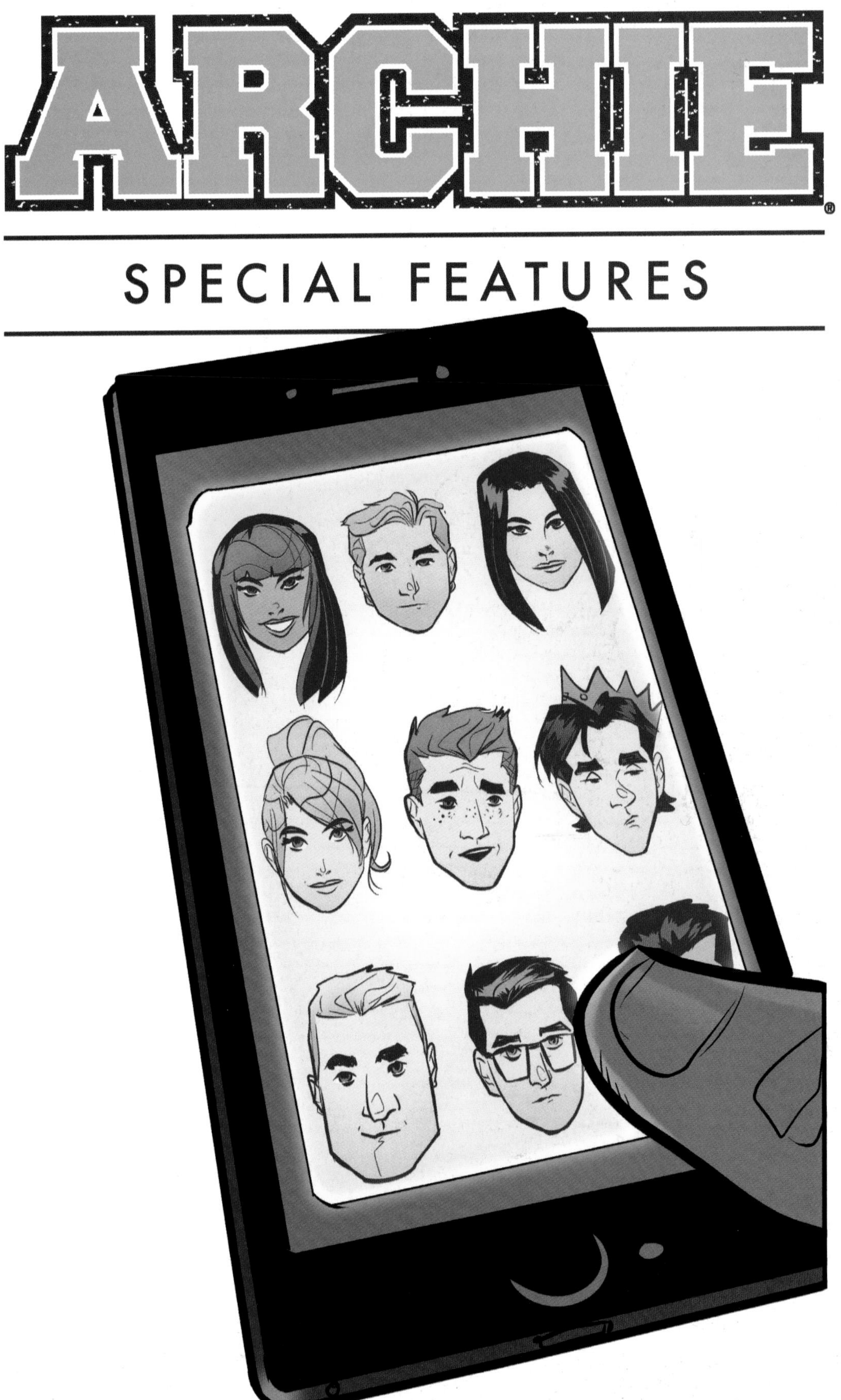

# ARCHIE®

## COVER GALLERY

In addition to the amazing main covers we have for each issue, we also receive gorgeous artwork from an array of talented artists for our direct market exclusive covers. Here are all of the main and variant covers for each of the five issues in Archie Volume Three.

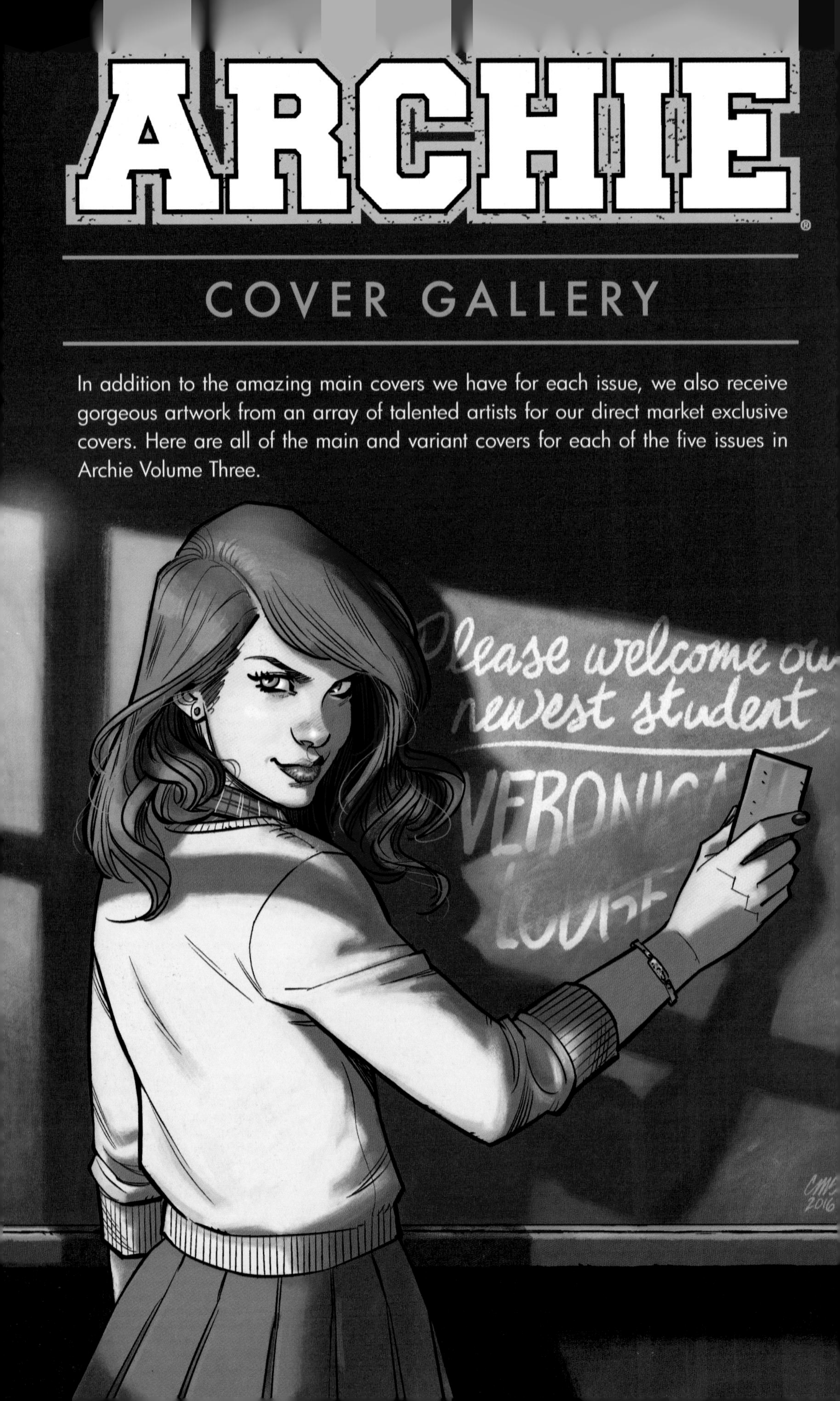
newest student

ISSUE
THIRTEEN

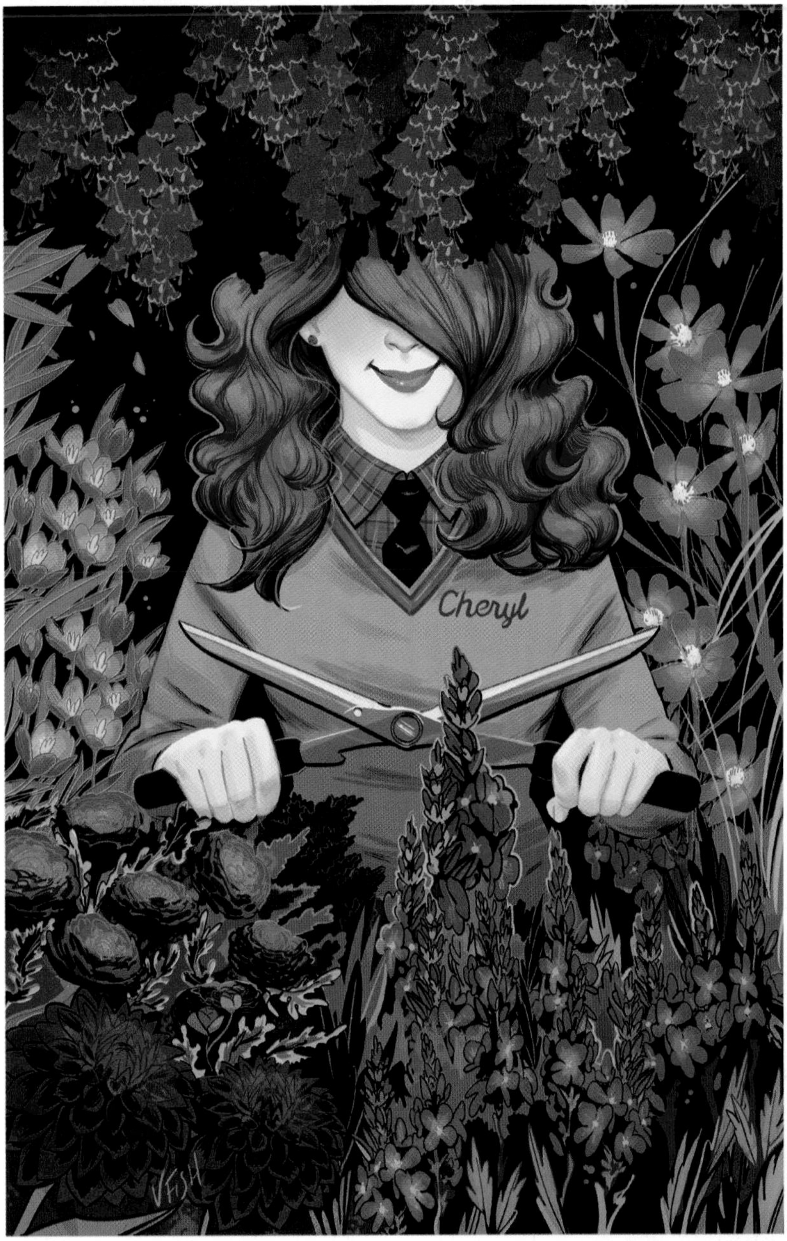
Cheryl
VFISH

VERONICA
FISH

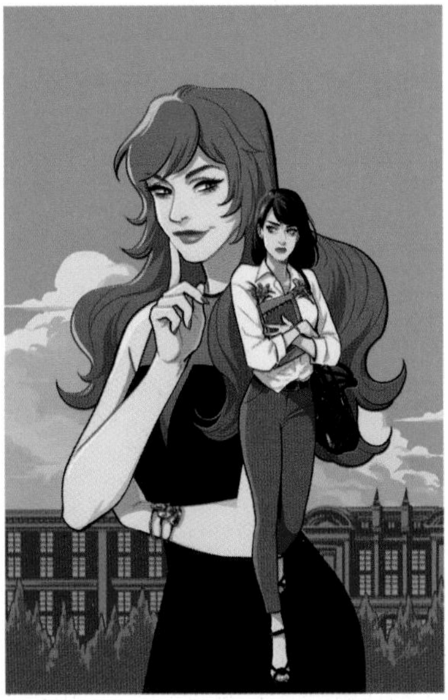

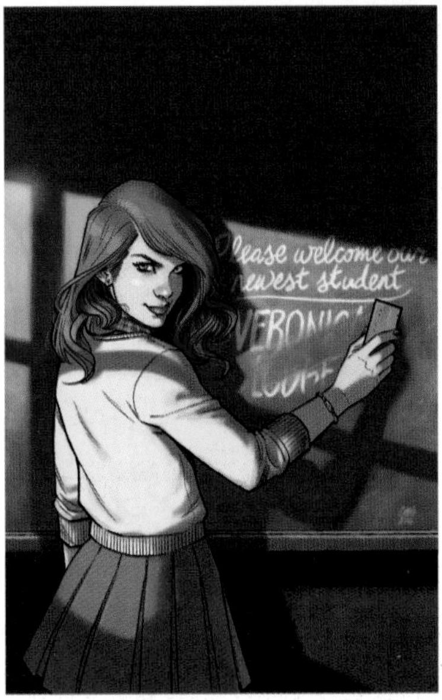
Please welcome our
newest student

(L)
AUDREY
MOK

(R)
CAMERON
STEWART

ISSUE
FOURTEEN

JOE
EISMA

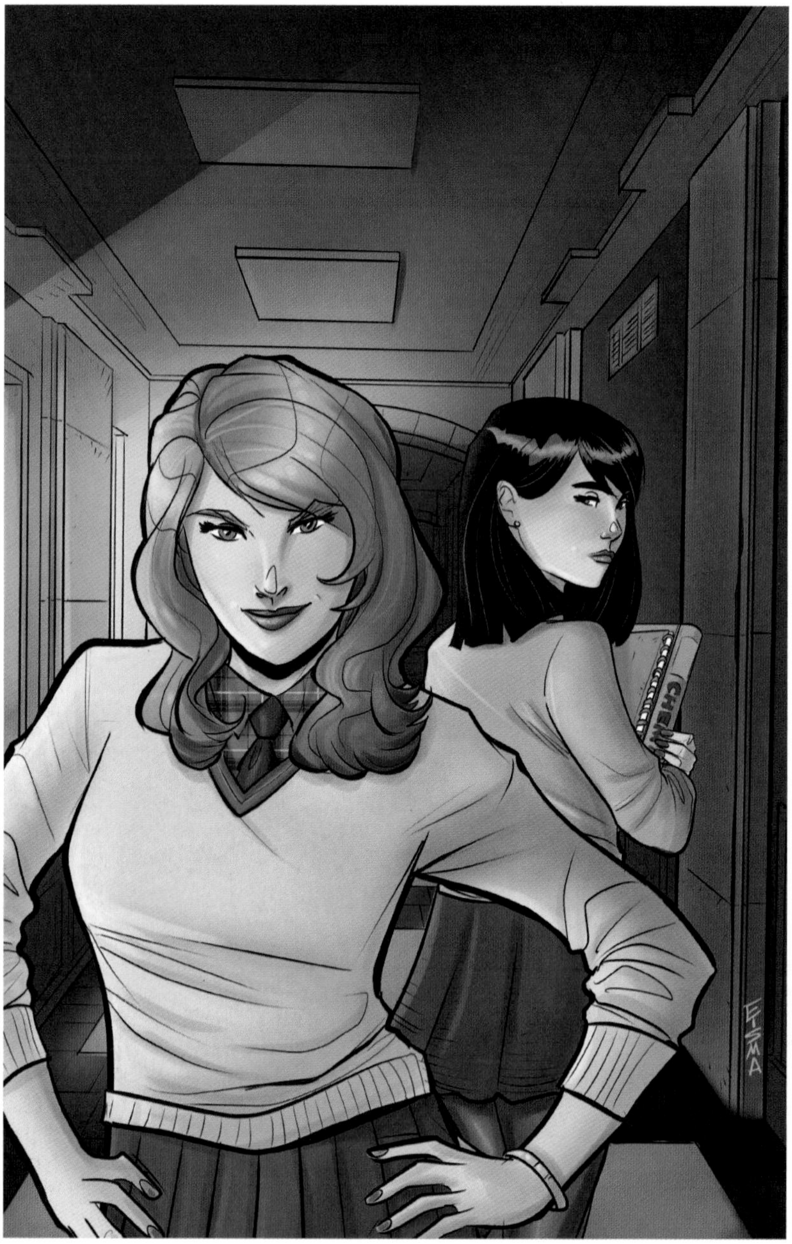

(L)
DEREK
CHARM

(R)
ALITHA
MARTINEZ

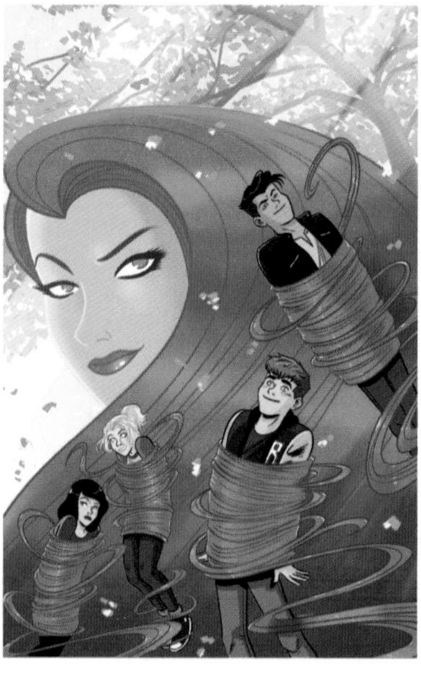

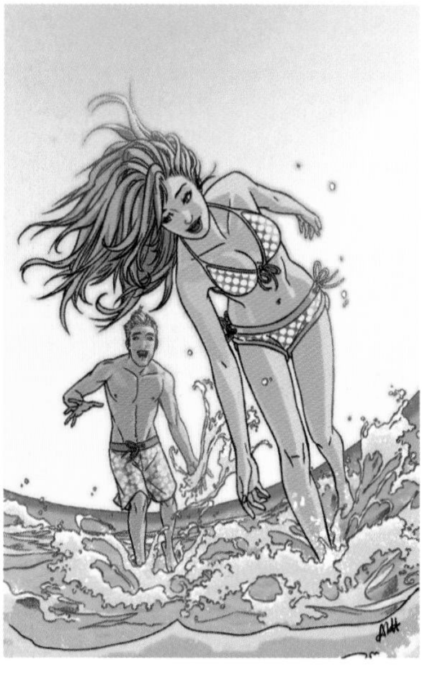

# ISSUE FIFTEEN

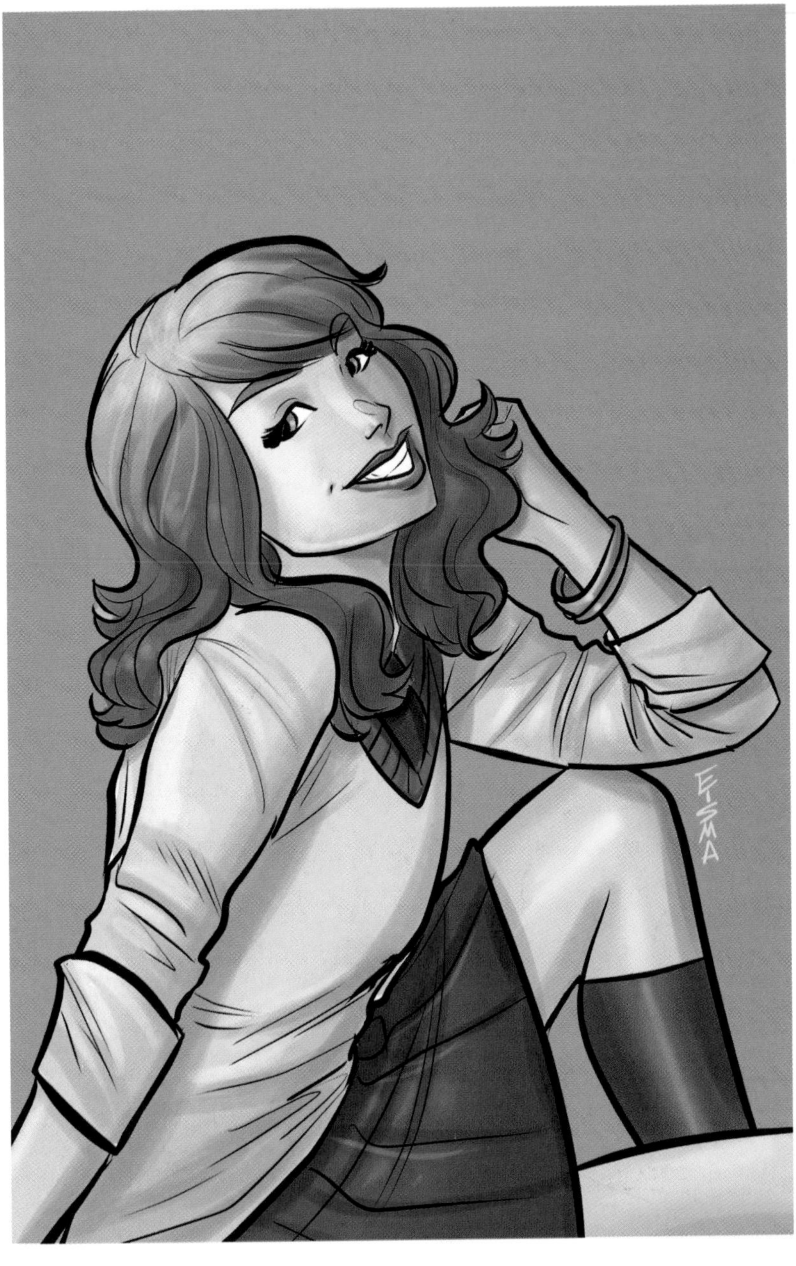
EISMA

JOE EISMA

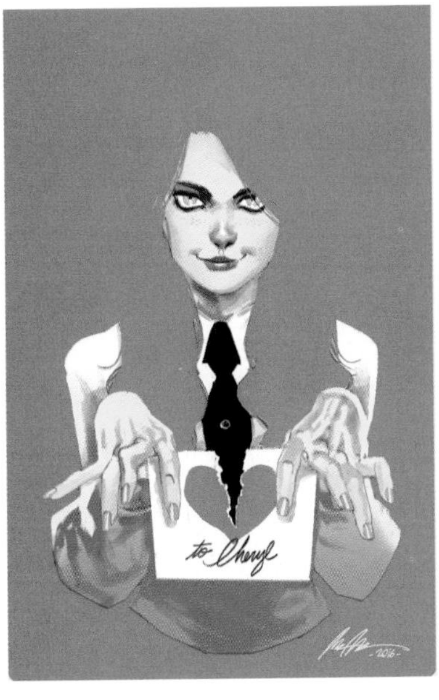
to Cheryl

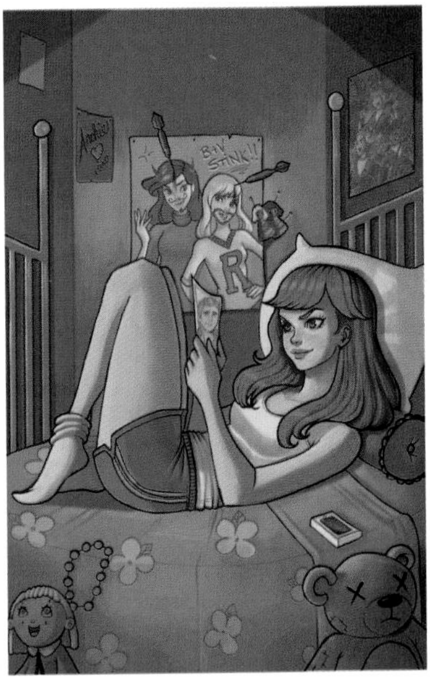

(L)
RAFAEL ALBUQUERQUE

(R)
CHRISSIE ZULLO

ISSUE
SIXTEEN

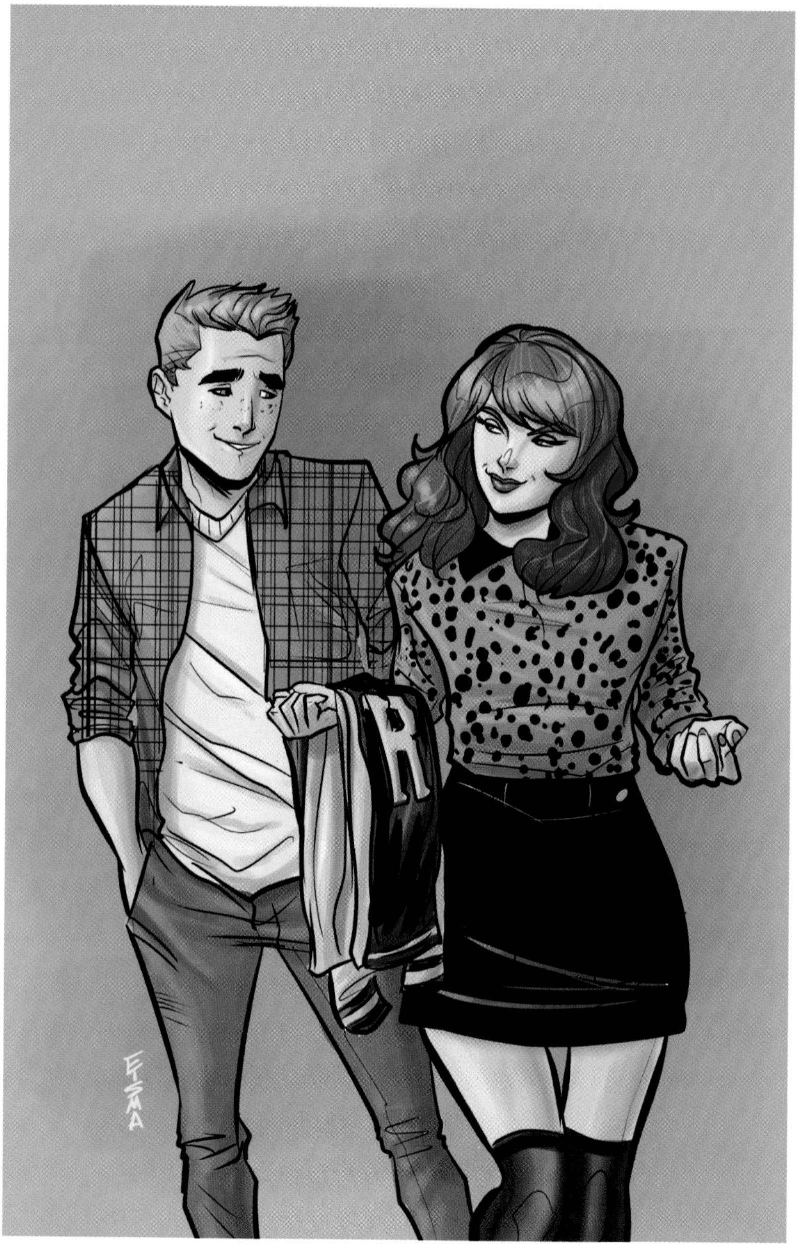

JOE
EISMA

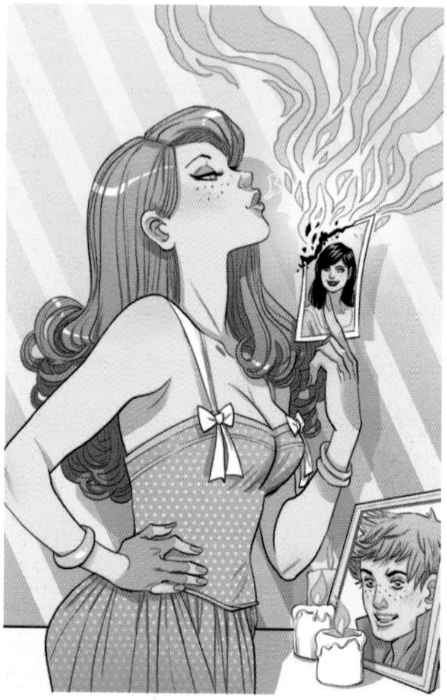

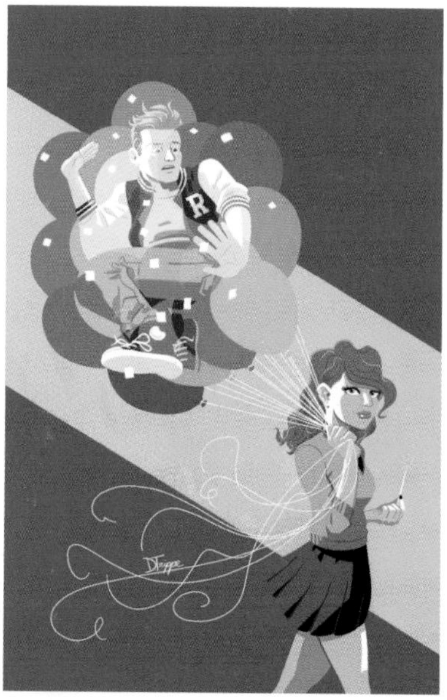

(L)
MARGUERITE
SAUVAGE

(R)
DEAN
TRIPPE

ISSUE
SEVENTEEN

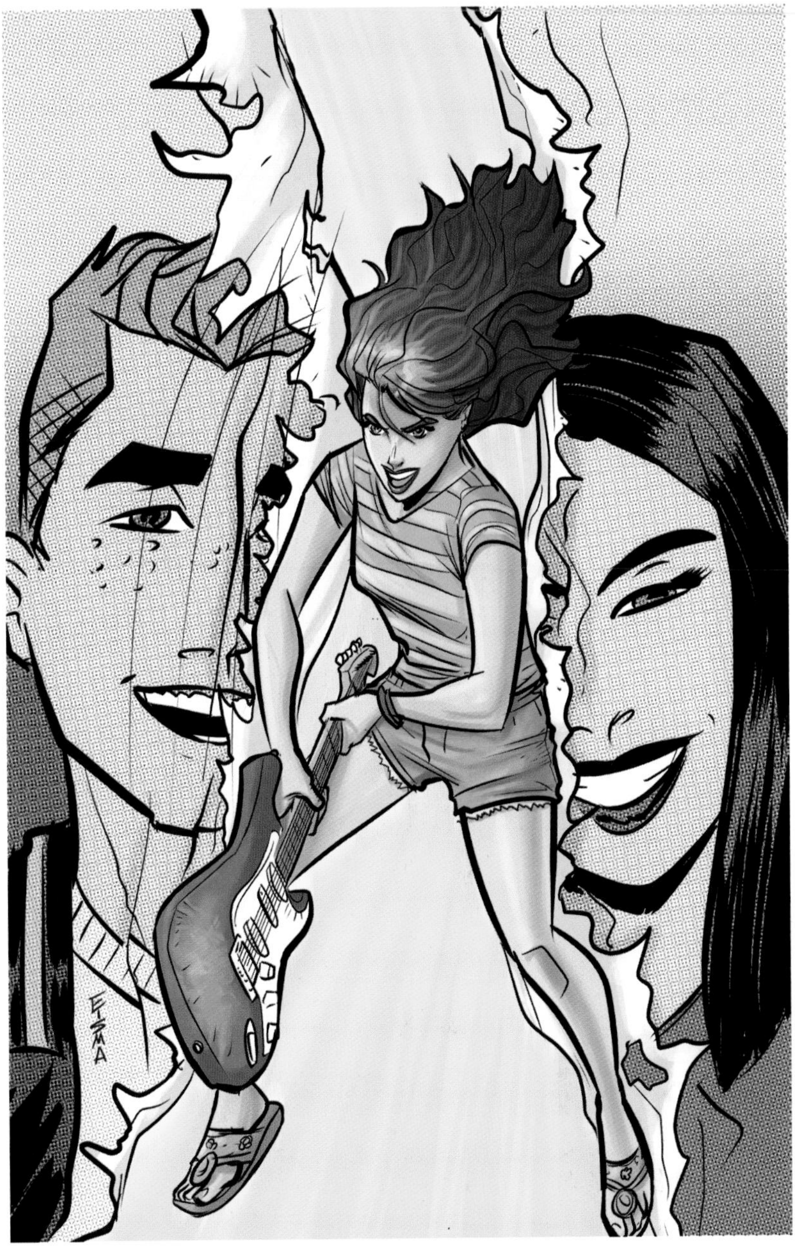
EISMA

JOE
EISMA

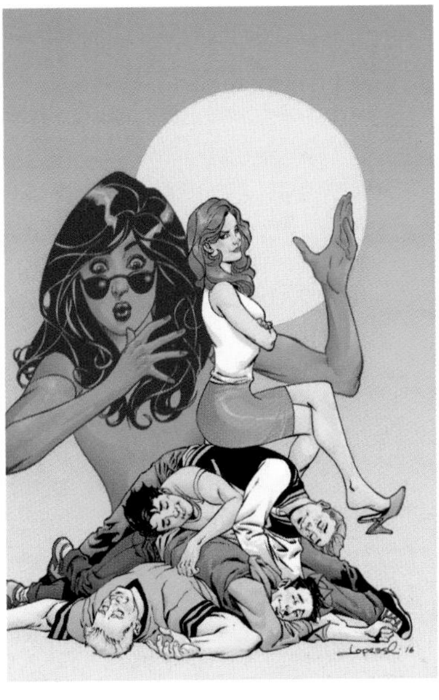

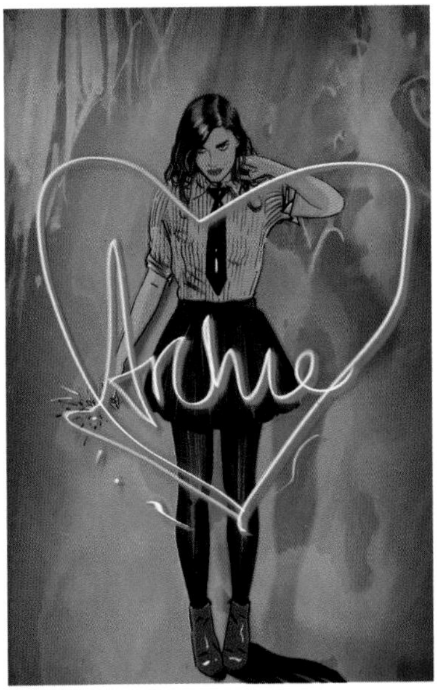
Archie

(L)
AARON
LOPRESTI

(R)
TULA
LOTAY

## ARCHIE ANDREWS

Archie Andrews is well liked in his hometown of Riverdale—though his clumsiness tends to anger some. At school he is popular for his guitar playing skills, athletic endeavors and overall likeable demeanor. He and his long-time girlfriend Betty Cooper recently broke up, leaving him broken-hearted and confused—until Veronica Lodge moved to Riverdale. Since her arrival, Archie's world has been turned upside down: he's fallen head-over-heels in love, almost lost two of his best friends, nearly single-handedly took down a local newspaper empire, landed himself in the middle of a heated political campaign, formed a band, dealt with the crushing hardship of having a long-distance relationship and almost became a pawn in a rich family's revenge scheme. Now that he and Veronica are back together, nothing can go wrong—right?

## VERONICA LODGE

Veronica Lodge moved to Riverdale and took the entire town by storm. She comes from big money, thanks to her tycoon father Hiram Lodge. Her focus is always on the finer things in life, from the fanciest threads to the most exclusive restaurants. When her family moved to Riverdale, she never thought she'd fit in with the frighteningly average teens there, but she soon found out that her peers were anything but. Falling in love with the affable (albeit klutzy) Archie Andrews, Veronica's discovered that there really is some charm to small-town life. Just when things seemed to be working out, her father up and shipped her off to a boarding school in Switzerland, where she dominated at school but found a new rival in the devious Cheryl Blossom. Thanks to Veronica's wits and resources, she knew exactly how to restore order.

# WHO'S WHO

## CHERYL BLOSSOM

The feisty Cheryl Blossom has a life story that closely mirrors Veronica Lodge's—but what Cheryl lacks in Veronica's compassion she more than makes up for in cleverness. She's rich, powerful and always has a few tricks up her sleeve—commanding respect and followers everywhere she goes. Cheryl ruled the Lyceé Camembert—a boarding school in Switzerland—until Veronica Lodge arrived on the scene. After the Lodges forced her family out of Switzerland and into Riverdale, Cheryl's even more hell-bent on getting revenge than ever before. She's going to make sure she gets what she wants, and she doesn't care who she takes down in order to do so.

## JASON BLOSSOM

Twin brother of Cheryl Blossom, Jason is never one to pass up a good opportunity to get in on a nefarious plan—fortunately that's what his sister excels at! After Lodge Enterprises bought out Blossom Tech—Jason's father's company—the twins were forced to move to the small town of Riverdale. Jason's blood is far too rich for suburban life, so he makes it his mission to plot, plan and make as much trouble as he can, just to shake things up and keep life interesting.

## BETTY COOPER

Betty is the quintessential girl-next-door. She is cute, sweet and earnest and she's always ready to help out those who are in need—whether it's volunteering at the hospital or fixing up Archie's broken down jalopy. She excels in school, sports and extracurricular activities. Her kindhearted ways have endeared her to everyone in Riverdale. However, her heart was in pieces after she broke up with her long-time boyfriend Archie Andrews. It's taken a while for her to recover, but after many tears and battles—and an ill-fated relationship with fellow Riverdale High student Sayid Ali—Betty's finally ready to move on and find happiness.

## JUGHEAD JONES

Jughead Jones's favorite activities are eating, sleeping and eating again. Besides his tremendous appetite, Jughead is best known for his grey beanie cap; he rarely goes anywhere without it. Best friend of Archie Andrews, Jughead is Archie's polar opposite: aloof, analytical and avoids drama at all costs. Under his casual demeanor lies an incredibly sharp wit and a compassionate soul, meaning that he often has to act as Archie's voice of reason. While Archie's heart (and often times mind) were far away from Riverdale while Veronica was abroad, Jughead did everything in his power to keep Archie grounded and out of trouble.

## REGGIE MANTLE

Reggie Mantle is a self-absorbed, wisecracking schemer. He's the rival of many at Riverdale High, especially Archie Andrews. The many practical jokes and ruthless plots he plays on other students make him more infamous than popular. There could be more to Reggie than just his egotistical and manipulative ways, but he won't let it show that easily. His plans to foil Archie and Veronica's relationship backfired, landing him in hot water with both his father Richard Mantle, the editor of the Riverdale Gazette, and Mr. Lodge. Reggie's also hiding a well-kept secret that only a few people know about, and he'll do whatever it takes to keep that information private.

# SPECIAL PREVIEW

# REGGIE AND ME

STORY BY
TOM DeFALCO

ART BY
SANDY JARRELL

COLORING BY
KELLY FITZPATRICK

LETTERING BY
JACK MORELLI

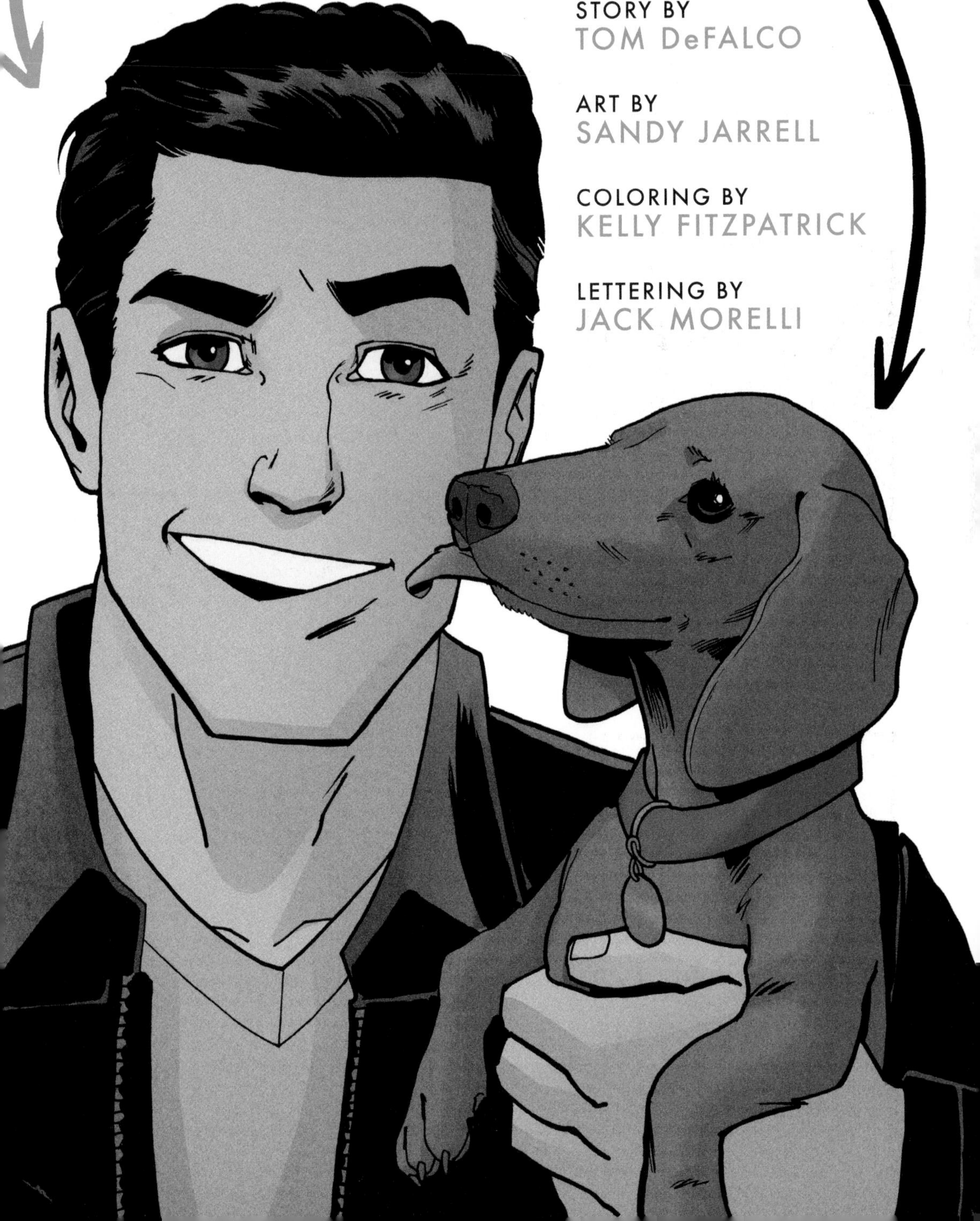

# ISSUE ONE

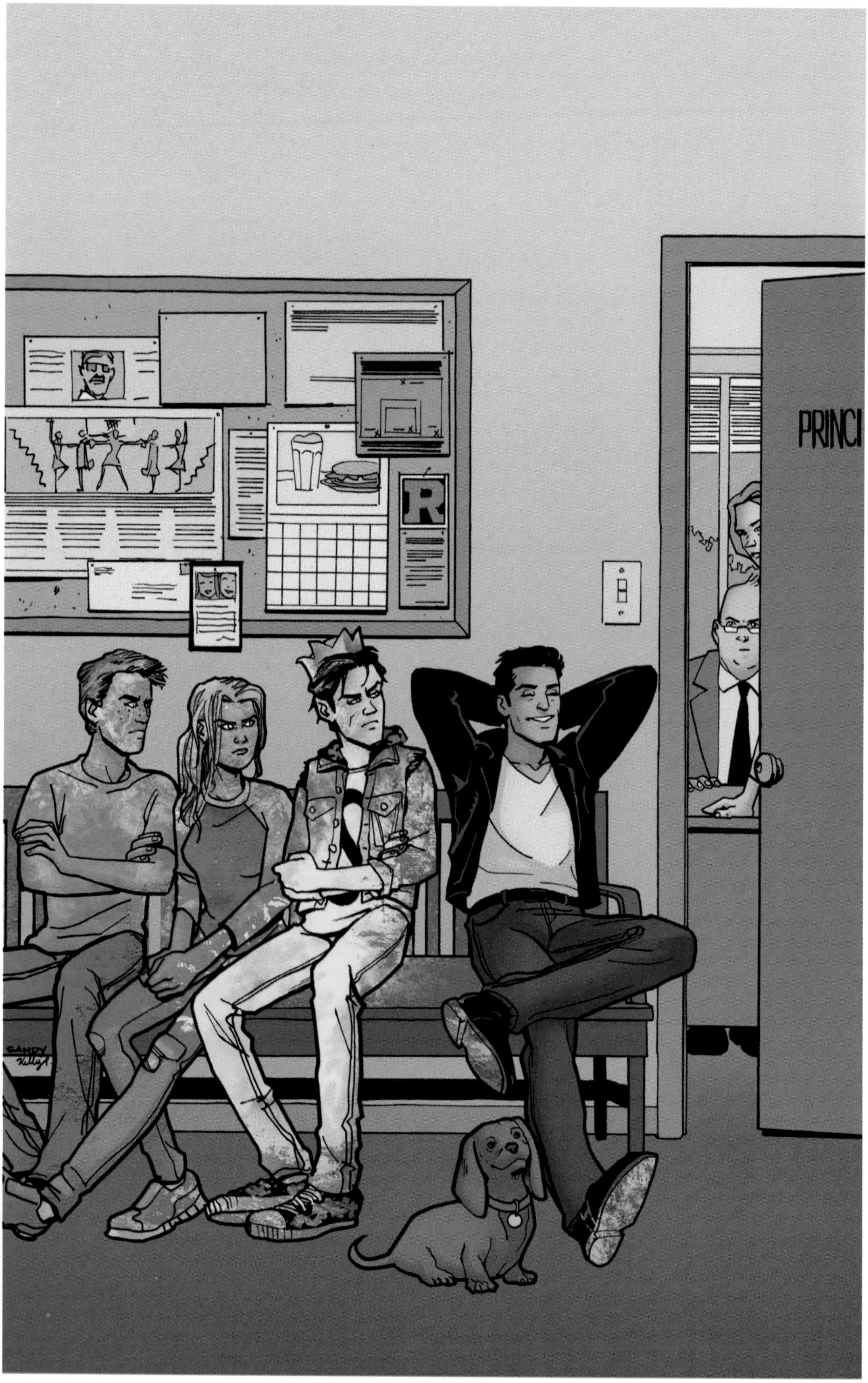
PRINCI

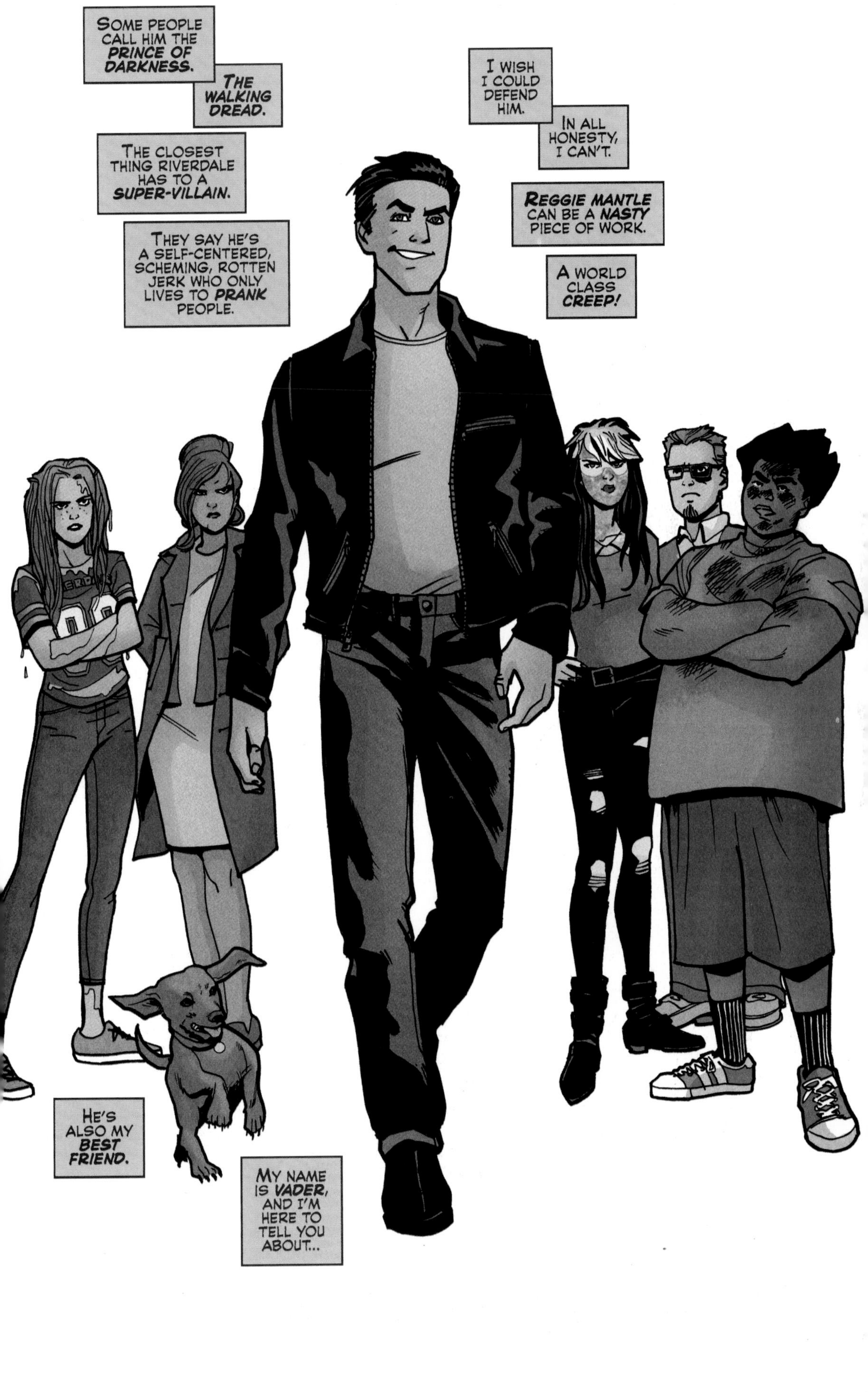

SOME PEOPLE CALL HIM THE PRINCE OF DARKNESS.
THE WALKING DREAD.
THE CLOSEST THING RIVERDALE HAS TO A SUPER-VILLAIN.
THEY SAY HE'S A SELF-CENTERED, SCHEMING, ROTTEN JERK WHO ONLY LIVES TO PRANK PEOPLE.
I WISH I COULD DEFEND HIM.
IN ALL HONESTY, I CAN'T.
REGGIE MANTLE CAN BE A NASTY PIECE OF WORK.
A WORLD CLASS CREEP!
HE'S ALSO MY BEST FRIEND.
MY NAME IS VADER, AND I'M HERE TO TELL YOU ABOUT...

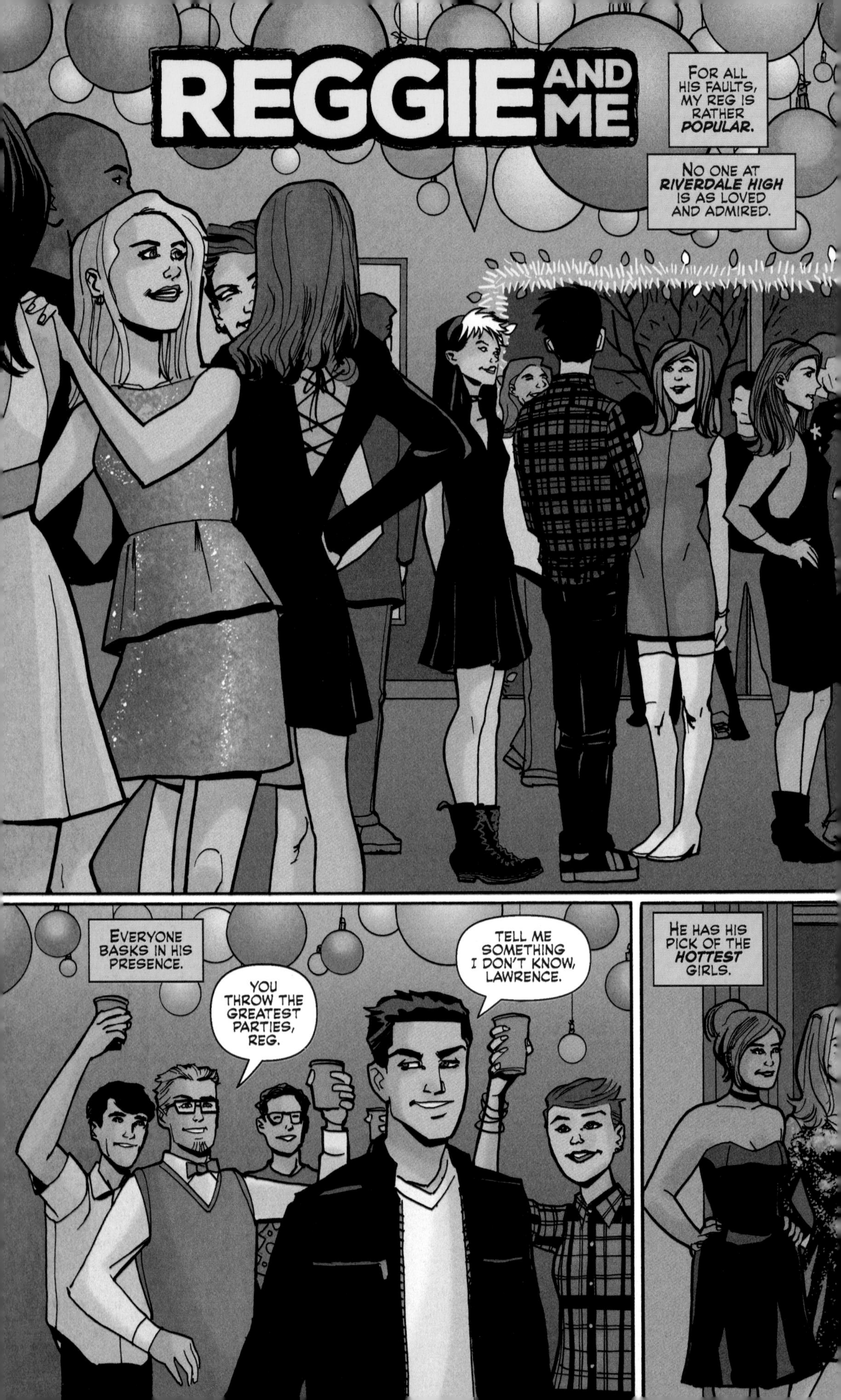
REGGIE AND ME
FOR ALL HIS FAULTS, MY REG IS RATHER POPULAR.
NO ONE AT RIVERDALE HIGH IS AS LOVED AND ADMIRED.
EVERYONE BASKS IN HIS PRESENCE.
YOU THROW THE GREATEST PARTIES, REG.
TELL ME SOMETHING I DON'T KNOW, LAWRENCE.
HE HAS HIS PICK OF THE HOTTEST GIRLS.

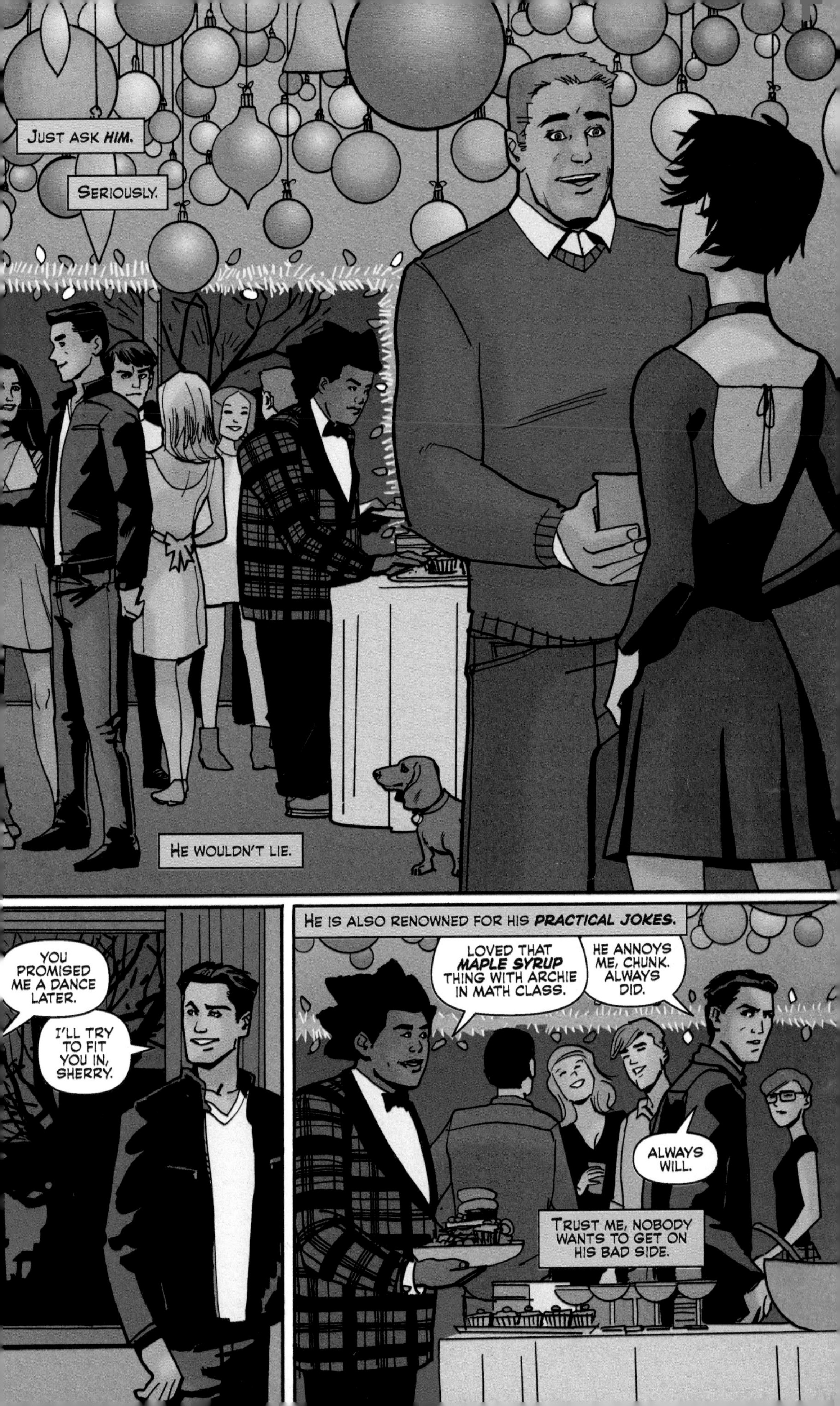

JUST ASK HIM.
SERIOUSLY.
HE WOULDN'T LIE.
YOU PROMISED ME A DANCE LATER.
I'LL TRY TO FIT YOU IN, SHERRY.
HE IS ALSO RENOWNED FOR HIS PRACTICAL JOKES.
LOVED THAT MAPLE SYRUP THING WITH ARCHIE IN MATH CLASS.
HE ANNOYS ME, CHUNK. ALWAYS DID.
ALWAYS WILL.
TRUST ME, NOBODY WANTS TO GET ON HIS BAD SIDE.

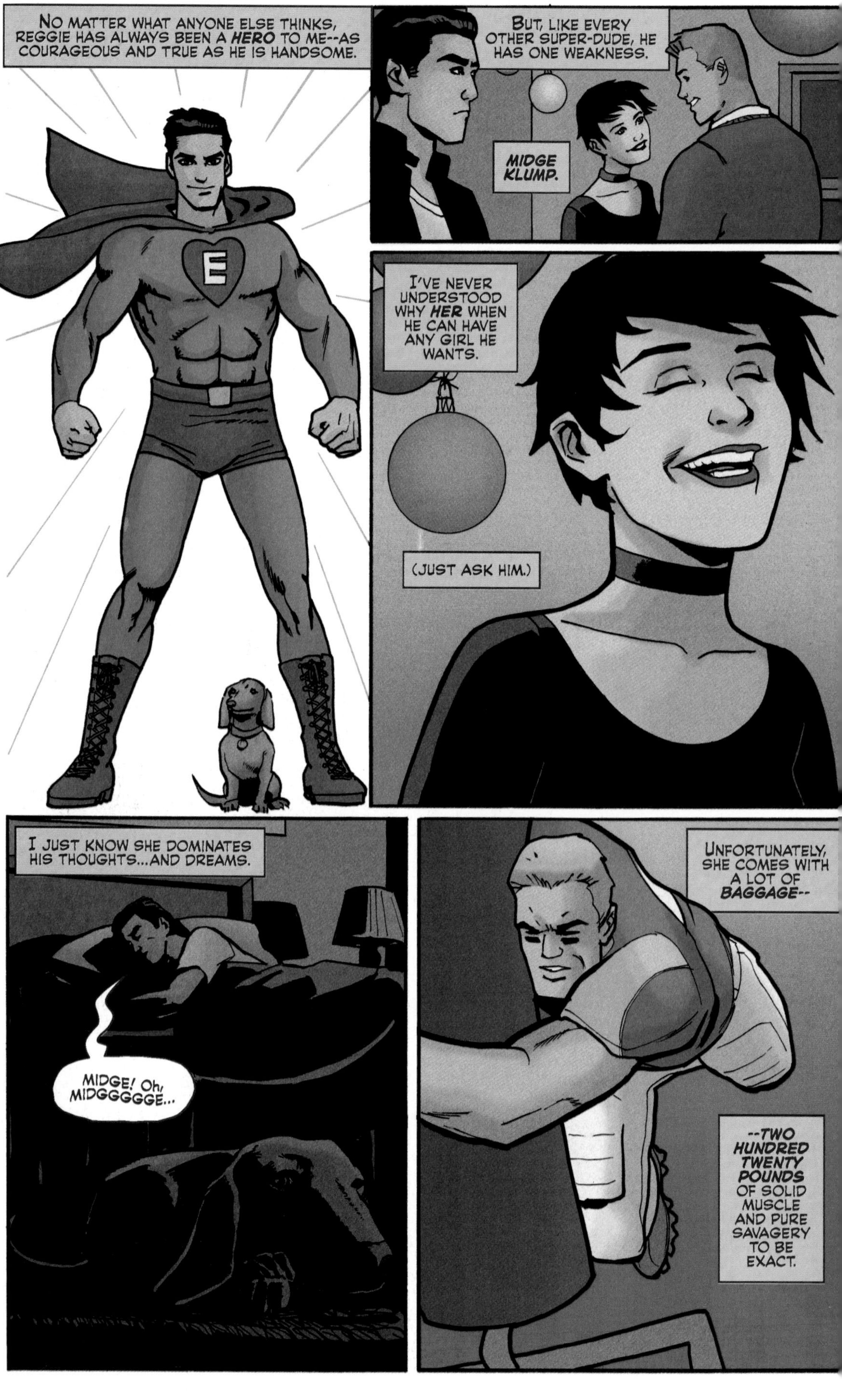
NO MATTER WHAT ANYONE ELSE THINKS, REGGIE HAS ALWAYS BEEN A HERO TO ME--AS COURAGEOUS AND TRUE AS HE IS HANDSOME.
BUT, LIKE EVERY OTHER SUPER-DUDE, HE HAS ONE WEAKNESS.
MIDGE KLUMP.
I'VE NEVER UNDERSTOOD WHY HER WHEN HE CAN HAVE ANY GIRL HE WANTS.
(JUST ASK HIM.)
I JUST KNOW SHE DOMINATES HIS THOUGHTS...AND DREAMS.
MIDGE! Oh, MIDGGGGGE...
UNFORTUNATELY, SHE COMES WITH A LOT OF BAGGAGE--
--TWO HUNDRED TWENTY POUNDS OF SOLID MUSCLE AND PURE SAVAGERY TO BE EXACT.

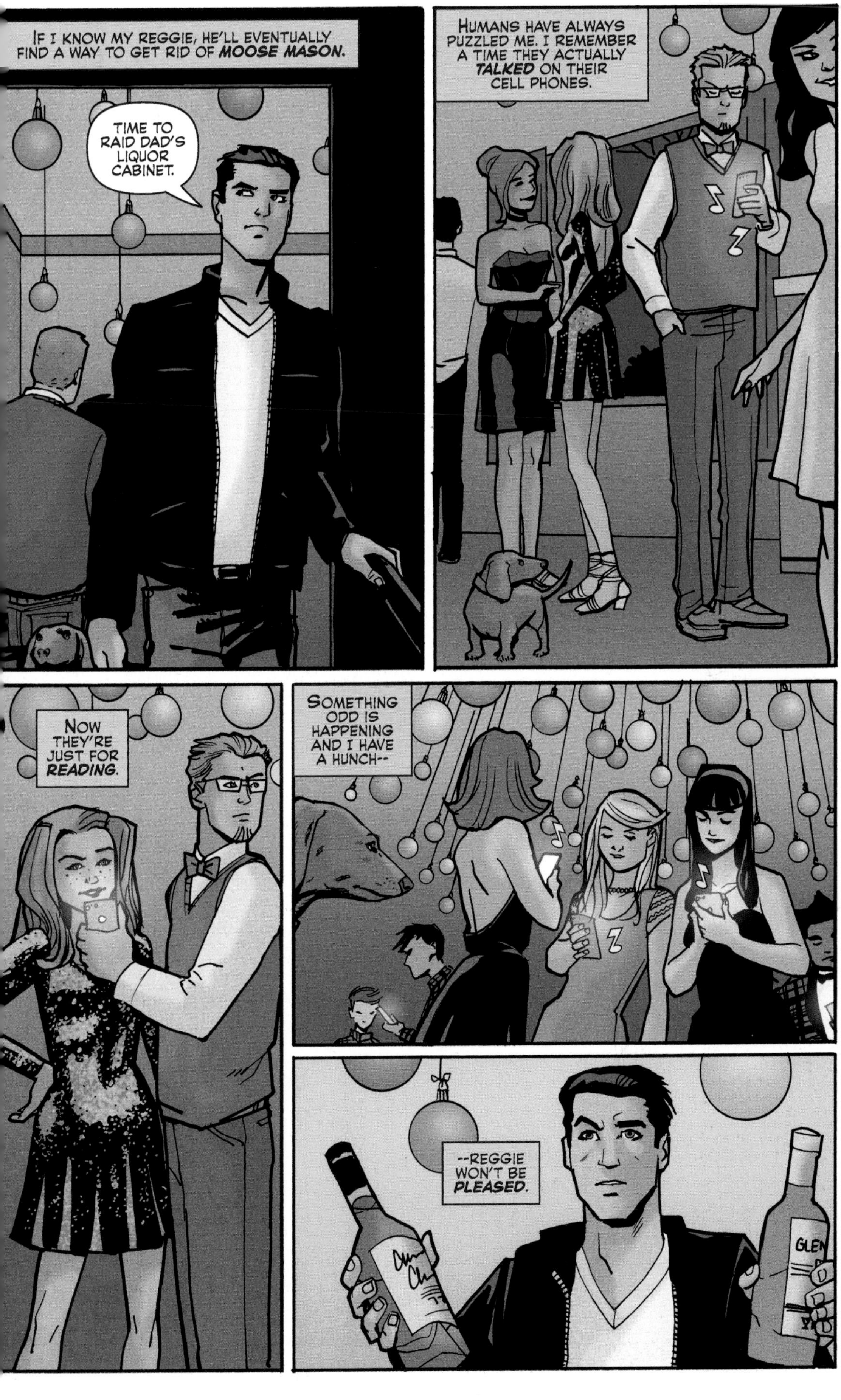
If I know my Reggie, he'll eventually find a way to get rid of *Moose Mason*.
Time to raid Dad's liquor cabinet.
Humans have always puzzled me. I remember a time they actually *talked* on their cell phones.
Now they're just for *reading*.
Something odd is happening and I have a hunch--
--Reggie won't be *pleased*.
GLEN

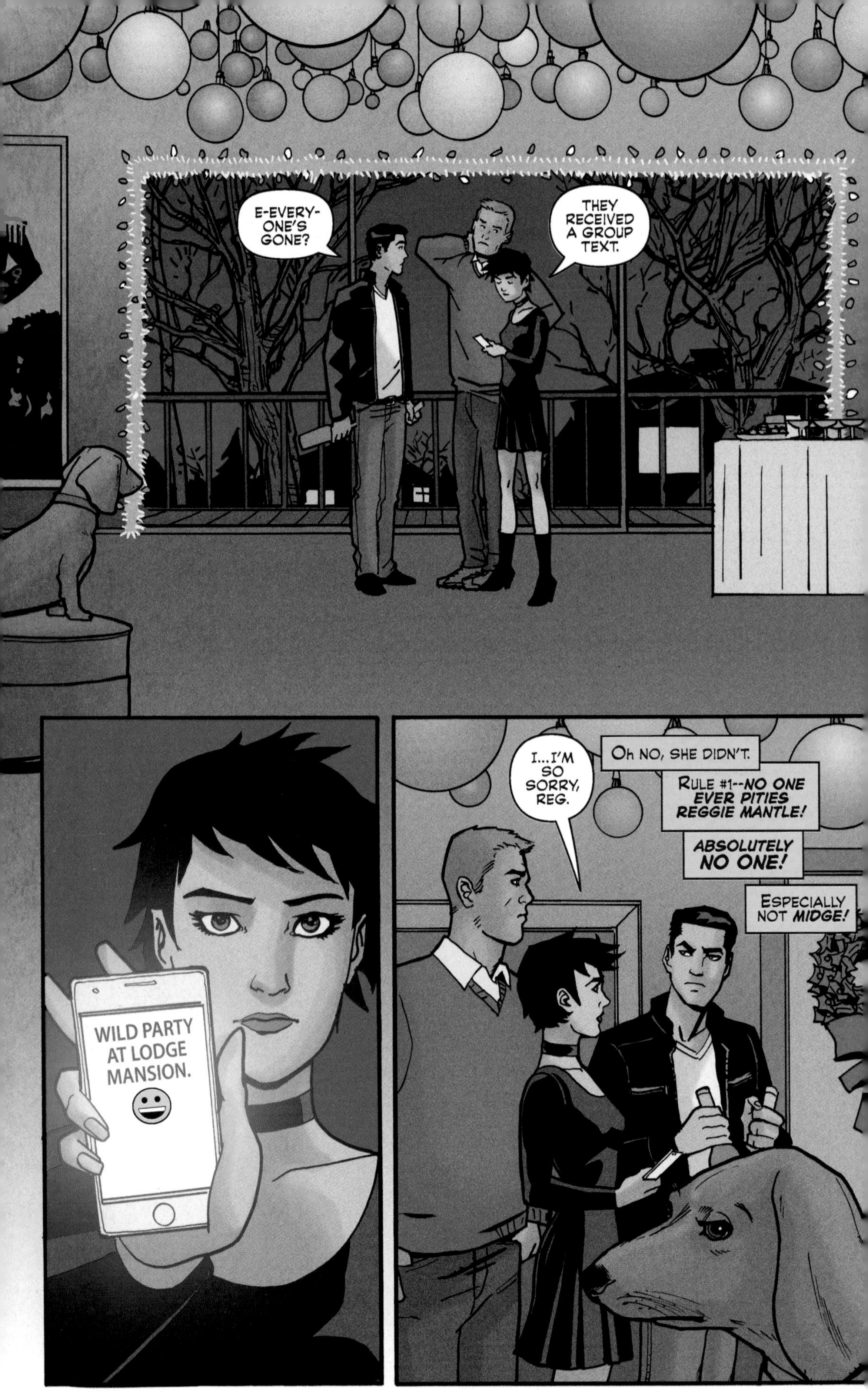

E-EVERY-ONE'S GONE?
THEY RECEIVED A GROUP TEXT.
WILD PARTY AT LODGE MANSION.
I...I'M SO SORRY, REG.
Oh NO, SHE DIDN'T.
RULE #1--NO ONE EVER PITIES REGGIE MANTLE!
ABSOLUTELY NO ONE!
ESPECIALLY NOT MIDGE!

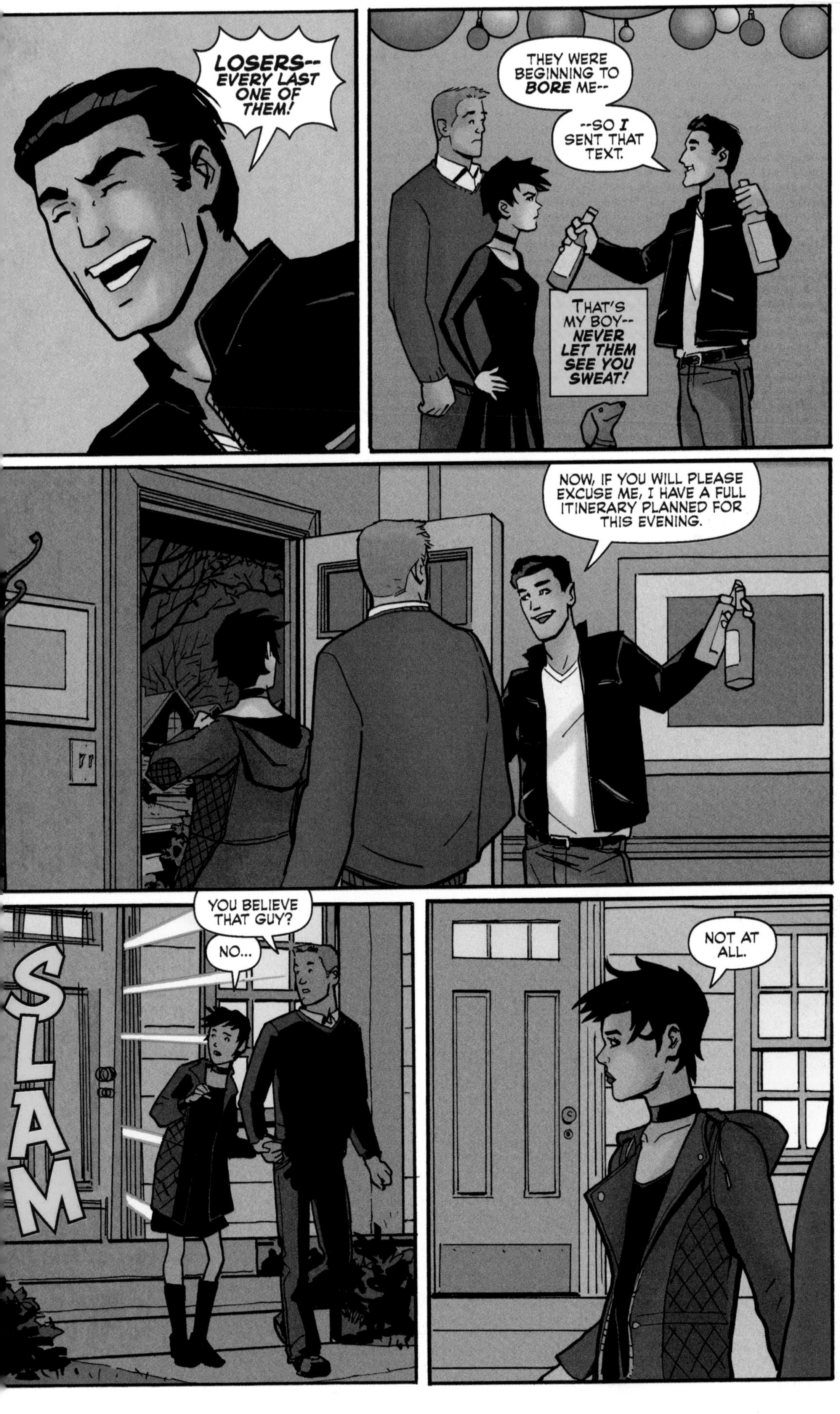
LOSERS-- EVERY LAST ONE OF THEM!
THEY WERE BEGINNING TO BORE ME--
--SO I SENT THAT TEXT.
THAT'S MY BOY-- NEVER LET THEM SEE YOU SWEAT!
NOW, IF YOU WILL PLEASE EXCUSE ME, I HAVE A FULL ITINERARY PLANNED FOR THIS EVENING.
SLAM
YOU BELIEVE THAT GUY?
NO...
NOT AT ALL.

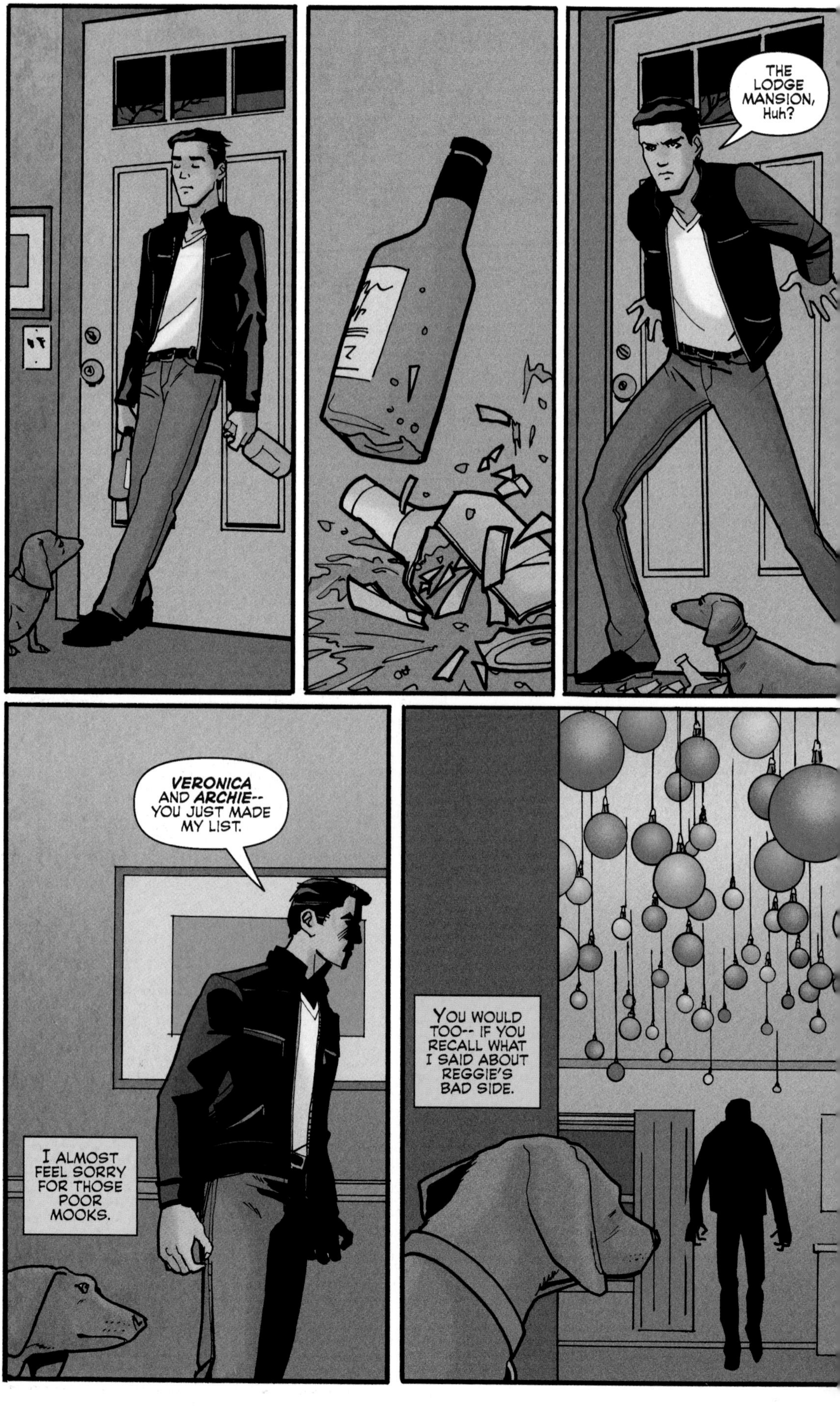
THE LODGE MANSION, Huh?
VERONICA AND ARCHIE-- YOU JUST MADE MY LIST.
I ALMOST FEEL SORRY FOR THOSE POOR MOOKS.
YOU WOULD TOO-- IF YOU RECALL WHAT I SAID ABOUT REGGIE'S BAD SIDE.

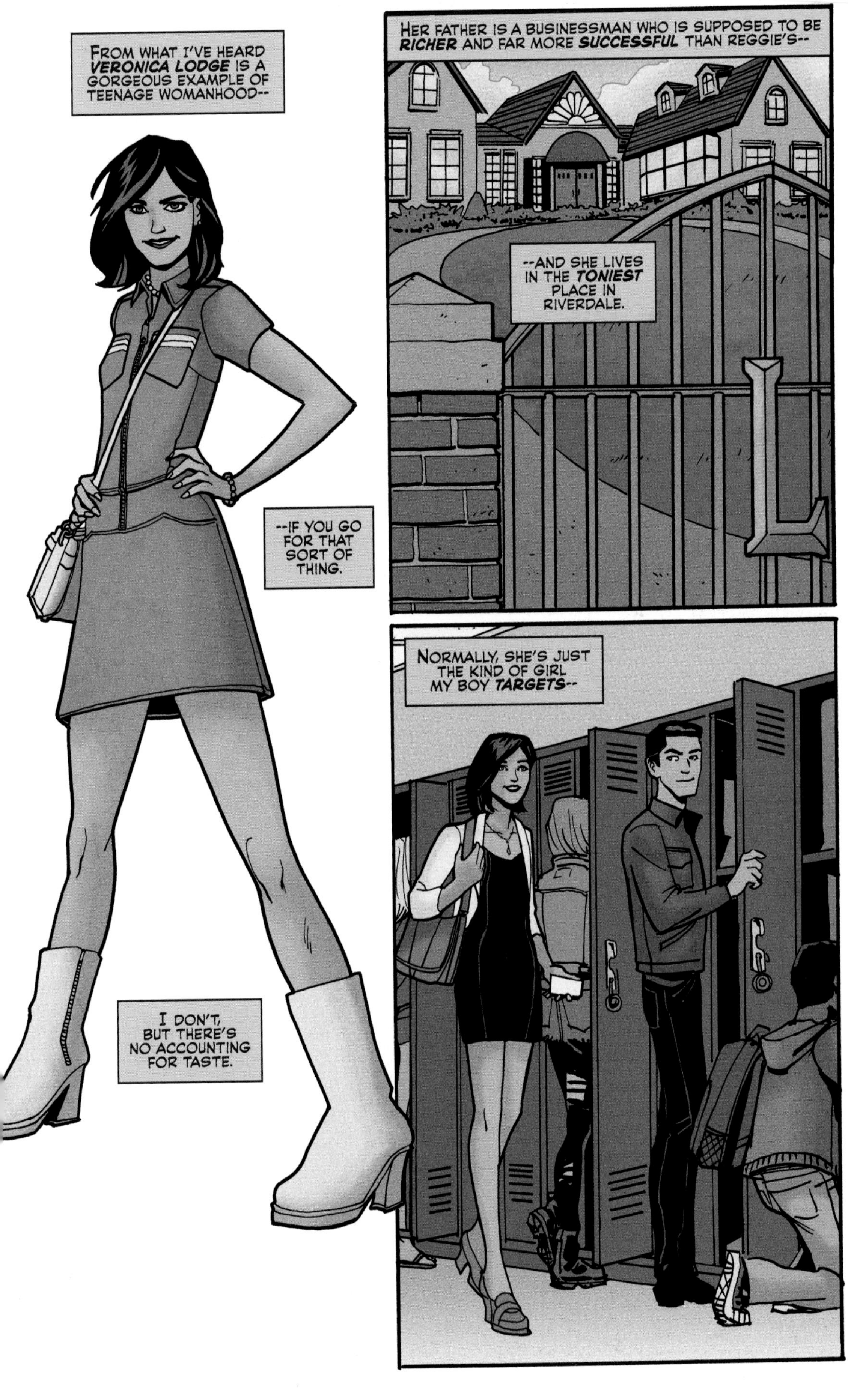

FROM WHAT I'VE HEARD VERONICA LODGE IS A GORGEOUS EXAMPLE OF TEENAGE WOMANHOOD--
--IF YOU GO FOR THAT SORT OF THING.
I DON'T, BUT THERE'S NO ACCOUNTING FOR TASTE.
HER FATHER IS A BUSINESSMAN WHO IS SUPPOSED TO BE RICHER AND FAR MORE SUCCESSFUL THAN REGGIE'S--
--AND SHE LIVES IN THE TONIEST PLACE IN RIVERDALE.
NORMALLY, SHE'S JUST THE KIND OF GIRL MY BOY TARGETS--

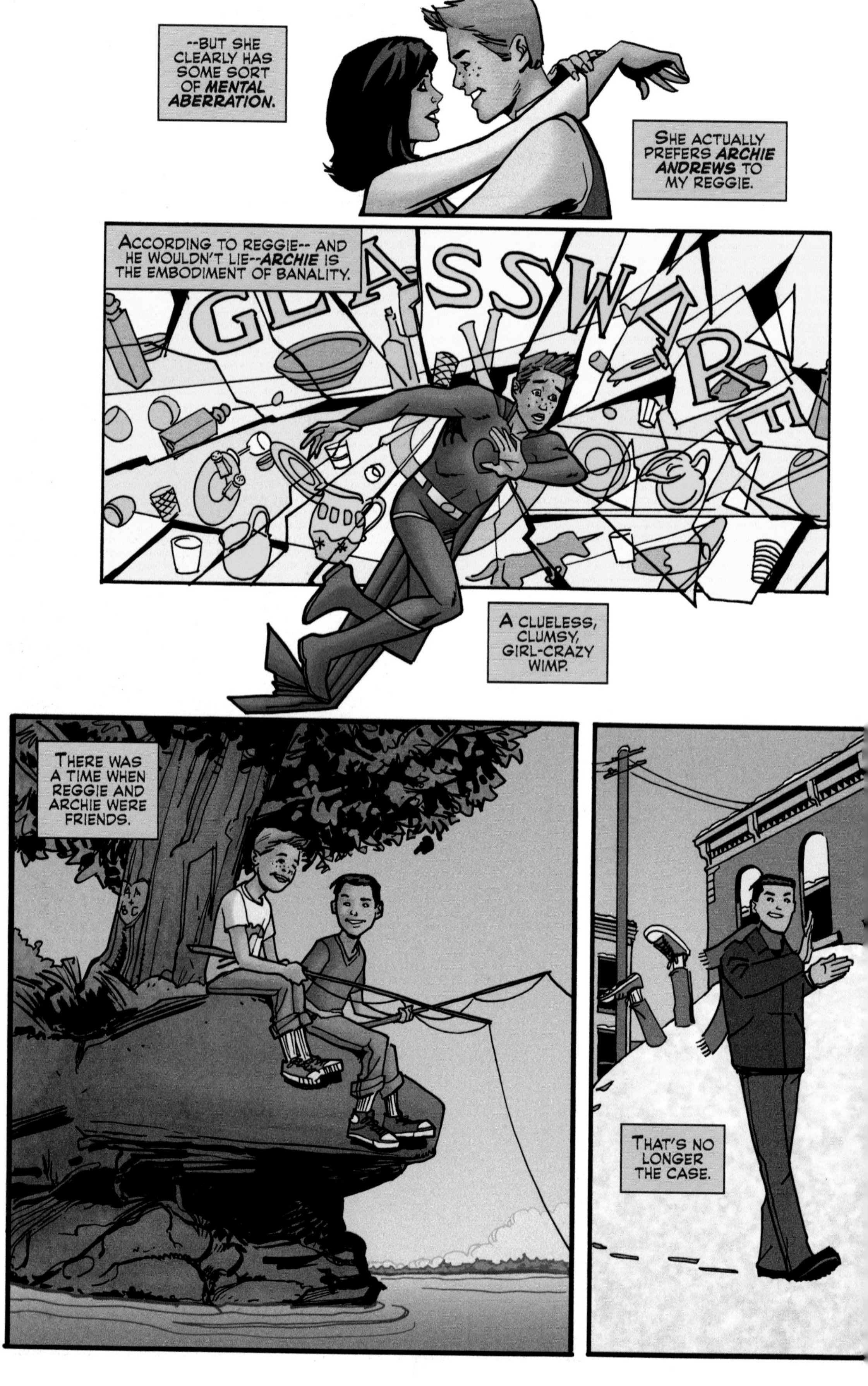
--BUT SHE CLEARLY HAS SOME SORT OF MENTAL ABERRATION.
SHE ACTUALLY PREFERS ARCHIE ANDREWS TO MY REGGIE.
ACCORDING TO REGGIE-- AND HE WOULDN'T LIE--ARCHIE IS THE EMBODIMENT OF BANALITY.
GLASSWARE
A CLUELESS, CLUMSY, GIRL-CRAZY WIMP.
THERE WAS A TIME WHEN REGGIE AND ARCHIE WERE FRIENDS.
THAT'S NO LONGER THE CASE.

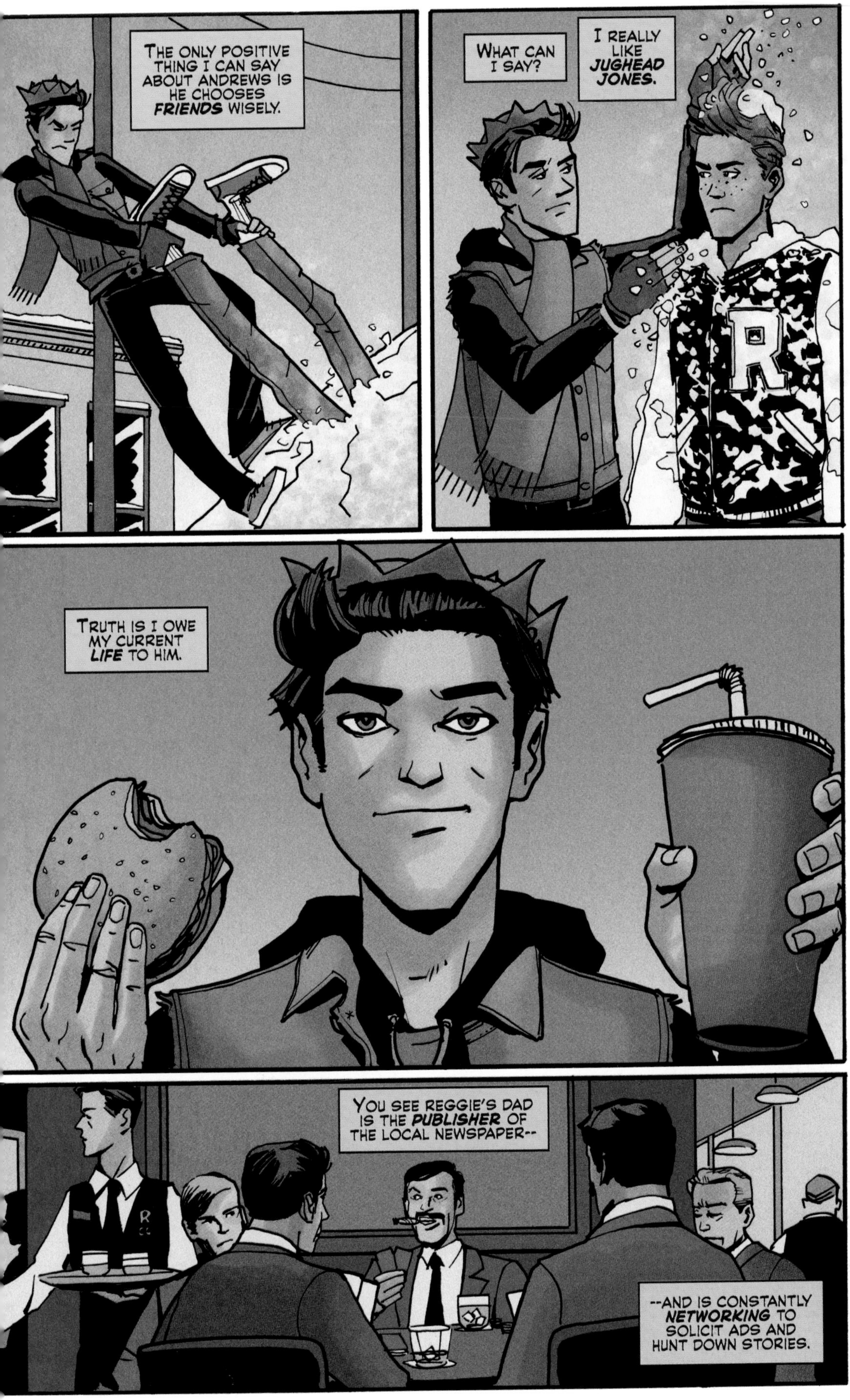

THE ONLY POSITIVE THING I CAN SAY ABOUT ANDREWS IS HE CHOOSES FRIENDS WISELY.
WHAT CAN I SAY?
I REALLY LIKE JUGHEAD JONES.
TRUTH IS I OWE MY CURRENT LIFE TO HIM.
YOU SEE REGGIE'S DAD IS THE PUBLISHER OF THE LOCAL NEWSPAPER--
--AND IS CONSTANTLY NETWORKING TO SOLICIT ADS AND HUNT DOWN STORIES.

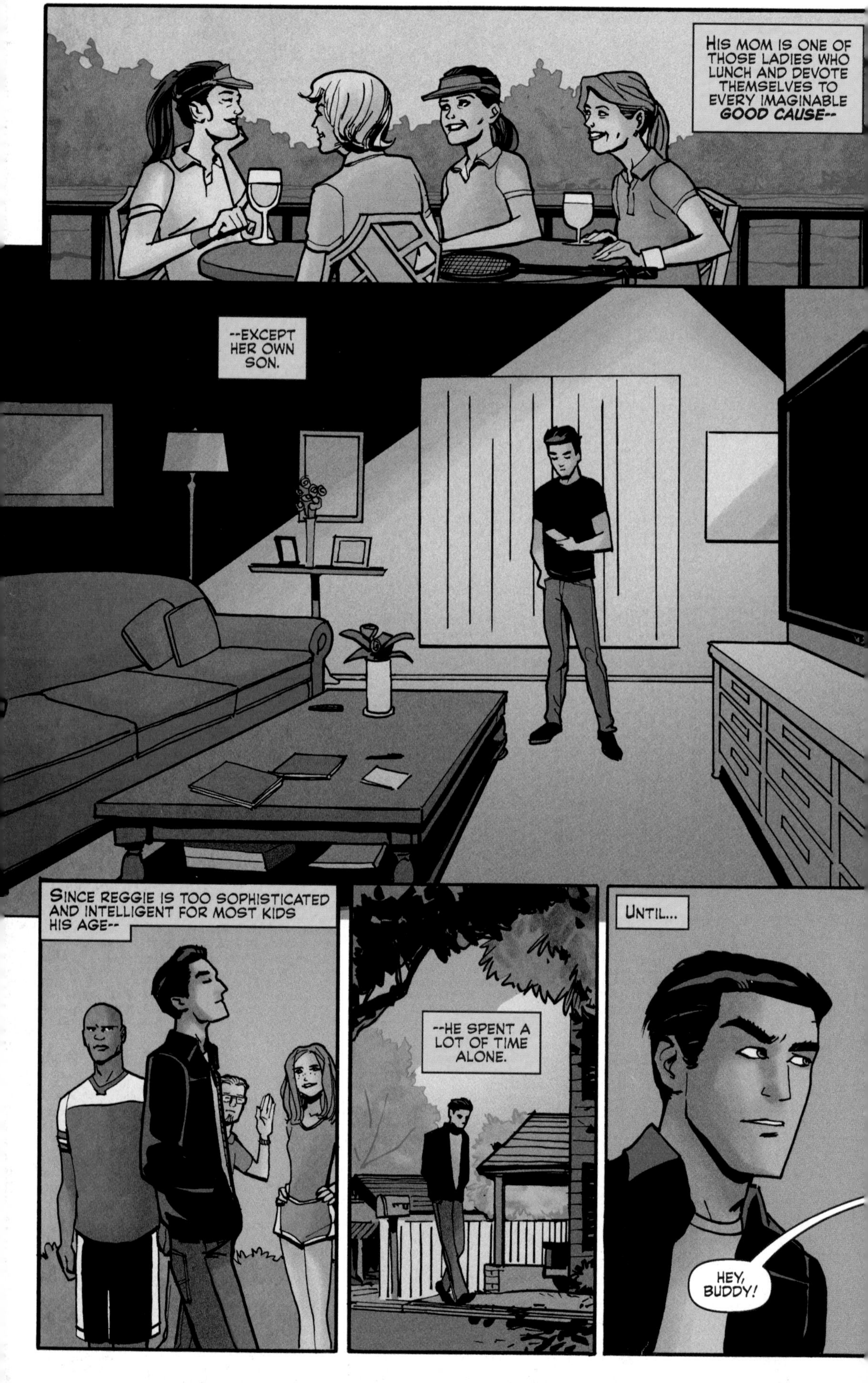
HIS MOM IS ONE OF THOSE LADIES WHO LUNCH AND DEVOTE THEMSELVES TO EVERY IMAGINABLE GOOD CAUSE--
--EXCEPT HER OWN SON.
SINCE REGGIE IS TOO SOPHISTICATED AND INTELLIGENT FOR MOST KIDS HIS AGE--
--HE SPENT A LOT OF TIME ALONE.
UNTIL...
HEY, BUDDY!

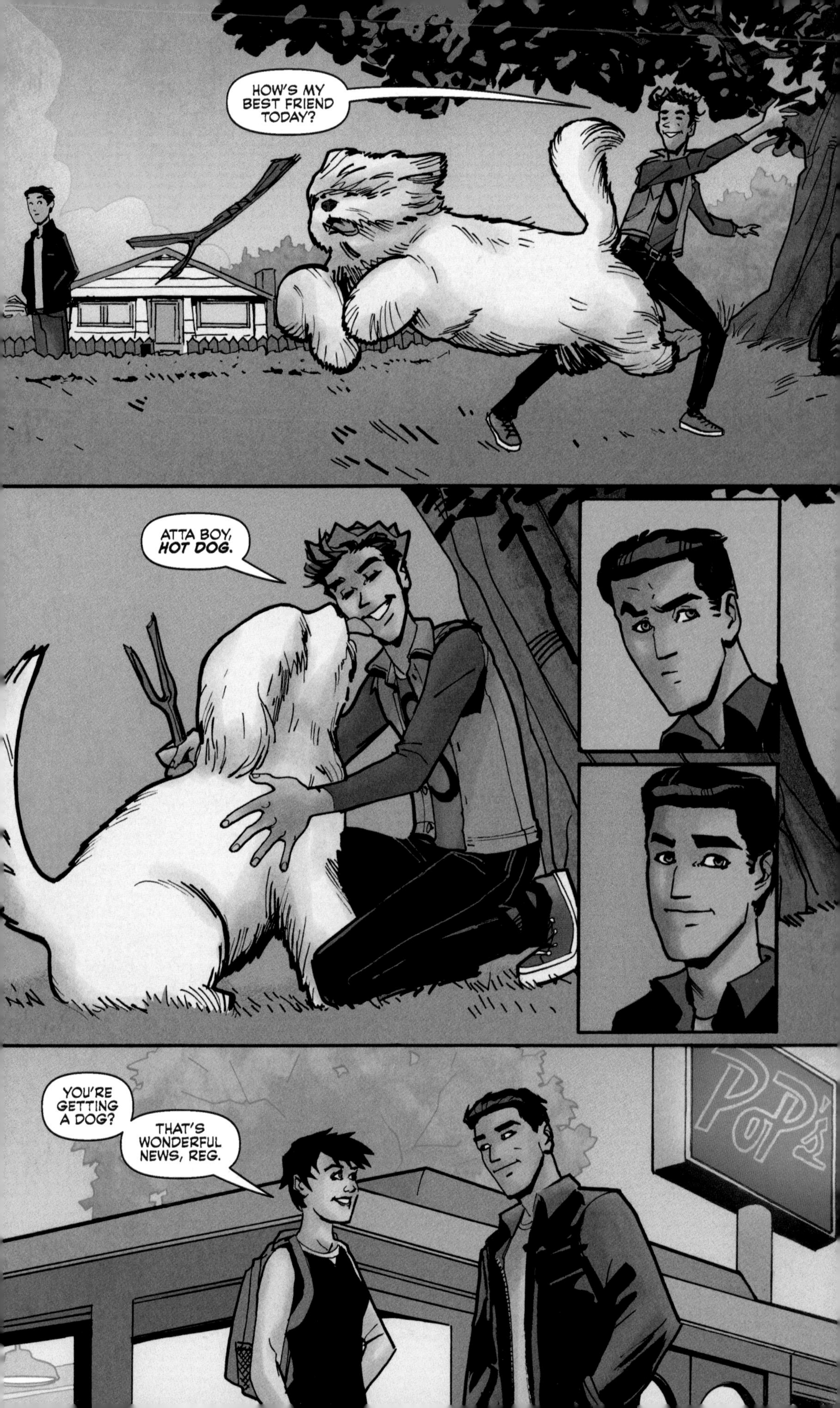

HOW'S MY BEST FRIEND TODAY?
ATTA BOY, *HOT DOG.*
YOU'RE GETTING A DOG?
THAT'S WONDERFUL NEWS, REG.
POP'S

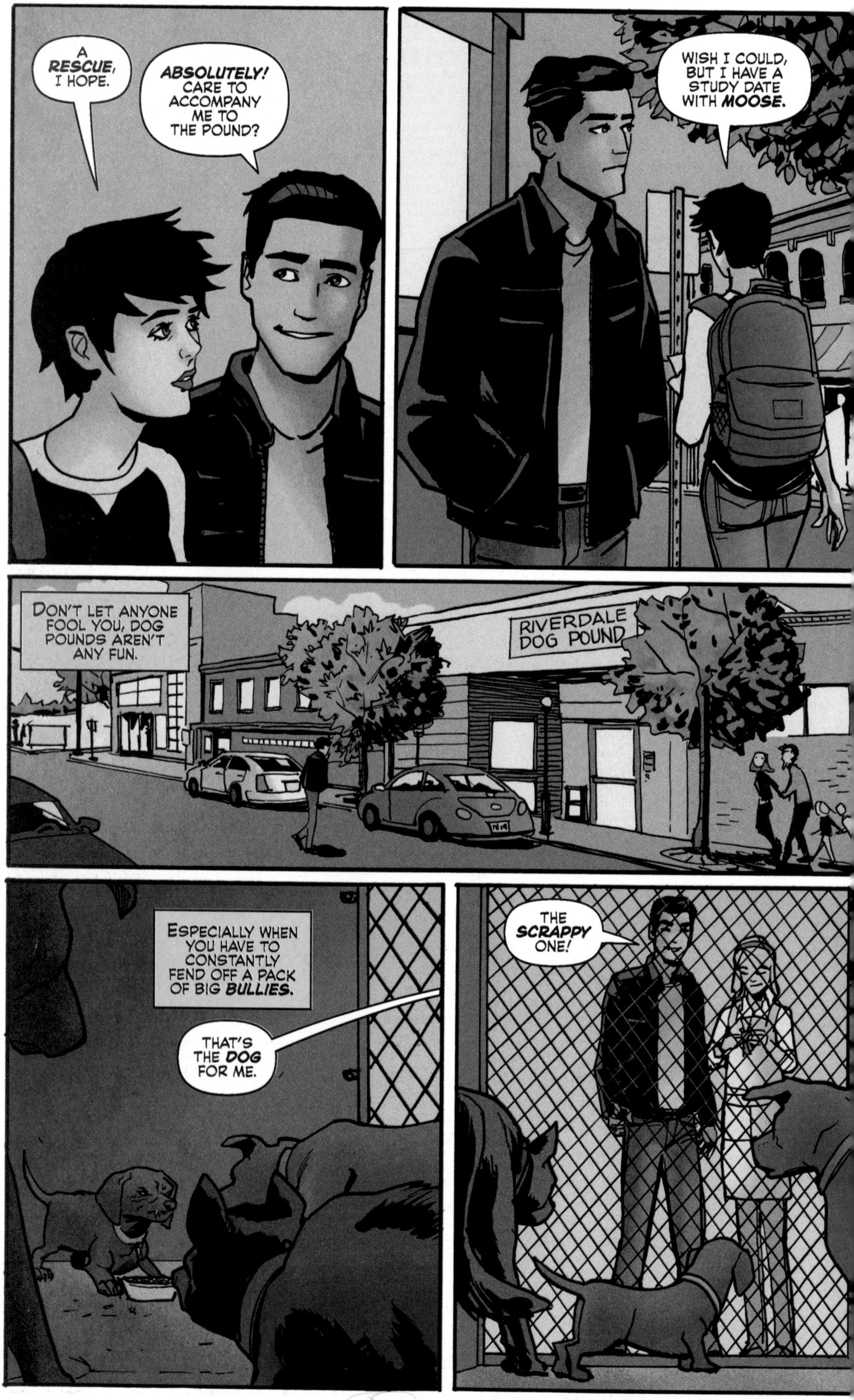
A RESCUE, I HOPE.
ABSOLUTELY! CARE TO ACCOMPANY ME TO THE POUND?
WISH I COULD, BUT I HAVE A STUDY DATE WITH MOOSE.
DON'T LET ANYONE FOOL YOU, DOG POUNDS AREN'T ANY FUN.
RIVERDALE DOG POUND
ESPECIALLY WHEN YOU HAVE TO CONSTANTLY FEND OFF A PACK OF BIG BULLIES.
THAT'S THE DOG FOR ME.
THE SCRAPPY ONE!

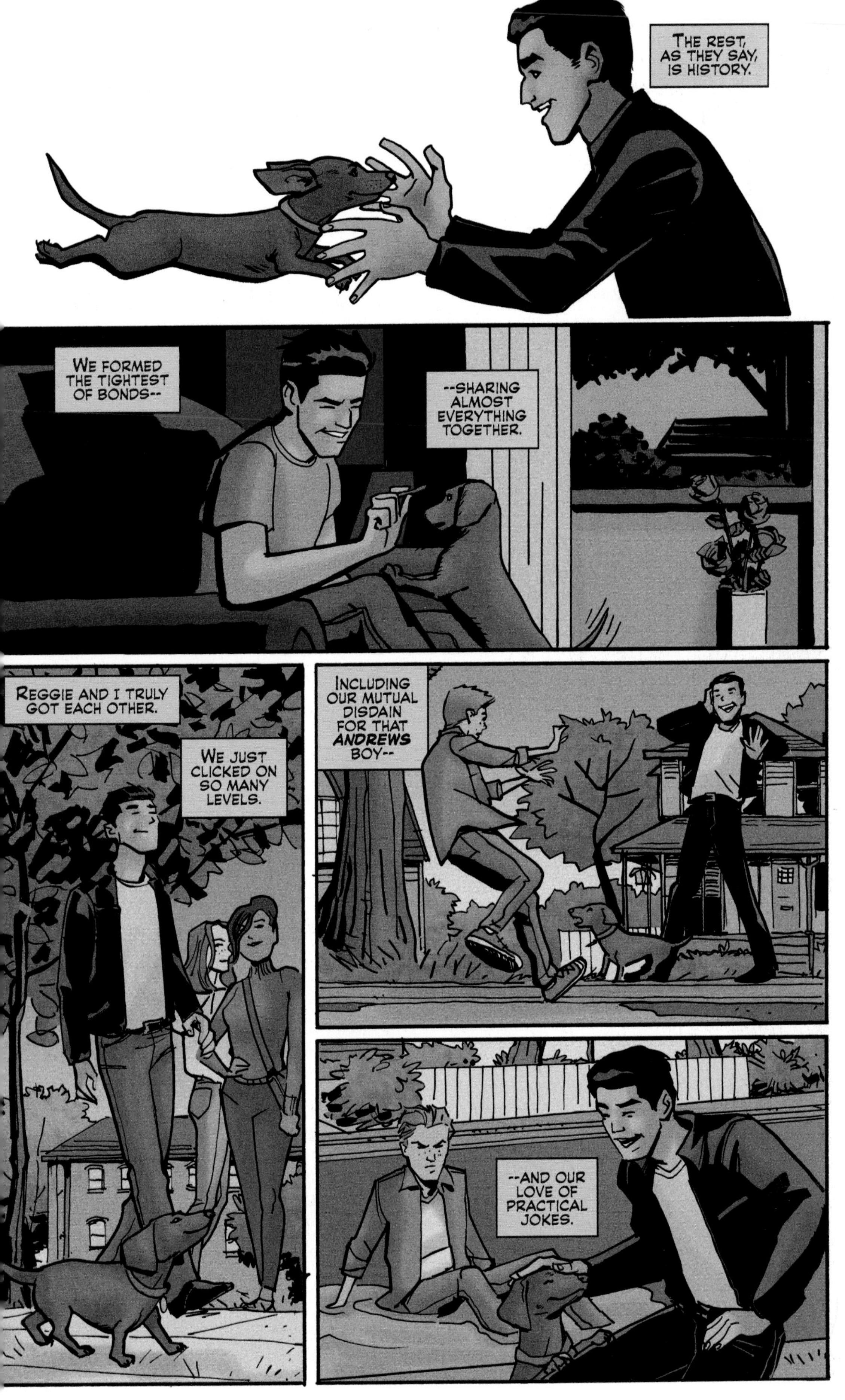
THE REST, AS THEY SAY, IS HISTORY.
WE FORMED THE TIGHTEST OF BONDS--
--SHARING ALMOST EVERYTHING TOGETHER.
REGGIE AND I TRULY GOT EACH OTHER.
WE JUST CLICKED ON SO MANY LEVELS.
INCLUDING OUR MUTUAL DISDAIN FOR THAT ANDREWS BOY--
--AND OUR LOVE OF PRACTICAL JOKES.

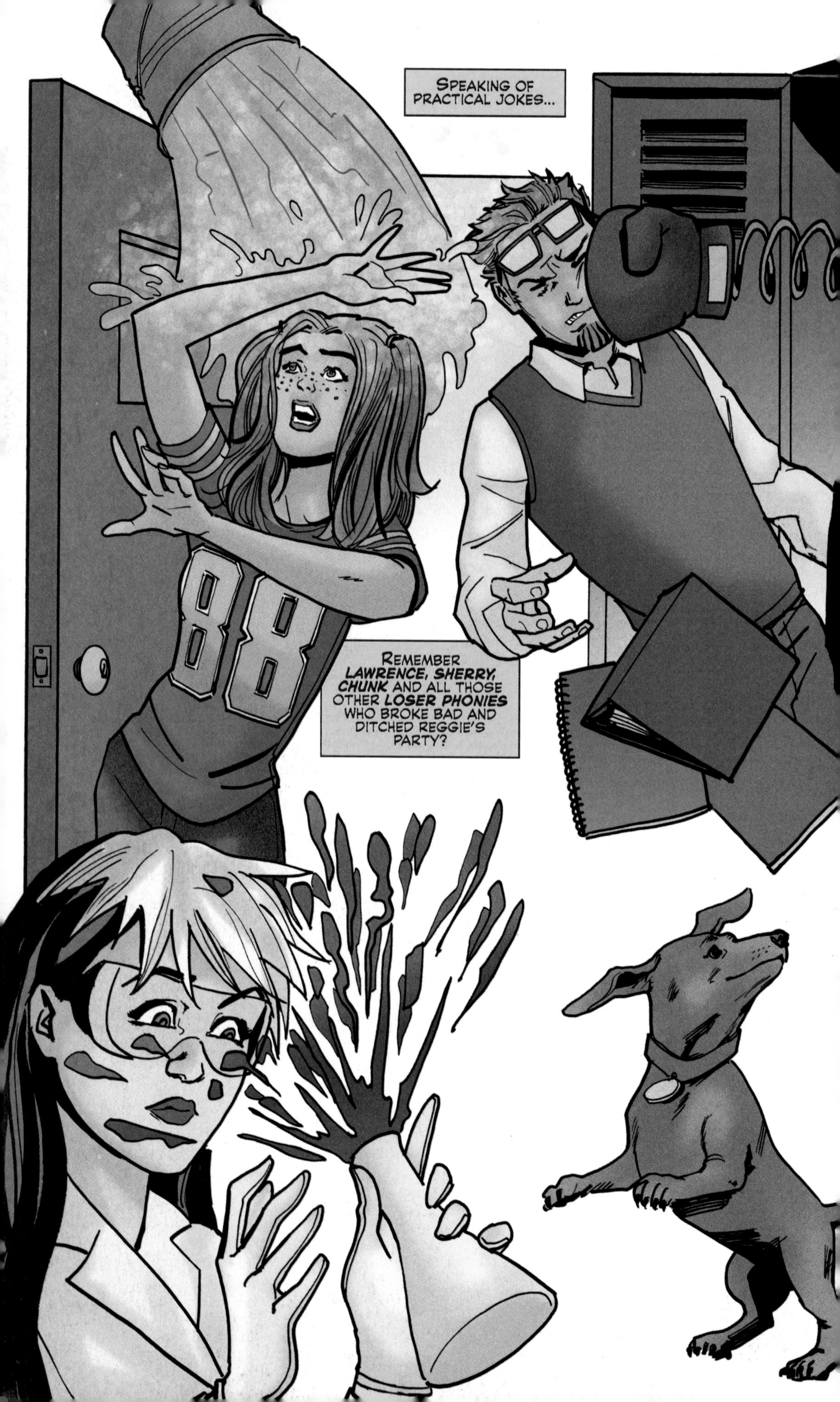
SPEAKING OF PRACTICAL JOKES...
REMEMBER **LAWRENCE, SHERRY, CHUNK** AND ALL THOSE OTHER **LOSER PHONIES** WHO BROKE BAD AND DITCHED REGGIE'S PARTY?

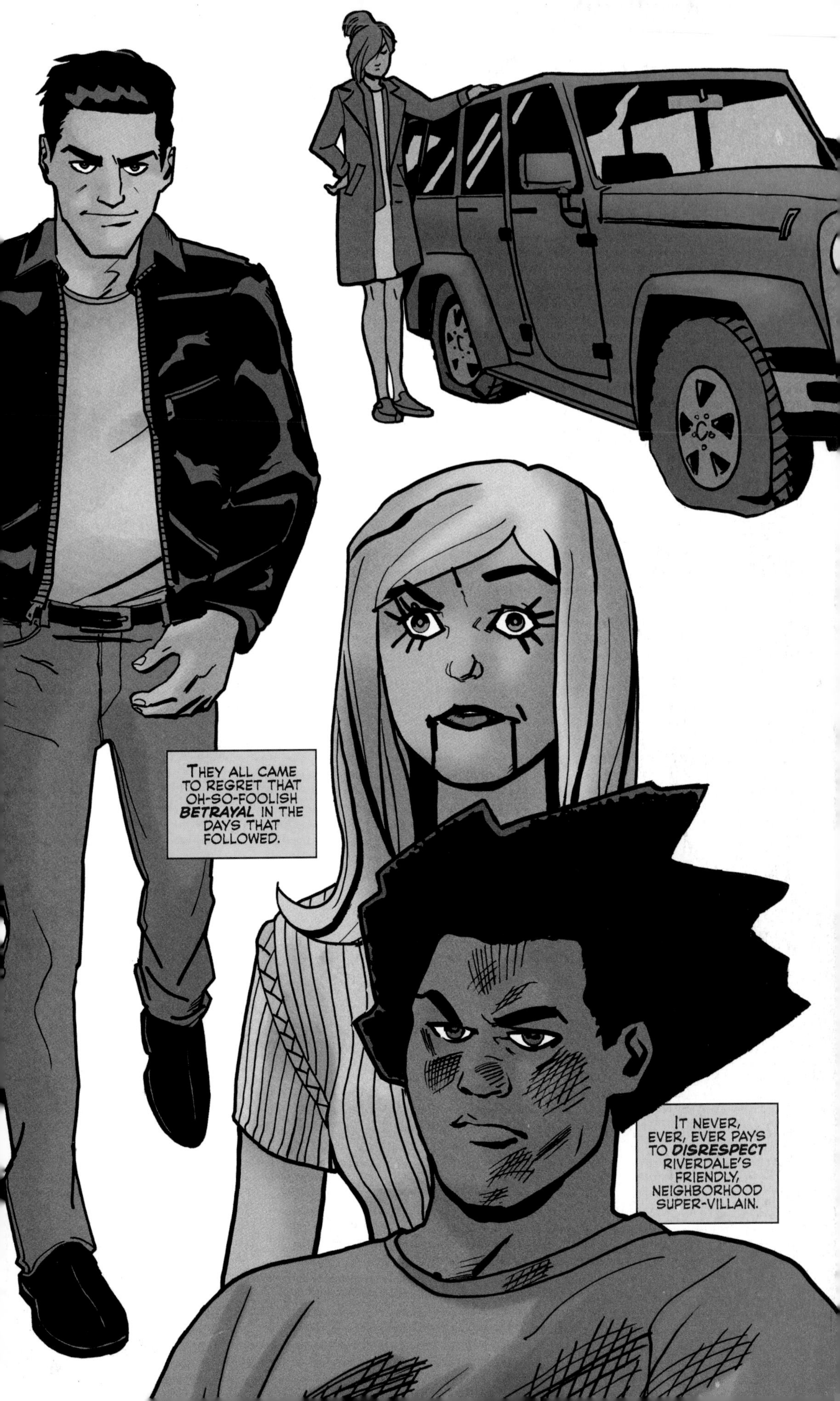
THEY ALL CAME TO REGRET THAT OH-SO-FOOLISH BETRAYAL IN THE DAYS THAT FOLLOWED.
IT NEVER, EVER, EVER PAYS TO DISRESPECT RIVERDALE'S FRIENDLY, NEIGHBORHOOD SUPER-VILLAIN.

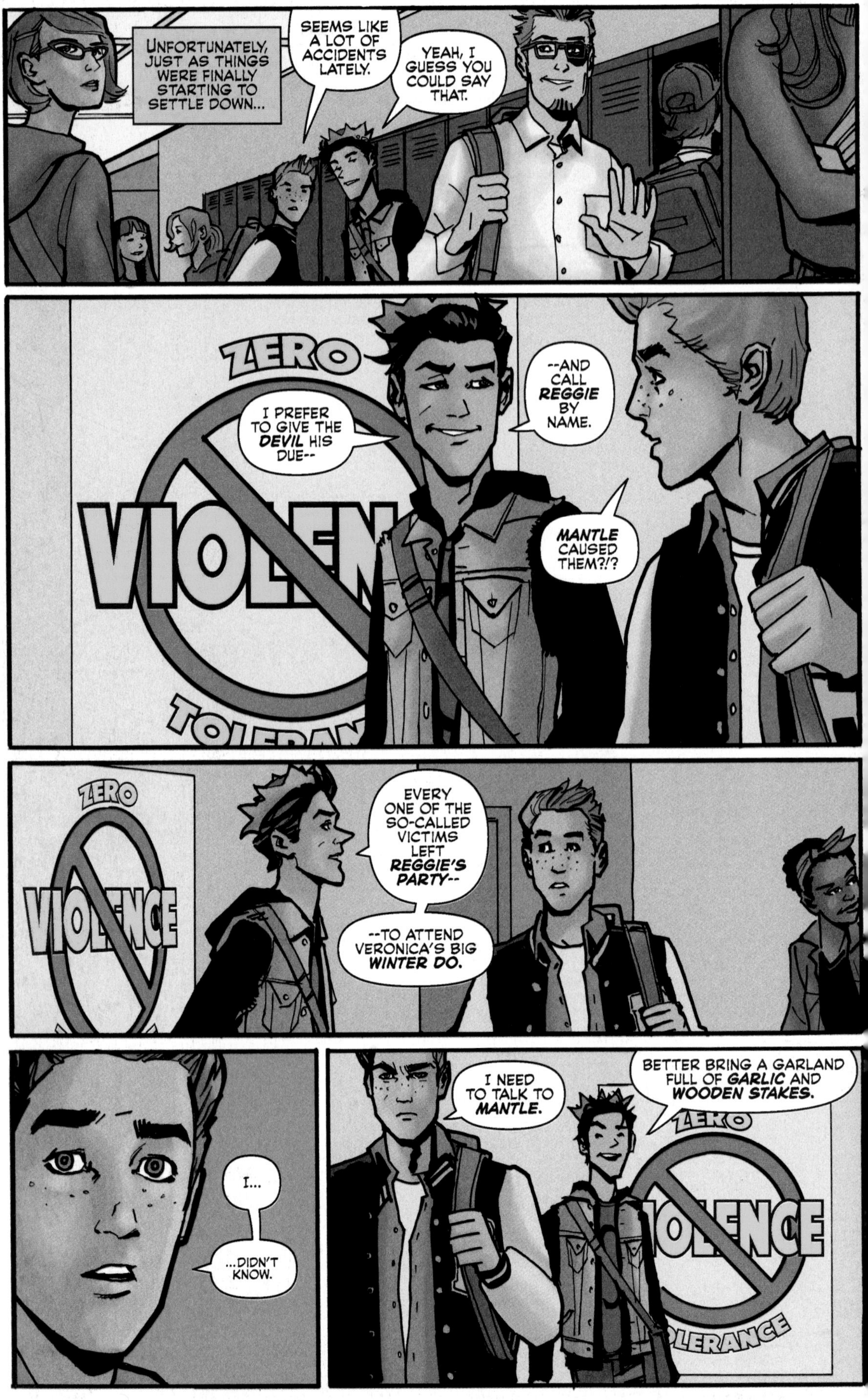
UNFORTUNATELY, JUST AS THINGS WERE FINALLY STARTING TO SETTLE DOWN...
SEEMS LIKE A LOT OF ACCIDENTS LATELY.
YEAH, I GUESS YOU COULD SAY THAT.
ZERO
VIOLEN
TOLERAN
I PREFER TO GIVE THE DEVIL HIS DUE--
--AND CALL REGGIE BY NAME.
MANTLE CAUSED THEM?!?
ZERO
VIOLENCE
EVERY ONE OF THE SO-CALLED VICTIMS LEFT REGGIE'S PARTY--
--TO ATTEND VERONICA'S BIG WINTER DO.
I...
...DIDN'T KNOW.
I NEED TO TALK TO MANTLE.
BETTER BRING A GARLAND FULL OF GARLIC AND WOODEN STAKES.
ZERO
IOLENCE
OLERANCE

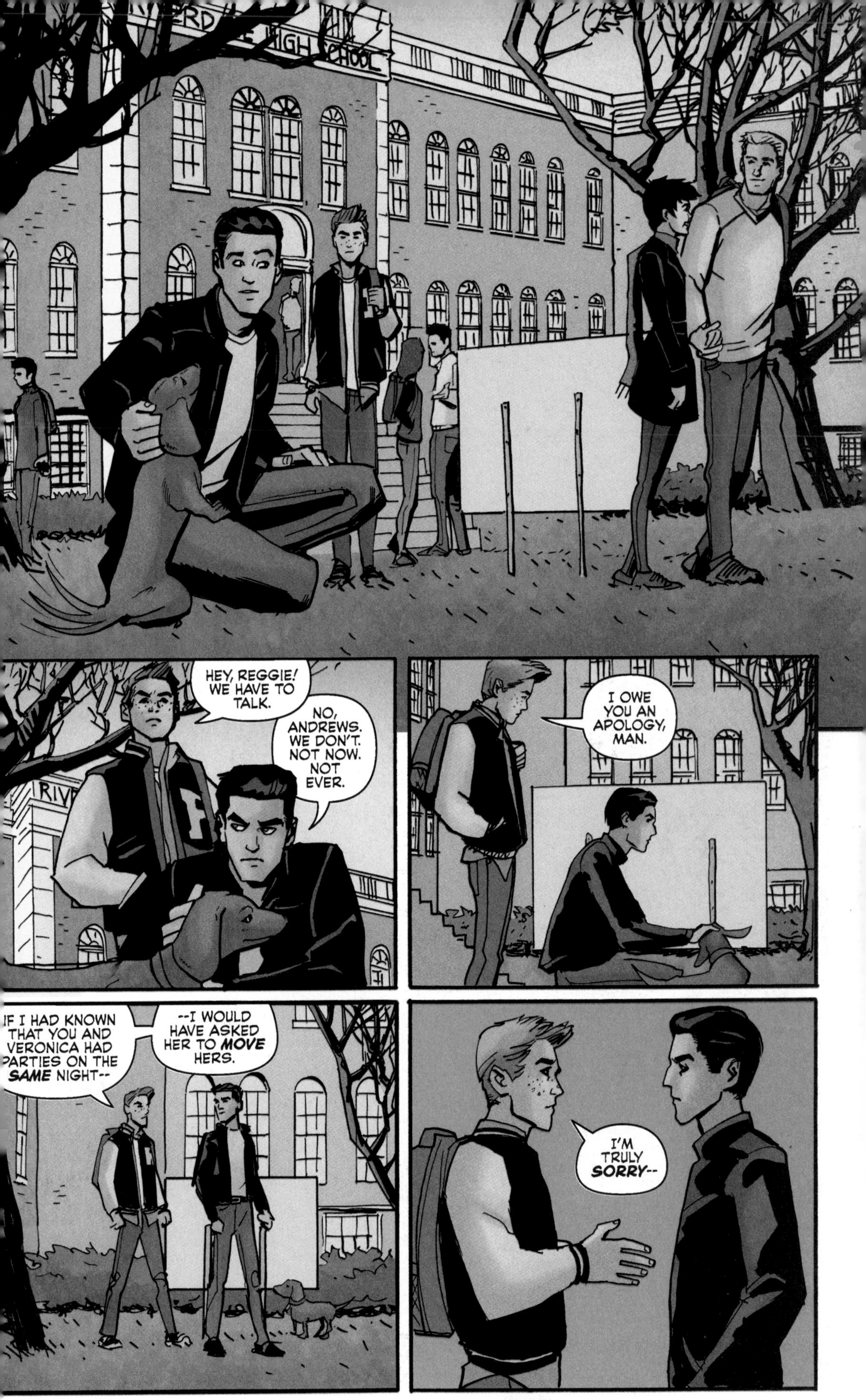

HIGH SCHOOL
HEY, REGGIE! WE HAVE TO TALK.
NO, ANDREWS. WE DON'T. NOT NOW. NOT EVER.
I OWE YOU AN APOLOGY, MAN.
IF I HAD KNOWN THAT YOU AND VERONICA HAD PARTIES ON THE **SAME** NIGHT--
--I WOULD HAVE ASKED HER TO **MOVE** HERS.
I'M TRULY **SORRY**--

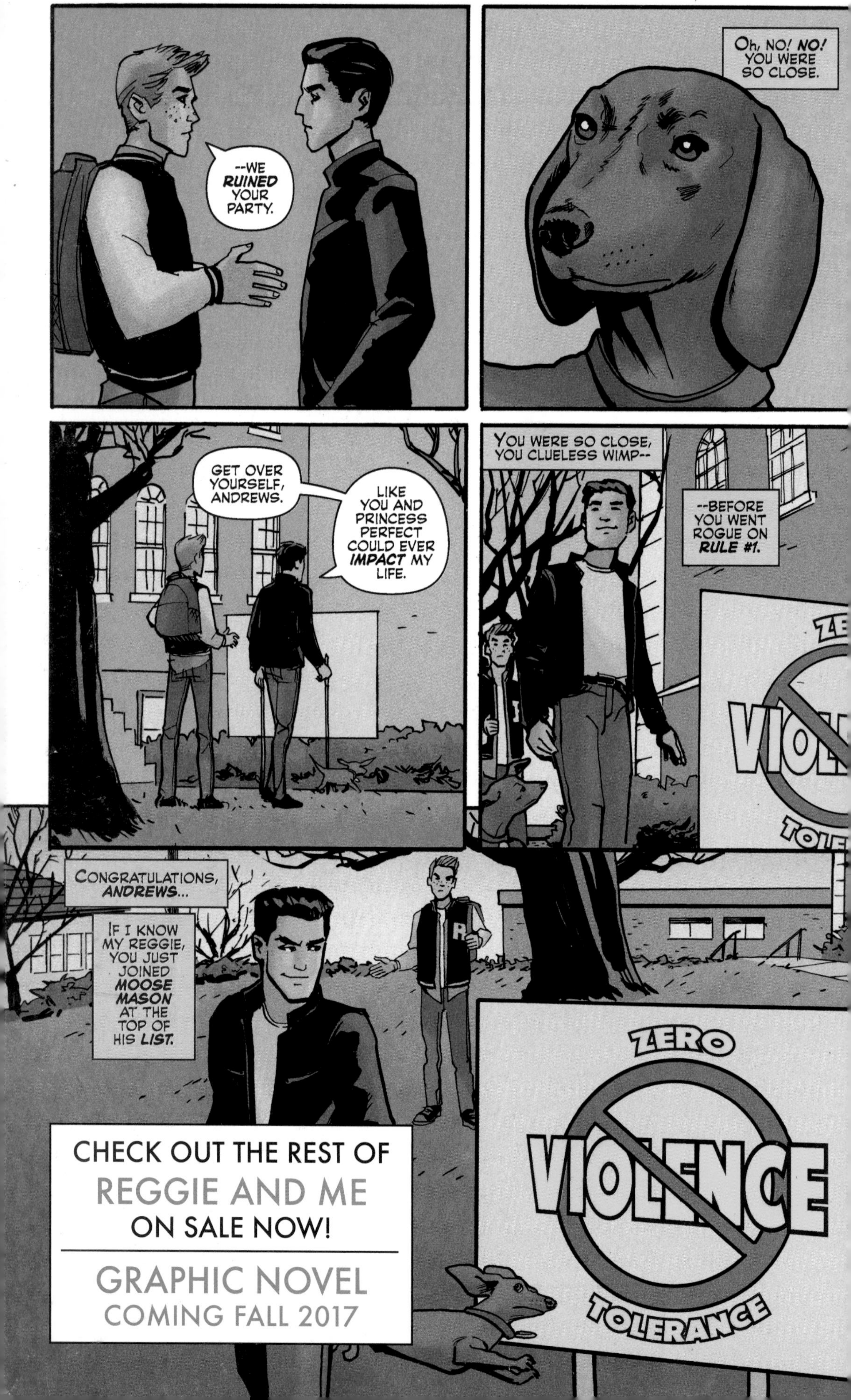
--WE RUINED YOUR PARTY.
Oh, NO! NO! YOU WERE SO CLOSE.
GET OVER YOURSELF, ANDREWS.
LIKE YOU AND PRINCESS PERFECT COULD EVER IMPACT MY LIFE.
YOU WERE SO CLOSE, YOU CLUELESS WIMP--
--BEFORE YOU WENT ROGUE ON RULE #1.
CONGRATULATIONS, ANDREWS...
IF I KNOW MY REGGIE, YOU JUST JOINED MOOSE MASON AT THE TOP OF HIS LIST.
ZERO
VIOLENCE
TOLERANCE
CHECK OUT THE REST OF
REGGIE AND ME
ON SALE NOW!
GRAPHIC NOVEL
COMING FALL 2017